ST. IRENAEUS OF LYONS

Against the Heresies

Ancient Christian Writers

THE WORKS OF THE FATHERS IN TRANSLATION

No. 64

ST. IRENAEUS OF LYONS: AGAINST THE HERESIES

Book 3

TRANSLATED AND ANNOTATED

BY

DOMINIC J. UNGER, OFM Cap, WITH AN

INTRODUCTION AND FURTHER REVISIONS

BY

IRENAEUS M. C. STEENBERG

THE NEWMAN PRESS
New York/Mahwah, NJ

COPYRIGHT © 2012
BY
CAPUCHIN PROVINCE OF MID-AMERICA

INTRODUCTION COPYRIGHT © 2012
BY
IRENEAUS M. C. STEENBERG

Library of Congress Cataloging-in-Publication Data

Irenaeus, Saint, Bishop of Lyons.
    [Adversus haereses. English]
    Against the heresies/St. Irenaeus of Lyons; translated and annotated by Dominic J. Unger with an introduction and further revisions by Irenaeus M. C. Steenberg.
        p. cm.—(Ancient Chiristan writers; no. 55-)
    Translation of: Adversus haereses.
    Includes biblioghaphaical references and index.
    ISBN 0-8091-0454-7 (v. 1)
    ISBN 978-0-8091-0589-2 (v. 3)
    1. Gnosticism—Controversial literature—Early works to 1800. 2. Theology, Doctrinal—Early works to 1800. I. Unger, Dominic J. II. Dillon, John J. III. Title. IV. Series: Ancienct Christian writers; no. 55, etc.
    BR60.A35 no. 55, etc.
    [BR65.I63]
    270 s—dc20
    [239'.3]
                                                                            91-40838
                                                                            CIP

Published by The Newman Press
an imprint of Paulist Press
997 Macarthur Boulevard
Mahwah, New Jersey 07430

www.paulistpress.com

PRINTED AND BOUND IN THE UNITED STATES OF AMERICA

CONTENTS

DEDICATION

For Thomas G. Weinandy, OFM Cap,
friend to Dominic Unger, OFM Cap, and myself,
who has long been waiting for this book

ACKNOWLEDGMENTS

I would like to acknowledge the assistance and support of Rev. Dr. Thomas G. Weinandy, OFM Cap, Dr. Alexis Torrance, and above all Rev. Dr. John J. Dillon for their assistance in reading through, correcting, and commenting on earlier drafts of this volume. Any mistakes that remain are my own. I should also like to thank Mr. Paul McMahon and Dr. Nancy de Flon at Paulist Press for their excellent editorial work in bringing the volume to press.

I.M.C.S.
September 2011

LIST OF ABBREVIATIONS

Given the relative infrequency with which bibliographic sources are repeated in the notes, we have elected in the present volume to keep abbreviations to a minimum. Titles of books and journals are normally given in full, with the following exceptions:

ACW	Ancient Christian Writers (Westminster, MD/ London/New York/Paramus, NJ/Mahwah, NJ, 1946–)
ANF	The Ante-Nicene Fathers (Buffalo, NY, 1885–96; repr., Grand Rapids, MI, 1951–56)
Arm.Iren.	Armenian version of Irenaeus's *Adversus haereses*
CCSL	Corpus christianorum, series latina
DACL	*Dictionnaire d'archéologie chrétienne et de liturgie* (Paris, 1907–53)
GCS	Die griechischen christlichen Schriftsteller der ersten drei Jahrhunderte (Leipzig, 1897–)
Gos.Tr.	*Gospel of Truth* (NHC I,3 and XII,2)
Grabe	The edition of *Adversus haereses* by Joannes Ernestus Grabe (Oxford, 1702)
Harvey	The edition of *Adversus haereses* by W[illiam] Wigan Harvey, 2 volumes (Cambridge, 1857)
Lat.Iren.	Latin version of Irenaeus's *Adversus haereses*
LXX	Septuagint
Massuet	The edition of *Adversus haereses* by René Massuet (Paris, 1713). Reprinted in MG 7.
MG	Patrologia graeca, ed. J. P. Migne (Paris, 1857–66)
ML	Patrologia latina, ed. J. P. Migne (Paris, 1844–64)
NHC	Nag Hammadi Codices
NT	New Testament
OT	Old Testament
SC	Sources chrétiennes (Paris, 1942–)

Stieren   The edition of *Adversus haereses* by Adolphus
             Stieren, 2 volumes (Leipzig, 1848–53)

A similar pattern has been followed with regard to patristic texts, and normally full details are provided *in situ* in the notes. However, the following are repeated with enough frequency to warrant standard abbreviations:

Clement, *1 Cor.*	Clement of Rome, *First Epistle to the Corinthians*
Eusebius, *HE*	Eusebius of Caesaria, *Historia ecclesiastica*
Irenaeus, *AH*	Irenaeus, *Adversus haereses* (*Against the Heresies*)
Justin, *1 Apol.*	Justin Martyr, *First Apology*
Justin, *Dial.*	Justin Martyr, *Dialogue with Trypho*
Tertullian, *De praesc.*	Tertullian of Carthage, *De praescriptione haereticorum*

INTRODUCTION

An earlier volume in this series provided a critical translation of and commentary on Book 1 of St. Irenaeus of Lyons' *magnum opus*, the *Refutation and Overthrow of Knowledge Falsely So-called* (usually abbreviated *Against the Heresies*).[1] This was a complement to the ACW series' earlier publication of the *Proof of the Apostolic Preaching*,[2] as the next phase in providing a critical English translation of the whole Irenaean corpus. While some considerable time has elapsed since those volumes appeared, work has continued on the project. The present volume offers a critical translation and thoroughgoing commentary on Book 3, perhaps one of the more significant portions of Irenaeus's lengthy opus, and work is nearly complete on Book 2. Given the intensity of interest in Irenaean studies today, together with the ongoing lack of a critical English edition with full linguistic notes and comparisons, we hope the present volume will prove a useful contribution to an expanding field.

THE TEXT

Translating Book 3: The Current Edition and Its Predecessors

Adversus haereses 3, among the most important portions of Irenaeus's lengthy tract, has had a long history of development in modern textual provision, specifically through the Sources chrétiennes. That series' vol. 34 (1952) first provided the scholarly translation of F. Sagnard, including a critical study of the text and copious notes. Sagnard was to produce no further Irenaean volumes for the SC, but the more expansive project of A. Rousseau and L. Doutreleau fleshed out its offerings with, eventually, critical editions of all five books. Some two decades after Sagnard had published his text of *AH 3*,

1

the revised and more elaborate edition of Rousseau/Doutreleau appeared in two volumes as SC 210, 211 (1974), providing not only a critical Latin text with full apparati but also complete reference to the Greek, Armenian, and Syriac fragments, as well as a fine (though not perfect) French translation and even, as per these scholars' custom, a remarkable (if not unproblematic) Greek retroversion of the entire book.[3] This edition has become the standard critical text for Irenaeus, superseding Sagnard's earlier work, and is unlikely to be replaced as such unless some new manuscripts or other materials are found. In our present translation, the editions of both Sagnard and Rousseau/ Doutreleau have been employed, particularly for comparison's sake when the two editions differ in critical source reading or translation. Since the latter editions print in their pages all the fragmentary excerpts from the Greek and other extant ancient translations, we have felt no need to reiterate them in the present volume, unless specifically warranted in the commentary. Students and scholars keen to examine directly the fragmentary excerpts mentioned in the notes will find them quite readily in the SC volumes.

We have continued to use the chapter and paragraph divisions of Migne, by now firmly established as standard among scholars. In some cases we have slightly modified paragraph divisions in the English translation, though never in such a manner as to alter the numeration. Following the pattern begun with Book 1, we have abandoned the chapter titles of older manuscripts (never original to Irenaeus, but maintained in many editions out of custom) for descriptions of our own, which we hope might be of more practical aid to the study of the text.[4]

The present translation has had a long history of its own. D. Unger, OFM Cap, as part of his larger project of producing a critical English translation of the whole *AH*, produced his draft version of Book 3, typeset in the early 1970s. His death in 1981, however, both cut short the project and deprived the academic and religious worlds of a dedicated and enthusiastic Irenaean scholar. But his work was to continue past his death. In 1992, J. Dillon published Unger's edition of *AH* 1, greatly updated, corrected, and modified, as the previously mentioned ACW 55. That volume was in some ways as much Dillon's as Unger's, given the substantial amount of reworking that had to be done in light of scholarly advances since the latter's death, especially in the realm of so-called "Gnostic" studies. Its importance as an edition was quickly established, as the attentiveness to detail and consistency in translation revealed just how lacking were the scant English editions previously available—the primary of which, namely, that presented in ANF 1, is both outdated in language and uncritical in form.[5] Unger's original conviction, that a heady commentary on the text was as much needed as a good translation, seems also to have been proved true, for the Unger/Dillon edition of *AH* 1 has become the standard volume for modern students and scholars.

Unger's design continues with the present text, as with the forthcoming volumes to complete the project and offer in similar form all five books of the *Adversus haereses*. In preparing each of these, we have been privileged to have before us the drafts done many years ago by Unger, both of the text and of his commentary. His insight into Irenaeus's thought and language became ever more apparent as we worked through somewhat faded, typeset documents, now decades old, which still in many ways seem current and apt. His is a strong witness to an era of scholarship that, regrettably, seems to be fading: Unger's mastery of Latin was superb, as was his grasp of Greek and various other ancient languages, and his breadth of exposure to and familiarity with the patristic witness was remarkable. His comprehensive approach to Irenaeus's vocabulary and usage is attested by his regular comments to the effect that, for example, "Irenaeus uses this term 72 times"—observations made in an era before computerized word searches and exhaustive concordances (Reynders' *Lexique comparé* was already recognized as having notable deficiencies).

Nonetheless, scholarship trudges on. Since Unger produced his draft translations and commentaries, scholarship into Irenaeus and, more broadly, second-century thought and history, has continued to advance with ardent step. The Sources chrétiennes had not fully completed their editions as Unger undertook his task, the result being that almost as soon as he had finished his drafts, they were in need of substantial revision. Texts he had viewed as final had changed, and precisions of vocabulary could be seen with new clarity. The full critical corpus had now to be taken into account, and the extensive scholarly notes of Rousseau and Doutreleau consulted. As regards the commentary, the find at Nag Hammadi was still underappreciated for its relevance to Irenaean study, due in large part to the delays caused by feuds over its texts and their rights. If scholars are still today coming to appreciate what this find means for our understanding of

"Gnosticism" and various other historical and philosophical/theological currents in the early Christian era, so much the more was this appreciation lacking at the time of Unger's writing. This deficiency was largely corrected in Dillon's work on *AH* 1, where the Nag Hammadi find has the most direct relevance; but scholarship in other areas has also advanced. The dominant (and largely negative) views toward Irenaeus put forward by W. Bousset, F. Loofs, and A. Harnack have since been effectively overturned by such scholars as G. Wingren, P. Bacq, Y. de Andia, and J. Fantino. The acute studies of Bacq (1978) and M. A. Donovan (1997), in particular, revealed a structure and design to Irenaeus's great polemical work hitherto unrecognized by most scholars—the latter directly analyzing our present Book 3 through this lens.[6] From the 1960s though the 1980s, A. Orbe produced an almost continuous stream of texts on Irenaeus, from multi-volume books to journal articles the length of books (including a study on the subject of Christ's anointing by the Spirit spanning a rather astounding 700+ pages[7]), which, while they may rightly come under some criticism for their speculative tendencies, nonetheless have exercised a profound influence on our understanding of the bishop of Lyons. More recently, such scholars as J. Behr, C. R. Smith, R. F. Brown, I. M. MacKenzie, and E. Osborn have focused in more tightly on such aspects as Irenaean anthropology, asceticism, chiliasm, necessitarianism, and other theological points. Indeed, Irenaeus has today become something of a "golden child" of early patristic study, and research into his life, times, thought, and influence has flourished over the past thirty years as never before.

All of this scholarly activity has meant that Unger's work could not simply be typeset and published: the project that lay beneath it had to be continued. The nature of his translation—which attempted to be a fully critical edition, comparing all available manuscript evidence for every line and every variation of the text—had to be applied to the increasingly accurate critical editions produced since his day, and his attention to detailed critical commentary had also to be carried on to accommodate significant advances in scholarly study. Thus, our work on Unger's project has involved a thoroughgoing reworking of his original drafts and notes. For the present volume, this has meant an extensive correction of his translation, which has been changed in one manner or another at almost every section (the Rousseau/Doutreleau SC volumes on *AH* 3 were published in 1974;

Unger had seen them and was aware that they would necessitate serious revision to his drafts, but he was not able to take them fully on board before his death). His style was laudable, very much an English-language equivalent of Irenaeus's tone and mannerisms in the originals, and we have attempted to keep to this as much as possible. Many changes, however, have been made in the areas of terminological consistency throughout the full scope of the translation, as well as accurate renditions of Irenaeus's names for his opponents (ensuring, for example, that *haeretici* is translated not as "Gnostics" but as "heretics").

As to the commentary, Unger's breadth of scriptural awareness provided him with the tools to reference biblical quotations and allusions throughout, and these we have hardly had to touch—though we have made corrections and added a few references he seems not to have noticed. Elsewhere, his draft commentary has been either discarded or essentially written anew. In matters of linguistic commentary, for example, Unger regularly took issue with renditions—whether source or translation—in the SC volumes being produced while he wrote, with regard to which SC was ultimately proved correct in later volumes; or, as was the case more than once, we have deemed SC's (or another source's) rendition accurate, in spite of Unger's objections. Provision of revised and new notes is more pertinent, though, to matters of theological and historical commentary. Unger wrote notes of extensive length (one so long that it was extracted and published independently as an article in its own right[8]) on items which, in his day, were new and worthy of extended comment (e.g., the priority of Matthew in Irenaeus's dating of the Gospels), but which have since become common stock and require only brief mention. Elsewhere, currents in the scholarship of his day have largely been dismissed or proved wrong, such as his conviction that Irenaeus was commenting on the Montanists in *AH* 3.11.9. Further, there is the simple fact that scholarship has continued to explore Irenaeus's thought and world in new and creative ways since Unger's lifetime, and there are an abundance of themes we felt worthy of comment that Unger himself did not treat. Irenaean anthropology is a matter of profound interest in present-day studies, as are elements of his cosmology, Christology, and trinitarian language, and his views on Mary the Mother of God.

The result of all these circumstances is that the present volume is very much a "collaborative effort" between Unger and the present author. While we have felt very strongly that we are carrying on

Unger's work and bringing this scholar's contribution before the eyes of a new generation, we would not wish to hide that this is in some ways as much a new edition as it is the presentation of an old.

THE CONTENT OF *ADVERSUS HAERESES* 3

Given that the pertinent need of the moment is of a careful text, and as our commentary is itself quite lengthy, the decision has been made not to preface the volume with too much introductory material, which would in any case necessitate reduplicating a great deal of what is explained thoroughly in the notes. Rather, it seems pertinent to offer a brief word on the central themes treated here in Book 3, giving the reader a sense of the major contours Irenaeus wishes to trace out in the text and the way in which they reveal aspects of his larger thought. This will be followed by an outline of the contents of *AH* 3, so that the reader may locate passages of interest and read the more detailed commentary provided in the notes.

The Overarching Theme: One and the Same God

The central theological theme of *AH* 3 is stated most succinctly by Irenaeus in 3.10.6, at the end of a lengthy discourse on the testimony of Luke and Mark: "So it is one and the same God and Father who was announced by the prophets, handed down by the Gospel, whom we Christians worship and love with our whole heart as the Creator of heaven and earth and of all things in them." Irenaeus's concern, across the book, is to demonstrate this center and heart of the *regula fidei*, and it is enunciated in various ways throughout the volume. As he notes in the preface, the teachings of the Valentinians and other groups (whom he has considered in Books 1 and 2) are varied and contradictory; but the teaching of the apostles, the teaching of the Church, is singular and true. In the previous books, Irenaeus had made it his purpose to adumbrate and expose the variant teachings of those many others, all of whom in one way or another contradict what is here his central point: God is the Creator, and this same Creator-God is one and the same with the Lord Jesus "loved with the whole heart" by the Christians. Now, in Book 3, he turns to a task that is less exclusively heresiological and polemical: "in this third book we shall adduce proofs from the Scriptures" (3.Praef.). It is in the sacred writings—the Law, the Prophets, and here in Book 3 chiefly the Gospel and Acts of the Apostles—that this great theological vision is enshrined and exposed to the faithful, and part of Irenaeus's interest in this book is in seeking out "the power of the Gospel" that "the Lord of all things gave to His apostles," through whom Christians know the doctrine of God's Son (ibid.).

This is not to say that the content of *AH* 3 is not polemical, nor has Irenaeus here abandoned his broader heresiological project. As he makes explicit, the scriptural exploration found in the current book is to be added to the expositions of Books 1 and 2, enabling the reader, in the mix, to "resist [heresies] confidently and most insistently in favor of the only true and living faith, which the Church received from the apostles and distributes to her children" (3.Praef.). But what begins to emerge in Book 3 is a focus less on what others are doing and teaching wrongly (though this remains present) than on what the apostles first, and the Church now, does rightly. We have here a testimony to the apostolic inheritance and transmission of the one Gospel, harmonizing with the ancient Scriptures and passing down to all future generations the right belief in the saving Son who, crucified and risen, is at one and the same time the Lord, Creator of heaven and earth.

The Faith Received and Transmitted: The Fourfold Gospel

This focus brings Irenaeus to consider the nature of the "true and living faith" (3.Praef.), and how it has been received in the Church. Two interconnected themes trace out this vision: first, the reception and transmission of the text, not only of the ancient Scriptures but also of the apostolic witnesses of the one Gospel; and second, the receptive, transmitting nature of the Church, which receives that one Gospel and, like a nurturing mother, distributes it to her children.

The textual discussion comes first, attracting Irenaeus's direct attention from chapter 1 onward. He stresses that the Gospel was first preached orally, and only later written down, that it might become "the foundation and pillar of our faith" (see 1 Tim 3:15[9]). The Gospel has its ultimate source in Christ, the eternal Word, who reveals it to His apostles through word and experience; and this word and experience are the inheritance they pass on to their own successors. Thus, for Irenaeus, the oral origins of the Gospel are part and parcel of the common voice of the Church's true witness—for the four gospel accounts do not emerge out of independent textual or historical traditions, but out of the same, common oral preaching that was the product of the apostolic experience of Christ. So it is that, with respect to the written volumes of the evangelists, "all these have handed down to us that there is one God, the Creator of heaven and earth...and one Christ, God's Son" (3.1.2)—that is, they each proclaim that common foundation of the true faith that is Irenaeus's focus in this book.

In the same way, Irenaeus is keen to identify and stress the apostolic origins of each account of what he does not call "the four Gospels" (as we are wont to do today), but, rather, the "fourfold Gospel which is held together by the one Spirit" (3.11.8)—stressing its common and divinely united proclamation. He is not interested in these apostolic origins on grounds that apostolic "authority" is categorically distinct from the inspirational testimony of other writers or disciples of the Lord, but because such fourfold testimony, born of the apostolic experience—of Christ's life, the cross, the resurrection—is authentically an expression of the one Gospel that Christ Himself was and that He preached to those closest to Him. It is not a speculation or reflection—pious or otherwise. What is proclaimed is the experience of the living Lord, rather than the "wisdom" that each "discovers by himself" (see 3.2.1).

This emphasis grounds Irenaeus's extended treatment on the lineage of the fourfold Gospel currently in the Church's possession. Like many others of the early period, Irenaeus takes for granted a Matthean primacy, stating that Matthew first wrote in Hebrew. Mark is taken to have written down Peter's witness, and Luke Paul's; and John is said to have written the fourth testimony to the Gospel at "Ephesus of Asia." In our notes we trace out some of the chronological implications of Irenaeus's treatment of this lineage; but it is worth remembering at every point in the discussion that he is chiefly concerned with what this lineage has to say about the common witness of the fourfold testimony, grounded in apostolic experience. Considerations of precise chronologies, geographies, and so forth, while certainly attracting Irenaeus's interest (and sometimes giving rise to symbolic points of emphasis), are not his primary concern.

This stress on the apostolic origins as well as the uniform nature of the one Gospel, also drives Irenaeus to—famously—delineate for the first time a "closed canon" of four gospel texts (at 3.11.8). There are many practical reasons why Irenaeus would have felt compelled to produce a definitive and closed listing of Gospels for the Church (e.g., a response to Marcion, a general need to address the promulgation of new texts in the late second century), and we must not ignore these. However, Irenaeus also has theological motivations here. His parallelisms to the "four zones in the world in which we live, and four cardinal winds," together with "four pillars" that support this great foundation, have appeared unsatisfactory to some readers; yet Irenaeus's emphasis is on the universality of the fourfold Gospel, drawing from a series of examples the fact that this number, four, is indicative of a cosmic embrace of all creation. There are four directions, four winds; but there are also four faces in the scriptural vision of the creatures in Ezekiel 1:6–10, and these faces—lion, calf, man, and eagle—symbolize the four dimensions of Christ's nature that are brought out in the fourfold evangelical testimony: the lion (John), His powerful, sovereign, and kingly nature; the calf (Luke), His ministerial and priestly nature; the man (Matthew), His incarnate recapitulation; and the eagle (Mark), His spiritual anointing (3.11.8). There are also four principal covenants that God has made with the human race (with Adam, Noah, Moses, and the Gospel). But Irenaeus's *Demonstration* 34 reminds us that the chief fourfold image for the Christian is of Christ crucified: the four dimensions of the cross are symbolic of the Savior's embrace of all creation and history. So the delimited, closed, fourfold canon of the one Gospel, for all the practical reasons it was surely desirable in the period, stood on theological legs as well.

The Faith Ensured: The Succession of Apostolic Proclamation

A theme that had been stressed throughout Books 1 and 2 of the *AH* was that text, as a thing unto itself, is insufficient to right understanding. The Valentinians, like so many others, often use the same texts as the Christians Irenaeus represents (though at times they also introduce others), but from these they elicit quite different readings. So it is that, in Book 3, he wishes to stress that while the Scriptures and the fourfold Gospel may indeed be the perfect testimony to the true faith, they are so in their right proclamation and approach. Thus, the Gospel, which is the textual fruit of the apostolic experience of the crucified and risen Christ, is received into the communion of the faithful in the ongoing "tradition that derives from the apostles and is guarded in the Churches by the succession of presbyters" (3.2.2). The phrases "apostolic tradition," "tradition of the apostles," and similar terms are spackled throughout the book for precisely this reason. The tradition of the apostles is authentic encounter with the true Christ. It is not the embodiment of some set of doctrinal suppositions apart from the scriptural testimony embraced by the Church, a kind of "second authority"; rather, it is the very context of continued apostolic encounter—that the Christ met and known in the Scriptures, in the ecclesiastical worship and sacramental life of the Christians, remains one and the same with the true Christ known to the apostles, who have handed that experience down to future generations.

This emphasis in Irenaeus grounds a passage that has traditionally been one of the most disputed in his corpus: the succession list of bishops in Rome provided in 3.3.1–4. On grounds that "in a volume of this kind it would be too long to list the successions of all the Churches" (3.3.2), Irenaeus provides a listing of the bishops of Rome, from the Church's dual-apostolic founding (by Peter and Paul) through to the bishop current at the time of Book 3's composition, Eleutherus.[10] How one is to interpret Irenaeus's descriptions of the Roman Church as "the greatest and most ancient," as possessing "greater authority" (3.2.2), has been hotly contested in scholarship—usually with confessional bias barely (if at all) concealed in the treatments. In our notes we draw attention to a few points of clarification (e.g., that Irenaeus knew quite well that the Roman Church was not the "most ancient" in any chronological sense); but we have tried not to carry forward what has, at this stage in Irenaean scholarship, become a somewhat tired and rather fruitless debate.

Of a few things we can be certain. Irenaeus does not provide his succession list as an attempt at historical dating (and there are problems with the chronology implied in his listing, at the very least). Nor is Irenaeus interested in providing a listing to demonstrate (much less establish) an inheritance of power or authority. His interest is—as the positioning of the listing in the book makes quite clear—in demonstrating that the apostolic experience of Christ that grounds the right proclamation of the one Gospel is to be found today through the inheritance of the successive communion of presbyter-bishops. The succession list is fundamentally exegetical. It is, in its vertical dimension (of lineage back to the apostles) together with the horizontal (the common voices of all the Churches), the assurance of what Mary Ann Donovan called the "one right reading" of the scriptural Christ in the Church today. Only this makes sense of Irenaeus placing the succession list between his introduction to the harmony of truth in the fourfold Gospel in 3.1–2 and his actual treatment of Gospel testimony in 3.5 onward. It makes little sense to think that Irenaeus would here insert an otherwise disconnected treatise on ecclesiological authority and structure; and in fact Irenaeus expressly indicates that he is not doing so. The conclusion of the succession list is capstoned with the statement that "truth…can be obtained easily from the Church; for the apostles most abundantly placed in her, as in a rich receptacle, every thing that belongs to the truth, so that *every one who desires can take* from her *the drink of life*" (3.4.1; cf. Rev 22:17; John 7:37). He then goes on to stress that the succession list he has provided has a practical scriptural-exegetical purpose ("If there is a dispute about some small question, ought we not to have recourse to the most ancient Churches, in which the apostles had lived, and take from them what is certain and clear in regard to the question under discussion?"), and even to stress that if the apostles had not left any written documents as Scriptures, the Christian would still possess the tradition of their experience, enshrined in the Church, which would proclaim one and the same Gospel (cf. 3.4.1, 2).

Scholars will surely continue to debate the nature and merits of the Roman succession list in *AH* 3.3 for some time; but it is clear that, when one takes it as an integral part of the Gospel discussion of the book as a whole, and not as an extractable treatise on episcopal authority, its more authentic contours become clear.

Ecclesiology

The fact that the succession list of 3.3 is not an ecclesiological statement per se is not to say that Book 3 has nothing to say on matters ecclesiological. There are numerous statements on the nature of the Church that are important and revealing. We have already had occasion to mention Irenaeus's words in the preface, where he describes the Church in maternal terms as the one who "received [the living faith] from the apostles and distributes [it] to her children." She is also "a rich receptacle" into which the apostles placed "every thing that belongs to the truth," and the sole "entrance to life"

(3.4.1). She has been entrusted to the care of those whom the apostles raised up in their tradition (ibid.). She ensures that "the tradition that derives from the apostles is of such a nature in the Church and continues among us" (3.5.1), and indeed manifests this tradition of truth to the whole world (cf. 3.3.1). She has a practical dimension, which requires "administrating" by her bishops (see Irenaeus's description of Bishop Linus of Rome in 3.3.3); and through their testimony she speaks to her children (so the characterization of the Roman Church "writing a letter to the Corinthians" in the hand of Bishop Clement). She is of common and unified testimony everywhere, but there are hierarchies to her ordering and authority—so Irenaeus's famous (and famously disputed) statement that "with this [the Roman] Church, because of her greater authority, it is necessary that every Church, that is, the faithful who are everywhere, should agree, because in her the apostolic tradition has always been safeguarded by those who are everywhere" (3.3.2). Yet, once again, this "greater authority" is understood by Irenaeus not in political terms but in terms of the authentic manifestation of apostolic testimony to the scriptural Christ.

"One and the Same" Lord as God

It is this proclamation of the scriptural Christ that is at the heart of the book. Having set out the context by which the Gospel has been received, preserved, and handed down in the Churches, and having established the framework by which the faithful can be assured that she proclaims the right reading of that Gospel and all the Scriptures, Irenaeus stresses time and again that thus Christ is proclaimed without error; for the Church, having received the truth, does not hand out error, "nor would His disciples have named any other God or called any other Lord besides Him who is truly God and Lord of all" (3.5.1). Going through the fourfold Gospel in some detail, and relating its proclamations to the ancient Scriptures as well as the testimony of the apostles (in the Acts and other documents), Irenaeus traces out his foundational theme that "it is one and the same God and Father who was announced by the prophets, handed down by the Gospel" (3.10.6). The apostles only proclaim one as true Lord, and it is this Son, who is also God (and Irenaeus several times ascribes the title *Theos/Deus* directly to the Son). This Son reveals the Father, as well as the Spirit, and the Spirit makes Him known as true Lord and King, anointing Him for the redemptive work of salvation (cf. 3.8, 9). In the incarnation, passion, and resurrection there is definitively something new; but this newness in Christ is of His working within the economy in a new way, not of His being something different from what He has always been. "By these important testimonies, therefore, the Gospel shows that the God who spoke to the fathers is the one who made the law through Moses, through which law we know that He spoke to the fathers. This same God, by virtue of His great goodness, poured out upon us His mercy" (3.10.2)—namely, by "visiting us from on high" (see Luke 1:78) in the incarnation.

The Nature of the Incarnation

It can rightly be said that the second half of *AH* 3 concerns itself with what we might consider the implications of the incarnation, and Irenaeus speaks in detail about what is known of the one Son through the apostolic testimony born of the experience of His life and teaching, the cross, and the resurrection in glory.

That the Word of the Father who became flesh is one and the same with the Creator of the cosmos is a consistent refrain (see explicit discussions in 3.11; 3.16). As such, Irenaeus identifies in Him "two generations": He "possessed in Himself the generation from the most high Father" and "He experienced the noble birth from the Virgin" (3.19.2). This is important enough for Irenaeus to state it a second time: "So this Son of God, our Lord, was both the Word of the Father and the Son of Man. Since He had a human generation from Mary, who was of the human race and was herself a human being" (3.19.3). Irenaeus is not here speaking of a kind of christological chronology (i.e., that "before" the Son was generated of the Father, and "later" of the Virgin), but of a theology of the Son's truly redemptive incarnate life. The one encountered in the flesh is true Son of a true human woman, and the one thus encountered is eternal Son of the divine Father, one and the same Christ who thus makes the Father visible, humanly (3.19.1).

This Christ is also He who sends the Spirit, as proclaimed by Peter (3.12.1); but He sends the Spirit precisely because He has first been anointed by this selfsame Spirit of the Father (the theme of the whole of 3.17). "The Lord received this life as a gift from the Father, and He, by sending the Holy Spirit into the whole world, bestows it upon those who partake of Him" (3.17.2). So the Spirit and the Son, described elsewhere by Irenaeus as the two "hands" of the Father, are interconnected in the economy of redemption.[11] The Spirit descends upon the Son "when He had been made the Son of Man," and thus anoints the human Son with the Father's breath, which vivifies all human creatures from the first (cf. Gen 2:7). So the Spirit becomes accustomed, with Christ, "to dwell in the human race, and to rest among human beings, and to dwell in God's handiwork, thus fulfilling the Father's will in them and renewing them from their old selves for the newness of Christ" (3.17.1).

From 3.18.1 Irenaeus begins explicitly to reflect on the "why" of the incarnation—why the Son took human flesh and offered Himself at the cross. He had already emphasized (in 3.16.6–9) that this was to recapitulate and perfect the economy; and Irenaeus stresses here that He thus refashions humankind, which "had been dashed to pieces by its disobedience" and was unable to refashion itself (3.18.2). The Christ, truly passible in His humanity, is able to suffer the cross and the tomb and thus rise from the grave (3.18.3–6); and, so suffering as man in perfect obedience, He unites the suffering creature to the Father in the Spirit, causing him to participate anew in the divine life (3.18.7, 19.1). The abiding mercy of the Father is thus manifest (3.20.1–4), responding to the disaster of sin and transgression with the economy of self-sacrifice by which humanity may be restored in glory—and, "having been united with the Word of God and receiving adoption, might become a son of God" (3.19.1).

The Sign of the Virgin

A further central theme in Book 3 is that of "the sign of the Virgin" (3.21.1), which Irenaeus raises most expressly in chapters 21 and 22. Taking the authority of the Septuagintal testimony (see Isa 7:14) to Mary as παρθένος ("virgin") and not merely νεᾶνις ("maiden") as divinely assured (and so his accounting of the advent of the LXX in 3.21.2, 3), Irenaeus exegetes tremendous meaning from the various scriptural testimonies to her person. There is, first, the essential fact that from her the Son obtains genuine, true, and full humanity (cf. 3.21.5). This is followed by a reflection on Mary, who, by generating the Christ without husband, is thus literally the extension of "David's womb," an odd phrase found in Psalm 131(132):11 and which Irenaeus firmly believes was so uttered precisely to foretell the virgin birth (3.21.5). The "sign" of the Virgin is that of God's activity, that He effects the birth, "without a man producing it" (3.21.6)—thus affirming the truly divine nature of the human Son. Irenaeus further addresses the symbolism of the stone uncut by human hands (3.21.7; Dan 2:34, 45); the rod of Moses that became "enfleshed" (3.21.8; Exod 7:9–12); and he offers an extended treatment of the prophecy of Jeremias that the Messiah would be king, noting that Joseph, as a descendant of Jechonias (according to Matt 1:12), fell under the disinheritance of Jechonias and all his descendants (3.21.9; Jer 22:24, 25, 28–30; 43:30, 31 LXX). A son born of Mary by Joseph's paternity could thus not possibly be a true Messiah-King—further affirming the virgin birth.

Yet for all this, Irenaeus's real focus on the Virgin is theological. It is not merely that she is the fulfillment of prophecy and ensures the truly human reality of the Christ through her humanity, and His divinity through the miraculous virginal birth. More than this, she is actively engaged in the work of redemption of her Son. The Christ took from her the true likeness of the original handiwork, "that the same might be recapitulated, the likeness having been preserved" (3.21.10); and then, in likeness to the economy of that first fashioning, He lives out His perfect obedience to the Father in concert with her ready obedience to her Son. This leads Irenaeus into his detailed consideration of Mary as recapitulator of Eve, becoming "the cause of salvation for herself and the entire human race" (3.22.4), the one who unties the knot of disobedience by obedience.

The Eschatological Redemption of Adam

A final key theme in Book 3 is that salvation in Christ—fully an eschatological reality—extends cosmically across all creative history. Since the Word who is incarnate is the eternal Son, Creator God, His redemptive work is not restricted chronologically to those who encounter Him during or after His incarnate life. Christ, the new Adam, redeems the first Adam who had fallen in sin; for the whole economy of human existence constitutes His "coming to the lost sheep and making a recapitulation of so great an economy, and seeking out His handiwork" (3.23.1).

Chapter 23 in particular affords Irenaeus the opportunity to express a robust vision of the economic dimensions of the salvation offered in Christ, which sees all human history from Adam in terms of its central axis in Christ. God's cursing of the serpent and response to human sin prefigures His thwarting of sin yet redemption of the sinful creature (see 3.23.3); the comparison between Adam's response to his sin, and Cain's to his, foreshadows the healing nature of the New Adam's redemption (see 3.23.4, 5); etc. Even the expulsion from paradise and the new struggles to demarcate human existence after the transgression are tied intimately into the redemptive working of the Son, preparing humanity for its eventual regrafting into the life of the Father through His incarnation and the accustomization of the Spirit (see 3.23.6, 7; 3.13.6).

CONTENT OUTLINE

The above are the key themes in what is a densely packed and rich book. In order to provide the reader with a guide to how these fit together in the structure of Irenaeus's argument, as well as to identify the myriad other themes that emerge from the book, we provide the following outline of its contents.

3.Praef   Introduces the theme of Book 3: right proclamations from the Scriptures, to refute the wrong teachings of those groups described in *AH* 1–2, and the correct proclamation of the rule of faith, the "doctrine of God's son."

Reception of the apostolic Gospel

3.1   Gospel first preached orally, then handed down (*tradiderunt*, "traditioned") in the Scriptures, by the guidance of the Spirit. All four Gospel accounts are of apostolic origin.

3.2   Heretical variation: Truth not handed down through apostles, but delivered through a "living voice"; apostles and disciples mingled truth with remnants of the law; new groups have discovered the "hidden mystery."

Apostolic tradition through the succession of bishops

3.3.1   The Church throughout the world manifests the whole truth in the tradition of the apostles. The apostles left nothing hidden, but openly proclaimed all they had received.

The succession list of the Roman Church

3.3.2   Given space constraints, it is not possible to list the succession from the apostles of all the Churches; instead, that of the Church of Rome will be given. All Churches in Christendom agree in the faith with this Church.

3.3.3   The succession list of Rome, from Peter and Paul to Eleutherus, "the twelfth in line from the apostles" and pope contemporaneous with Irenaeus's writing.

3.3.4   Additional examples of apostolic succession: Polycarp; the Church in Ephesus.

The manner in which the truth is traditioned in apostolic succession

3.4   The apostles deposited in the Church, "as in a rich receptacle," the fullness of the truth; she is thus the sole entrance to true life. All disputes ought to have recourse to these centers of apostolic tradition, where the faith is preserved by the Spirit. Even the "barbarians" have come to believe rightly in Christ through the Spirit that preserves the truth found in the Church.

3.5   The apostles proclaimed the truth they had experienced and received; they did not accommodate themselves to the expectations or desires of their hearers. Proclamation of the truth, rather than error, is part of the healing ministry of the Church.

Scriptural refutations of various heretical points

3.6   The Scriptures only give the titles "God" and "Lord" to the true Creator and His Son. Various heretical misreadings of the Scriptures, which attempt to identify multiple beings called "Lord," are refuted. Irenaeus notes (3.6.3–5) that sometimes Scripture uses the title "Gods" with "a certain modification and indication" to refer to the children of God.

3.7   Paul's comment that "the God of this world has blinded the minds of unbelievers" (2 Cor 4:4) is misread by the heretics; the phrase must be read by transposing words, to reveal "the unbelievers of this world." Other examples of transposition in Paul are explored.

3.8.1   "You cannot serve God and mammon" (Matt 6:24) does
                not imply two Lords, as some of the heretics exegete it.

3.8.2, 3   Reference to the devil as "the strong man" is made rela-
                tive to humanity, not as indicating a being coeval in
                power to God. God created all things freely; expressions
                in Scripture use varying appellations to make pastoral
                points.

Specific teachings on God from the Gospel: Matthew

3.9.1   Matthew indicates that the Father of Jesus Christ is the
                same God that gave the promise to Abraham and sent
                John as forerunner.

3.9.2   The birth of Christ from David's lineage confirms the
                identity of God in the old and new covenants. The gifts
                of the magi symbolize the aspects of Jesus' person:
                myrrh for His sacrificial death, gold for His kingship,
                and frankincense for his divinity as God.

3.9.3   Jesus' baptism reveals His divinity and saving purpose;
                but it is not to be exegeted docetically or in a manner
                that separates Jesus and Christ. The prophets are called
                upon to show that the Spirit and Christ are united in
                mission and work.

Specific teachings on God from the Gospel: Luke and Mark

3.10.1, 2   The service of Zacharias in the temple, together with
                the commissioning of John the Baptist and the identity
                of the archangel Gabriel sent to the Virgin, confirm the
                identity of Jesus' Father with the God of Moses and the
                patriarchs.

3.10.3–6   Specific refutation of various heretical divisions of
                Christ and His Father from the Creator God of the old
                covenant, drawn from the prophecy of Zacharias; the
                angels' words to the shepherds regarding the city of
                David; the purification of Jesus in the temple; the
                prophetic words of Simeon and Anna; the testimony of
                the forerunner; and Christ's ascension to the Father.

Specific teachings on God from the Gospel: John

3.11.1   John, the author of the fourth Gospel account, specifically refutes the teachings of Cerinthus, the Nicolaitans, and others that the Father of Jesus and the Creator God are different divine beings. This is exegeted through a sustained focus by Irenaeus on the prologue to the Gospel.

3.11.2–4   The heretics ultimately deny any incarnational relation of God to creation, since they do not truly believe that "the Word became flesh" (John 1:14).

3.11.5, 6 Jesus' power over created elements (e.g., transforming the water into wine at Cana) reveals his identity as Creator Lord, the only-begotten of the Father.

The summary of the fourfold Gospel

3.11.7(a) The cardinal points of the fourfold Gospel: (1) one God is Maker of heaven and earth; (2) He was announced by the prophets; (3) He established the economy of the law through Moses; (4) He is the Father of the Lord Jesus Christ; (5) there is no other God besides Him.

3.11.7(b) The authority of this Gospel is so great that even the heretics do not dare abandon it, but instead manipulate it. Examples are given of the Ebionites, who use only one Gospel account (Matthew); Marcion, who alters another (Luke); and the followers of Valentinus, who incorrectly exegete John.

The necessity of the fourfold Gospel: a closed "canon" of four Gospel accounts

3.11.8, 9 It is not possible to have more, or less, than the four accounts of Matthew, Mark, Luke, and John. Their apostolic origin and authority (addressed in 3.1) are confirmed by symbolic, prophetic images: the four zones of the world; the four cardinal winds; the four pillars of the earth; the four faces of the animals seen in Ezekiel's vision. As these correlate to the "images of the dispensation of the Son of God," they demonstrate the whole of His being, as well as the catholic nature of the Gospel proclamation. Those who alter the Gospel by adding, removing, or changing the content of these books destroy the harmony and order arranged by God.

Teachings on God from the other apostles: from the Book of Acts

3.12.1   The pattern of "traditioning" the faith through apostolic succession is exemplified in the selection of a replacement for Judas; its sanctity is confirmed in the coming of the Spirit at Pentecost.

3.12.2–5   Peter's testimony that the blessing promised to the fathers was fulfilled in Jesus. Peter and John preached the same Gospel; theirs are the voices of the "Mother City," whose teaching, in fulfillment of the promises of the old covenant, predate heretical teachings and claims.

3.12.6–9   Claims that the apostles would only have been able or willing to teach belief in an old God are refuted. Multiple examples cited from the life of Peter, followed by examples from Philip and Paul.

3.12.10, 11 The martyrdom of Stephen, including his sermon, confirms that all the apostles announced one and the same God, who gave the promise to Abraham and fulfilled it in Christ.

3.12.12–15 Heretical concerns with divorcing the God of Jesus Christ from the Old Testament law are misguided.

It is not one apostle or another alone that taught the truth; the Gospel is found in the harmony of all

3.13   It was not Paul alone who possessed the truth, by virtue of receiving it through revelation.

3.14   This is proved through the example of Luke, Paul's companion, through whom alone many of the Gospel events are known. A long catalogue of such Luke-specific narratives is provided. The followers of Marcion and Valentinus are both berated for accepting only parts of Luke, but not the whole of the "complete [*perfecto*] Gospel."

3.15.1   Those who accept Paul cannot refuse to accept his testimony of Luke; and those who accept Luke's authority, cannot dismiss his words on Paul.

3.15.2, 3   It is the way of liars to distort the holistic testimony of the apostles. The heretics practice various types of scriptural subterfuge to promote their doctrines; nonetheless, the truth is simple and has been entrusted to children.

Jesus Christ is Himself the Word of God the Father

3.16.1   The Valentinians and others assert a multiplicity of "Saviors" and "Christs."

3.16.2   Exegesis from Matthew on "one and the same Christ Jesus," with a focus on the "human nature" of the Word through Mary.

3.16.3, 4   The same is attested in Paul, then Mark, then in Simeon and a multitude of other examples. Emphasis is placed on the human lineage of "one and the same Son" through David's line. Christ is the refreshment of the departed.

3.16.5, 6(a)   The crucifixion and resurrection confirm that the human Son is the divine Word, as anticipated by the Scriptures. Those who divide the Christ by forging multiple Saviors—such as the Valentinians and others mentioned—are antichrists.

Christ the Word is recapitulator of the economy

3.16.6(b)   The true Word has "grafted" Himself to humanity in the incarnation, recapitulating in Himself all things; so He is sovereign over heavenly as well as earthly realms.

3.16.7   All things are duly ordered and timed by the Father through the Son. The Virgin's eagerness at Cana is a lesson in accepting God's timing of the economy, as are various other testimonies from the Gospel.

3.16.8, 9   Those who divide the Christ are outside this economy; their teaching is homicidal. This is confirmed in the crucifixion and resurrection, as attested by Paul.

The Holy Spirit and the Son

3.17.1–3   It is not an aeonic power that descends on Jesus at His baptism, but the Holy Spirit. This Spirit becomes, with Christ, "accustomed to dwell in the human race" for its renewal. The Spirit is sent to all at Pentecost, "moistening" the soul for its growth as water from heaven, just as the body is washed in baptism (17.2). Christ receives this Spirit from the Father and sends it to the world (17.2). Humanity's need for the Spirit is prophesied in Gideon; humanity needs the Spirit so as to foster growth, and to have an Advocate in the face of the Accuser (Satan)—so Christ "entrusted his human nature to the Holy Spirit" (17.3).

3.17.4   The various heretics generally deny the place of the Spirit.

Why did the Word become man?

3.18.1   Christ's incarnation was not the beginning of the Word; He is eternal Son, always with the Father. The incarnation is the recapitulation of "the long unfolding of humankind," granting salvation through the restoration of being in the image and likeness, lost in Adam.

3.18.2   Humanity, "dashed to pieces" by disobedience, could not refashion itself; and the human race, dead in sin, could not receive salvation. So Christ accomplishes both in the incarnation: He lives as man to refashion obedience, and dies as man to conquer death and lift humanity up to new life.

The true sacrifice of the suffering Son

3.18.3–6   The impassible Word Himself suffers, having become passible in His anointed humanity. This is made clear by Paul as well as by the example of Peter's confession (see Matt 16:16). It is in this fact that Christ's exhortation for disciples to "take up their cross and follow Him" has meaning. So also the martyrs are "witnesses to the suffering Lord." Docetist claims deny the salvific work of the Son. In His obedience, suffering, death, and resurrection, Christ was "a man fighting for the fathers."

Union and participation

3.18.7   In the incarnation, Christ causes humans to "adhere to and be united with God." By this union, humanity partakes of imperishability and overcomes the enemy. The Son leads humankind back to friendship and concord with God. Humans can receive this "filial adoption" only by receiving participation in the Son—so Christ comes and lives through every age, uniting it to the Father in Himself. This the law alone could not accomplish; as humanity was bound to death, so death had to be overcome in a human being.

3.19.1   Those who assert that Jesus is "mere man" begotten of Joseph deny this economy and are not yet united to the Word of God, the "Word of imperishability" and freedom. Humans cannot receive imperishability and immortality unless they are united to imperishability and immortality; for this, the true Word had to unite Himself to man.

Christ's two generations ensure the power of His incarnate actions as salvific for all creation

3.19.2, 3   Christ has two "generations": His generation from the Father, and His generation from the Virgin. Thus Jesus Christ is at once man and Word. This gives His death and resurrection the power of new life for all humankind.

Why was God thus merciful toward humanity, which had been disobedient?

3.20.1, 2(a)   God has always been merciful to humankind's disobedience, for He has always foreseen the incarnation of His Word. This is typified in Jonas who, being swallowed up, yet secured the Ninevites' repentance. So humanity was swallowed up, that it might too receive salvation. As such, God allows humanity's long period of transgression, that the human race might learn by it of the greatness of God and his redemption.

3.20.2(b)   God manifests Himself in human persons, just as a physician proves himself among the sick—for God is the glory of humankind, and humankind is the vessel of His working.

3.20.3, 4   For this reason, many signs have been given in confirmation of the Word's coming among humanity. Chief among them is the "sign of the Virgin"; then also the prophets Isaias, Jeremias, Micah, Habakkuk, and others.

The sign of the Virgin

3.21.1   Continuing the above, the chief sign of the Lord's salva-
            tion is the Virgin; thus, those who interpret Isaias to read
            "a young girl" rather than "Virgin" distort the prophecy
            of the economy. This is confirmed by the reading of the
            "Jewish translation" into Greek (the LXX), made long
            before Christ's coming.

3.21.2, 3   A summary of the advent of the LXX under Ptolemy,
            proving its character and contents as divine in origin,
            translated "through the inspiration of God." With this
            translation—which proves the coming of God's Son—
            all the apostles agree; and the translation is in agree-
            ment with the apostolic tradition.

3.21.4–9   The prophets, in concert with the apostles, preached
            through them that the fullness of time for adoption had
            come. By the Holy Spirit, these clearly show that Christ's
            birth will be from a true virgin, and that by His birth
            from her He will be both God and man. Numerous
            examples are shown, to confirm such a virginal birth:

            • the prophecies of Isaias (21.5, 7)
            • the lineage of David (21.5, 6)
            • Daniel's vision of a stone uncut by human hands
              (21.7)
            • the casting of Moses' rod (21.8)
            • Jeremias's account of the disinheritance of
              Jechonias, who is Joseph's ancestor (21.9)

Proof through the recapitulative economy

3.21.10   As Adam was fashioned of "untilled earth," so Christ is
            born similarly, of a Virgin; thus He recapitulates the
            ancient economy fully in Himself.

3.22.1, 2   As such, Christ receives from the Virgin, just as Adam
            received attributes from the untilled soil. From Mary
            Christ receives true human nature, thus joining Himself
            truly to His creation. So He eats, sleeps, fasts, sorrows,
            and so on.

3.22.3, 4   The recapitulative nature of the economy confirms this.
            Christ joins the ends to the beginnings, Himself to Adam

as Mary to Eve. Thus Mary plays an active role in redemption, being a new "cord" untying the "knot" tied by Eve.

The ends united with the beginnings: recapitulation and the restoration of Adam

3.23.1, 2   Given that all have their heritage in Adam as one blood and race, it is fitting that the salvation of humanity should—and must—extend as far back as Adam himself.

3.23.3–5   In anticipation of the future salvation he would receive in Christ, Adam's acts in Eden foretell his repentance and renewal. Unlike Cain, who compounded his sin with a lie, Adam shows repentance after his transgression; this is demonstrated through his response to God, the casting of blame, and the sewing of "garments of repentance."

3.23.6–8   God's response to Adam's sin foretells the incarnation of His Word: He removes humanity from paradise as a sign of the end of the dominion of sin. He establishes the curse against the serpent, foretelling the coming of the Word who will trample him underfoot—again demonstrating the connection of the incarnation to the beginnings in Eden; as such, those who deny the salvation of Adam (e.g., Tatian) deny the true economy and the Scriptures.

Summarizing the faith: receiving the true knowledge of God

3.24.1   The above constitutes the core of the rule of truth, the "nature of our Lord and the economy which He made for the sake of His own human race." This faith is received from the Church and safeguarded; it is, by God's Spirit, a deposit received in a vessel that always rejuvenates itself and the vessel that contains it. The Church's faith is the "life-breath of the first-fashioned," which vivifies its members and grants imperishability through the communion of Christ.

3.24.2   Those who alienate themselves from this truth are tossed to and fro by their own minds, lacking a stable doctrine and always seeking what they never find. But in the truth, God comes within reach of humankind's knowledge through His love—not a knowledge that allows His full nature to be known, but one that enables true relation and adoption. The true God bestows such gifts on His creatures, unlike the Epicurean God, who bestows nothing on his followers.

3.25.2–5   The true God is both just and good: these are not traits to be held in opposition or opposed to one another, as is the case among Marcion's followers. By "dividing God in two" along these lines, Marcion "destroys God on both counts." On such men God's judgment will fall, since they have not received and lived according to the goodness of His gifts. Plato proves the truth, that in God justice and goodness abide together.

3.25.6, 7   Lamentation over the foolishness of Valentinian and other heretical "cogitations." Yet the aim of this exposure is the conversion of their followers to the true God, for "we love them more than they think they love themselves." Love grounded in truth is salvific; it has only to be accepted—"consequently, we shall not grow weary in trying with all our might to extend a hand to them."

ST. IRENAEUS OF LYONS
AGAINST THE HERESIES

BOOK 3

PREFACE

My dear friend, you had given us orders to bring to light the "secret"—or so they think—tenets of the Valentinians, to show, too, how varied they are, and to add a refutation of them. So, beginning with Simon, the father of all heretics, we undertook both to expose them and to disclose their teachings and successions, and to refute all of them.[1] To accomplish this, though their exposé and the refutation from many angles belong to one work, we have sent you several books.[2] The first of these contains all their tenets and shows up the practices and characteristics of their conduct. In the second book their wicked doctrines were refuted and overthrown; they were laid bare and shown for what they really are. Now, in this third book we shall adduce proofs from the Scriptures, that we may not fall short in regard to any of the things you had ordered us to do; and so that, over and above what you awaited, you may have from us the means for exposing and refuting all those who in any way propose wicked teachings. For the *charity which is in God*, being *rich and without envy*,[3] grants more than anyone asks of it.[4]

Therefore, recall what we said in the first two books; and if you add to them the following, you will have from us a most complete refutation of all the heresies, and you will resist them confidently and most insistently in favor of the only true and living faith, which the Church received from the apostles and distributes to her children.[5]

For the Lord of all things gave to His apostles the power of the Gospel, and through them we, too, know the truth, that is, the doctrine of God's Son.[6] To them the Lord also said, *He who hears you hears me; and he who despises you, despises me and Him who sent me.*[7]

CHAPTER 1

FROM WHOM AND HOW THE
CHURCH RECEIVED THE GOSPEL

1. In point of fact, we received the knowledge of the economy of our salvation through no others than those through whom the Gospel has come down to us. This Gospel they first preached orally, but later by God's will they handed it on [*tradiderunt*] to us in the Scriptures, so it would be *the foundation and pillar of our faith*.[1] We are not permitted to say that they preached before they had received "perfect knowledge," as some dare to state, boasting that they are the correctors of the apostles. For, after our Lord had risen from the dead, and they *were clothed with power from on high when the Holy Spirit came upon them*, they had full assurance concerning all things, and had "perfect knowledge."[2] Only then did *they go forth to the ends of the earth, bringing* us *the good news* about the blessings that were sent from God to us and *announcing* heavenly *peace to men*, inasmuch as they collectively, and each of them individually, equally possessed the Gospel of God.[3]

Matthew, accordingly, produced a writing of the Gospel among the Hebrews in their own language, whereas Peter and Paul evangelized at Rome and founded the Church [there].[4] But after their departure, Mark, Peter's disciple and translator, handed down to us in writing what was preached by Peter.[5] Luke too, Paul's follower, set down in a book the Gospel that was preached by Paul.[6] Later, John likewise, the Lord's disciple who had also *rested on His breast*, issued the Gospel while living at Ephesus of Asia.[7]

2. All these have handed down to us that there is one God, the Creator of heaven and earth, who had been announced by the Law and the Prophets; and one Christ, God's Son.[8] Whoever does not give assent to these things despises the Father and is self-condemned, for he resists and opposes his own salvation—which is precisely what is done by the heretics.[9]

CHAPTER 2
PROOF THAT THE HERETICS FOLLOW NEITHER THE SCRIPTURES NOR TRADITION

1. Indeed, when they are exposed by means of the Scriptures, they turn round and make accusations against the Scriptures themselves, as if these were not correct or were not authentic and stated things variously,[1] and that the truth cannot be found in them by those who are ignorant of tradition. They claim the truth was not handed down by writings, but by a living voice, of which matter Paul said, *Yet among the mature we do impart wisdom—although it is not the wisdom of this world.*[2] And each one of them claims as this wisdom that which he discovers by himself, which is really a fiction, so that their truth may fittingly be in Valentinus at one time, at another in Marcion, at another in Cerinthus, finally in Basilides, or even in one who disputes against these and would not be able to say anything pertaining to salvation.[3] For each one of them, being totally corrupt, is not ashamed to deprave the rule of truth and preach himself.

2. When, however, we refer them again to the tradition that derives from the apostles and is guarded in the Churches by the succession of the presbyters, they are opposed to tradition and claim that they are wiser not only than the presbyters but even than the apostles, and have found the unadulterated truth.[4] In fact, they maintain that the apostles mixed with the Savior's words matter from the law, and that not only the apostles but the Lord Himself gave discourses derived at times from the Demiurge, at others from the Intermediate Region, and at yet others from the Highest Authority. They, however, know the *hidden mystery* without doubt, admixture, or adulteration.[5] That, indeed, is a most impudent blasphemy against their Creator. The result is that they no longer agree with either the Scriptures or tradition.

3. It is against such adversaries, my dear friend, that we must fight. Like slippery serpents they try to escape on all sides. For that reason we must resist them from all sides, for perhaps by confounding them with such resistance we might be able to bring some of them to convert to the truth. If it is not easy for anyone to make a soul that is held captive by error to repent, still it is not altogether impossible for error to flee when it is brought face to face with the truth.[6]

CHAPTER 3

APOSTOLIC TRADITION THROUGH THE
SUCCESSION OF BISHOPS FROM THE APOSTLES

1. All, therefore, who wish to see the truth can view in the whole Church the tradition of the apostles that has been manifested in the whole world. Further, we are able to enumerate the bishops who were established in the Churches by the apostles, and their successions even to ourselves.[1] These neither taught nor knew anything similar to what [the heretics] senselessly prate about. For if the apostles had known of any hidden mysteries that they taught to the "perfect" separately and privately from the rest, they would most certainly have handed them down to those to whom they entrusted the Churches themselves. For they willed that the men whom they left behind as their successors and to whom they gave their own teaching office should be perfect and blameless in every respect,[2] because if these men would stay on the right path, it would be a great profit; but if they would fall, it would be the greatest calamity.

2. Since, however, in a volume of this kind it would be too long to list the successions of all the Churches, we shall here address the tradition of the greatest and most ancient Church, known to all, founded and built up at Rome by the two most glorious apostles, Peter and Paul[3]—the tradition received from the apostles, as well as *the faith proclaimed* to men,[4] which has come down even to us through the successions of the bishops. In this way we confound all those who in any way whatever, either because of an evil self-complacency, or of vainglory, or of blindness and evil-mindedness,[5] gather in unauthorized assemblies. For with this Church, because of her greater authority, it is necessary that every Church, that is, the faithful who are everywhere, should agree, because in her the apostolic tradition has always been safeguarded by those who are everywhere.[6]

3. The blessed apostles, therefore, having founded and built up the Church, handed over to Linus the bishopric for administrating the Church. In his epistle to Timothy, Paul mentions this Linus.[7] Anacletus succeeded him; after him, in third place from the apostles, Clement acquired the bishopric.[8] He both saw the blessed apostles themselves and conferred with them, and still had the preaching of the apostles ringing in his ears and their tradition before his eyes. In

this he was not alone, for there were many others still left at that time who had been taught by the apostles.

It was under this Clement that no small dissension arose among the brethren at Corinth. The Church of Rome wrote a very forceful letter to the Corinthians, [thus] uniting them in peace, renewing their faith, and proclaiming the tradition which it had but recently received from the apostles.[9] This tradition proclaims one God almighty, the Creator of heaven and earth, the Fashioner of man, who brought on the flood and called Abraham, who led the people out of the land of Egypt, who conversed with Moses, who gave the law and sent the prophets, who prepared the fire for the devil and his angels.[10] All who wish can learn from this letter [scriptura] that this Father of our Lord Jesus Christ is announced by the Churches, and can understand the apostolic tradition of the Church,[11] since this letter is older than these men who now teach falsely, lying about another god above the Demiurge and the Creator of all things that exist.

Evaristus succeeded this Clement, and Alexander [succeeded] Evaristus. Xystus was appointed sixth in line from the apostles, and after him Telesphorus, who was also a most glorious witness.[12] After him came Hyginus, then Pius, and after him Anicetus.[13] Soter succeeded Anicetus; and now Eleutherus, the twelfth in line from the apostles, holds the title of the bishopric.[14] By this order and succession, the tradition that is in the Church from the apostles and the preaching of the truth have come down to us. And this is the fullest proof that it is one and the same life-giving faith that has been preserved in the Church from the apostles until now, and has been handed down in truth.[15]

4. Polycarp, likewise, not only was taught by the apostles and conversed with many of those who saw our Lord but also was appointed bishop of the Church at Smyrna in Asia by the apostles.[16] We, too, saw him in our early age, for he lived on a long time, and departed this life as a very old man, having most gloriously and most nobly suffered martyrdom.[17] He always taught the things that he had learned from the apostles, which he also handed on to the Church and which alone are true.[18] Of this all the Churches in Asia bear witness, as well as the successors of Polycarp until the present day. Now this man is a much more trustworthy and reliable witness of the truth than Valentinus and Marcion and the rest of the evil-minded men.

He it is who, while sojourning in Rome under Anicetus,[19] converted many to the Church of God, away from the heretics previously mentioned. He preached that he had received this one and only truth from the apostles, which he also handed on to the Church.[20]

There are those who heard him say that when John the disciple of the Lord was at Ephesus and went to take a bath, on seeing Cerinthus there, he rushed out of the bathhouse without having bathed. "Let us flee," he explained, "lest even the bathhouse collapse because Cerinthus the enemy of the truth is in there."[21]

Polycarp himself, when Marcion met him on one occasion and said, "Recognize us!" gave this reply: "I do recognize you as the first-born of Satan."[22] Such is the great discretion had by the apostles and their disciples, that they did not communicate even verbally with any of those who had adulterated the truth. In this regard Paul said, *As for a man who is factious, after admonishing him once or twice, have nothing more to do with him, knowing that such a person is perverted and sinful; he is self-condemned.*[23]

There exists also a very forceful letter of Polycarp written to the Philippians. From it those who wish and are concerned about their salvation can learn both the standard of his faith and the preaching of the truth. Moreover, the Church at Ephesus, which was founded by Paul but in which John remained till the time of Trajan, is also a true witness of the tradition of the apostles.[24]

CHAPTER 4
THE TESTIMONY OF THOSE WHO SAW THE APOSTLES, ON THE PREACHING OF THE TRUTH

1. Since there are, then, such great proofs, it does not behoove to seek further among others for the truth, which can be obtained easily from the Church; for the apostles most abundantly placed in her, as in a rich receptacle, every thing that belongs to the truth, so that *every one who desires can take* from her *the drink of life.*[1] For she is the entrance to life; all others are thieves and robbers.[2] For this reason we ought to avoid them; on the other hand, we ought to love with the greatest diligence whatever pertains to the Church, and to lay hold of the tradition of the truth.

What then? If there is a dispute about some small question, ought we not to have recourse to the most ancient Churches, in which

the apostles had lived, and take from them what is certain and clear
in regard to the question under discussion? What if the apostles had
not left us the Scriptures; ought we not, then, to follow the disposition
of tradition, which they handed down to those to whom they
entrusted the Churches?[3]

2. To this disposition many nations of the barbarians who believe
in Christ give assent, having salvation *written in their hearts through the
Spirit, without paper and ink*, and guarding carefully the ancient tradition.[4] They believe, namely, in one God the Creator of heaven and
earth and of all things which are in them,[5] and [in] Christ Jesus the
Son of God, who, because of *His surpassing love* toward the creature
He fashioned, accepted to be born of the Virgin.[6] And so, by Himself
He united man with God, suffered under Pontius Pilate, rose again,
was taken up in glory and will come in glory as Savior of those who are
saved and as Judge of those who are judged, hurling into eternal fire
those who disfigure the truth and the condemners of His Father and
of His own coming. Those who believed this faith, without writings,
are barbarians with respect to their language; but as regards doctrine
and practices and conduct they are most wise and pleasing to God on
account of the faith, conducting themselves as they do in all justice
and chastity and wisdom.[7]

If anyone speaking in their language were to tell them about the
fictions of the heretics, they would immediately stop up their ears and
flee far away, tolerating not even to listen to such blasphemous discourse. So, because of the ancient tradition of the apostles, they do
not allow even in the thought of their minds any of these heretics'
monstrous assertions whatever. In fact, among them there has been
neither an assembly [of the heretics], nor any instruction in doctrine
[by the heretics].[8]

3. Before Valentinus, of course, the Valentinians did not exist;
and before Marcion, there were no Marcionites. And the rest of the
evil-minded heretics whom we mentioned above did not exist at all
before the originators and inventors of their perverse systems.
Valentinus, indeed, came to Rome under Hyginus; he flourished
under Pius, and spent his time there until Anicetus. Cerdon, too, who
was prior to Marcion, lived under Hyginus, the eighth bishop.[9] He
came into the Church and made a confession, but continued on in
this wise: sometimes he taught in secret, then again made a confession. Finally he was exposed concerning what he was teaching falsely,

and he apostatized from the assembly of the brothers.[10] Marcion, who succeeded him, flourished under Anicetus, who was the tenth bishop.[11] The rest of the heretics who are called Gnostics[12] took their beginning from Menander, a disciple of Simon, as we have shown.[13] Each one of them became the father and pontiff of the doctrine that he espoused. But all of these appeared with their rebellion much later, namely, when the Church was already in the midst of its age.[14]

CHAPTER 5

BOTH CHRIST AND THE APOSTLES PRESENTED DOCTRINES IN TRUTH AND DID NOT ACCOMMODATE THEMSELVES TO THE VIEWS OF THEIR HEARERS

1. Since, therefore, the tradition that derives from the apostles is of such nature in the Church and continues among us, let us return to the proof from the Scriptures of the apostles, of those who wrote the Gospel. These wrote down the doctrine about God, proving that our Lord Jesus Christ is *the truth* and that *there is no deceit* in Him.[1] Just as David, too, prophesied His birth from the Virgin and His resurrection from the dead when he said, *Truth will spring up out of the ground.*[2] The apostles, being disciples of truth, are beyond all lying; for *a lie has no fellowship with the truth,* just as *darkness has no fellowship with light.*[3] [On the contrary,] the presence of the one excludes the other. Since, then, our Lord is the truth, He never told a lie. And so the one He knew to be the offspring of Degeneracy, He would certainly never have acknowledged as God, or as the God of all things, or the supreme King and His own Father. The Perfect [would] not [have confessed Himself to be] imperfect; nor the Spiritual, ensouled [*animalem*]; nor He who is in the Fullness [*Pleroma*], one who is outside of it. Nor would His disciples have named any other God or called any other Lord besides Him who is truly God and Lord of all, as these heretics who are most senseless sophists do, claiming that the apostles hypocritically fabricated their doctrine according to the capacity [to hear] and the answers expected by their questioners, blabbering blind things to the blind according to their blindness, to the weak according to their weakness, to the erroneous according to their error. Similarly, to those who thought that the Demiurge is the only

God, they announced him; to those who pondered the unnamable Father, they made the unutterable mystery [utterable] by parables and enigmas,[4] with the result that the Lord and the apostles would have enunciated doctrine not in keeping with the truth itself, but hypocritically and according as each hearer was able to grasp it.

2. That is, however, not the way of men who heal and give life, but of such as make [others] more sick and increase their ignorance. For such the law will be found very true, which pronounces accursed everyone who leads a blind man on the way astray.[5] For the apostles who were sent to search out these who had gone astray, to give sight to those who had lost their sight, to bring medicine to those who were ill, did, of course, not speak with them according to their opinion at that time, but according to the manifestation of the truth. For persons would not be doing the right thing, if they were to advise blind people who are about to fall over a precipice to keep on that most dangerous path, as if it were indeed the right path and they would happily come to their destination. What doctor who wishes to cure a sick person will act according to the desires of the sick person and not according to what is in keeping with medical science [*quod aptum est medicinae*]? But that the Lord came as Physician for those who were ill, He Himself testifies: *Those who are well have no need of a physician, but those who are sick. I have not come to call the righteous, but sinners to repentance.*[6] How, then, will the sick become strong, and how will the sinners repent? Is it by continuing in the very same things; or, on the contrary, by undergoing a great change and transformation of their former mode of living, by which they brought on themselves both a sickness that was not slight, and many sins? Ignorance, the mother of all these things, is driven out by knowledge. Therefore, the Lord brought knowledge to His disciples, by which He both cured the ailing and forced sinners away from sin. So He did not speak to them according to their former opinion, nor did He answer them according to the answers expected by the questioners, but according to the salutary doctrine, without hypocrisy or partiality.[7]

3. This is proved, likewise, from the Lord's discourses. He revealed the Son of God to those of the circumcision; the Christ, namely, who had been foretold by the prophets. That is, He manifested Himself as the one who would restore liberty to men, who would bestow on them the inheritance of incorruption.[8] The apostles, in turn, taught the Gentiles to forsake their empty woods and stones,

which they imagined were gods, and to worship the true God who established and made the entire human race, and by means of His creation nourished, increased and strengthened them, and bestowed on them existence.[9] [They also taught them] to await His Son, Jesus Christ, who *by His blood redeemed us* from the Rebellion [*Apostasia*], that we might be *a sanctified people*,[10] and that He would descend from heaven by the power of the Father and would also judge all people, and those who kept His precepts He would reward with God's blessings.[11] This [Christ] appeared in the last times as *the chief cornerstone* and gathered into one and united those *who were afar off with those who were near*, that is, the uncircumcised with the circumcised;[12] thus He *enlarged Japhet*, and established him *in the house of Sem.*[13]

CHAPTER 6

PROOF THAT IN THE SCRIPTURES NO ONE ELSE IS CALLED GOD AND LORD BUT THE ONLY TRUE GOD AND HIS WORD

1. Therefore, neither the Lord, nor the Holy Spirit, nor the apostles would precisely and absolutely ever have named "God" one who is not God, unless He truly was God. Nor would they, in their own name,[1] have called anyone Lord except God the Father who has dominion over all things, and His Son who received from His Father power over all creation,[2] as is expressed in this passage: *The Lord said to my Lord, sit at my right hand, until I make your enemies your footstool.*[3] This shows the Father speaking to the Son, who gave to Him the inheritance of the Gentiles and subjected to Him all enemies.[4] Since, therefore, the Father is truly Lord, and the Son truly Lord, the Holy Spirit deservedly designated them by the title "Lord." Again, in regard to the destruction of the Sodomites, Scripture says, *Then the Lord rained on Sodom and Gomorrha brimstone and fire from the Lord out of heaven.*[5] Here He points out that the Son, who also spoke to Abraham, had received power from the Father to condemn the Sodomites because of their wickedness.[6] The same is contained in this passage: *Your throne, O God, is forever; the scepter of Your kingdom is a scepter of equity. You have loved righteousness and hated wickedness; therefore, God, your God, has anointed you.*[7] The Spirit designates both of them by the title

"God": the Son who is anointed and the Father who anoints. Again, *God has taken His place in the council of the gods, and in the midst of the gods He holds judgment.*[8] He is speaking of the Father and the Son, and of those who received the filial adoption;[9] these, however, are the Church [*Ecclesia*], for she is God's assembly [*synagoga*], which God, that is, the Son, assembled by Himself. Of Him [the Spirit] also says, *The God of gods, the Lord has spoken, and He has summoned* the earth.[10] Which God? The one of whom He said, *God will come manifestly, yea our God, and He will not keep silence.*[11] This is the Son, who came to men by a manifestation of Himself. He it is who said, *I have shown myself to those who did not seek for me.*[12] Of what gods [is He God]? Of those of whom He said, *I have said, "You are gods, sons of the Most High."*[13] Of those, namely, who have received the grace of filial adoption, by virtue of which we cry, *Abba, Father.*[14]

2. So, as I have already stated, no one else is named God or called Lord except the God and Lord of all things, who also said to Moses, *I am who am.* And, *Thus you will say to the people of Israel: "He who is sent me to you."*[15] It is of Him that Jesus Christ our Lord is Son, who makes those *who believe in His name children of God.*[16] Again, the Son said to Moses, *I have come down to deliver this people,*[17] for He it is *who descended* and *ascended* for the salvation of men.[18] And so *He who is* was manifested as God by the Son of God, who is in the Father and has in Himself the Father.[19] The Father testifies to the Son and the Son announces the Father.[20] Also Isaias says, *And I am the witness, says the Lord God, and my servant whom I have chosen, that you may know and believe, and understand that I am He.*[21]

3. When, however, Scripture calls those gods who really are not, it does not, as I have already noted, present them as gods absolutely, but with certain modification and indication by which they are shown not to be gods. Thus does David say, *The gods of the nations are idols of the demons.*[22] And, *You shall not bow down to foreign gods.*[23] By the fact that he speaks of "gods of the nations," but the nations do not know the true God, and by the fact that he calls them "foreign gods," he excludes them from being [real] gods. But he, in his own name, tells us also what they are; for they are *idols of demons,* as he says. Isaias, too, excluded them from being gods: *Let all be put to shame who fashion a god and carve useless things, even I am witness says the Lord.*[24] He merely uses the name so that we might know of whom he speaks. Jeremias said the same thing. *The gods,* he said, *who did not make the heavens and the earth*

perish from the earth which is under the heavens.[25] By the fact that he added their ruin, he showed that they are not gods. Elias, also, having called all Israel to Mount Carmel and wishing to turn them from idolatry, said to them, *How long will you go limping with both hocks? There is one Lord God. Follow Him.*[26] Again at the [offering of] the holocaust, he spoke thus to the priests of the idols, *You shall call upon the name of your gods, and I will call upon the name of the Lord my God; and the God who hears today, He is God.*[27] By the fact that the prophet spoke these things he proved that they who were considered gods among them are not gods. Moreover, he turned them to the God in whom he believed and who truly is God, to whom he cried with this invocation, *O Lord, God of Abraham, God of Isaac, and God of Jacob, hear me today; and let all this people understand that You are the God of Israel.*[28]

4. Therefore, I too call upon You, *O Lord, God of Abraham, and God of Isaac and God of Jacob and Israel,* who are the Father of our Lord Jesus Christ, the God who because of the multitude of Your mercies has shown Your good pleasure toward us that we might know You; who made heaven and earth, who has dominion over all things; who are the only true God, above whom there is no other God. Through our Lord Jesus Christ grant the gift of the Holy Spirit;[29] and grant that everyone who reads this writing [*scripturam*[30]] may know You, that You alone are God, and may be strengthened in You, and may separate himself from every heretical, godless, and impious doctrine.[31]

5. Likewise, when the apostle Paul said, *Formerly...you were in bondage to beings that by nature were not gods; but now that you have come to know God,*[32] he separated those who were not [gods] from Him who is God. Again, when he said of the Antichrist, *who opposes and exalts himself against every so-called god, or object of worship,*[33] he pointed out those who are called gods, that is, idols, by those who are ignorant of God. To be sure, the Father of all things is called God, and that He is; and the Antichrist does not exalt himself above Him, but above those who are called gods but really are not. That this is true, Paul himself declares: *We know that an idol has no real existence, and that there is no God but one. For although there may be so-called gods in heaven or on earth...yet for us there is one God, the Father, from whom are all things, and for whom we exist; and one Lord, Jesus Christ, through whom are all things, and through whom we exist.*[34] He distinguished and separated those who are called gods, but really are not, from the one God the Father, from whom are all things, and he, in his own name, most firmly acknowledged the

one Lord Jesus Christ. In the clause *in heaven or on earth,* he does not speak of the makers of the world as these [heretics] explain. Rather, it is similar to what Moses said, *You shall not make to yourself a graven image of God, or any likeness of anything that is in heaven above or that is on earth beneath, or that is in the water under the earth.*[35] What the things in heaven are, he himself expounds, *Lest you lift up your eyes to heaven and when you see the sun and the moon and all the stars and all the hosts of heaven, you be drawn away and worship them and serve them.*[36] Even Moses himself, being a man of God, was presented to Pharaoh as a god.[37] But he was called neither Lord nor God by the prophets in the true sense of these terms, but he is called by the Spirit *faithful Moses, the minister and servant of God,*[38] and this he was indeed.

Chapter 7

What Is It That Paul Is Saying: "In Their Case, the God of This World Has Blinded the Minds of Unbelievers"?

1. They maintain that in his second letter to the Corinthians, Paul said openly, *In their case, the God of this world has blinded the minds of unbelievers,*[1] and therefore they claim that there is one God "of this world" and another who is above every dominion and principality and power.[2] But we are not at fault if these men, who assert that they know the mysteries which are above God, do not even know how to read Paul. For, in keeping with Paul's style, which makes use of transpositions [*hyperbatis*] as we have shown elsewhere by many examples, if any one reads it thus: *In their case, God,* and then puts punctuation and a slight pause, and reads the rest together, *of this world has blinded the minds of the unbelievers,* he will find the true sense. [The passage] would read thus: *God has blinded the minds of the unbelievers of this world.*[3] That is shown by distinguishing the phrases. For Paul is not speaking of *the God of this world,* as if he knew of some other above Him. God he acknowledges as God. But he does say that *the unbelievers of this world will not inherit the coming world of incorruption.*[4] But how *God has blinded the minds of unbelievers* we will demonstrate from Paul himself, as our study proceeds, so that we do not have to digress from our present topic too much.

2. From many other examples we can discover that the apostle frequently uses a transposed order of words because of the speed of his speech and the impulse of the Spirit that is in him. For example, in his letter to the Galatians he said, *Why then was the law of works? It was added...until the offspring should come to whom the promise had been made; it was ordained by angels through an intermediary.*[5] The order of the words is [properly] this: "Why then was the law of works?...It was ordained by angels, and was added through an intermediary, until the offspring should come to whom the promise had been made." Thus man asks the question, and the Spirit gives the answer.

Likewise, in his second letter to the Thessalonians, speaking of the Antichrist, he said, *And the lawless one will be revealed, and the Lord Jesus will slay him with the breath of His mouth, and destroy him by His appearing and His coming,...whose coming by the activity of Satan will be with all power and pretended signs and wonders.*[6] Here the order of the words should be: "And then the lawless one will be revealed..., whose coming, by the activity of Satan, will be with all power and pretended signs and wonders, and the Lord Jesus will slay him with the breath of His mouth, and destroy him with His appearing." Certainly, he does not say that the coming of the Lord will be by the activity of Satan, but the coming of the lawless one, whom we also call the Antichrist. So if one would not pay attention to the reading and indicate the breathing pause in that which is read, there would not only arise incongruences, but the reader would even blaspheme by saying the coming of the Lord will be by the activity of Satan. So, in such passages it is necessary to show the transposition by the [manner of] reading and preserve the logical meaning of the apostle. Consequently, in that passage above, we do not read about the God of this world, but about God, whom we truly call God. We will, however, hear about the unbelievers and blinded men of this world, that they will not inherit the future world of life.

CHAPTER 8
WHAT IS MAMMON? (MATTHEW 6:24)

1. So through the shattering of this calumny of theirs, it has been clearly shown that neither the prophets nor the apostles ever named any other God, or called any other Lord, except the true and

only God. Much less did the Lord Himself. He ordered *to render to Caesar the things that are Caesar's, and to God the things that are God's.*[1] Caesar He named Caesar, and God He acknowledged as God. Along the same line is this: *No one can serve two masters.* This is interpreted by Him when he says, *You cannot serve God and mammon.*[2] He acknowledged God as God, and He named that mammon which actually is such. He does not call mammon Lord when He says, *No one can serve two masters* [κυρίοις, lords]; but He teaches the disciples who serve God not to be subject to mammon or to be under its dominion. For He says, *Whoever commits sin, is the slave of sin.*[3] Therefore, just as He calls those who serve sin slaves of sin, but does not for that reason call sin itself Lord, so also those who serve mammon He calls the slaves of mammon, but does not call mammon Lord. The fact is that mammon, according to the Jewish language, which the Samaritans also use, is an avaricious person: one who desires more than he ought to have. But according to the Hebrew language with a suffix it is Mamuel, and means a gluttonous person, that is, one who cannot refrain from gluttony.[4] According to both of these meanings, then, one cannot serve God and mammon.

2. To continue, when the Lord spoke of the devil as the *strong man*, [He did] not [point him out as the strong man] in an absolute sense, but relative to us; whereas He did point out Himself as the strong man truly in every respect. He said, *In no other way can one plunder the goods of the strong man, unless he first binds the strong man…and then plunders his house.*[5] But we were his goods and his house when we were in rebellion, and really, the devil used us as he willed, and the unclean spirit dwelt in us. He was, indeed, not strong against Him who bound him and plundered his house, but against those men who were under his command, inasmuch as he had turned their mind away from God. These the Lord delivered. Jeremias says as much: *The Lord has ransomed Jacob, and has redeemed him from hands too strong for him.*[6] If, therefore, He had not pointed out him who binds and plunders his goods, but had only spoken of the strong man, then this would be an unconquered strong man. But He did add that it is the one who overcomes. For he who binds overcomes, while he who is bound is overcome. This He did without comparison, so that [the devil], rebel slave that he is, would not be compared to the Lord. For not only he, but none of the things that have been created and are in subjection can be compared

to the Word of God, *by whom all things have been made*, who is our Lord Jesus Christ.[7]

3. That all things, whether angels or archangels or thrones or dominions,[8] were established and created by God who is above all things, through His Word, has been pointed out by John. When he had said that the Word of God was in the Father,[9] he added, *All things were made through Him, and without Him was not any thing made.*[10] David too, when he enumerated his praises, mentioning by name all the things of which we have spoken, both the heavens and all their powers, added, *For He commanded and they were created; He spoke and they were made.*[11] Whom, then, did He command? The Word, no doubt, *by which,* he said, *the heavens were established and all their host by the breath of His mouth.*[12] That He made all things freely and just as He willed, David tells us, *But our God is in the heavens above and on the earth, He has made all things whatsoever He willed.*[13] But the things that were established are distinct from Him who established them; and the things that were created, from Him who created them. For He Himself is uncreated, without beginning and without end, in need of no one, self-sufficient, bestowing existence on all the rest. But the things made by Him have a beginning; and all things that have a beginning are also liable to dissolution, and are subject to, and in need of, Him who made them.[14] So it is necessary that these things have a different appellation among those who have even a modicum of sense for distinguishing such matters, so that He who made all things, together with His Word, is rightly called God and only Lord; but the things that were made are no longer able to share in that appellation, nor may they properly take the title that belongs to the Creator.

CHAPTER 9

THE TEACHING ABOUT GOD FROM THE APOSTLES WHO GAVE US THE GOSPEL, AND IN PARTICULAR MATTHEW'S WITNESS

1. We have, therefore, clearly demonstrated—and we shall demonstrate still more clearly—that neither the prophets nor the apostles nor Christ the Lord in His own name acknowledged any other as Lord or God but the one who is preeminently God and Lord.

The prophets and apostles acknowledged the Father and the Son, but no one else did they name God or acknowledge as Lord. The Lord Himself handed down to the disciples only the Father as God and Lord, who alone is God and Sovereign of all things. So, if we are truly their disciples, we must follow their testimonies, which are as follows.[1]

Matthew the apostle, for his part, acknowledged one and the same God, who had given the promise to Abraham that He would make his posterity as the stars of heaven;[2] and who through His Son Christ Jesus called us from the worship of stones to a knowledge of Himself, so that *those who were not a people* might be *a people;* and she who was *not loved* might *be loved.*[3] Matthew said that John, when preparing the way for Christ for those who boasted of carnal kinship but who had a capricious mind[4] filled with every evil, announced a repentance that would recall them from wickedness. He exclaimed, *You brood of vipers! Who has warned you to flee from the wrath to come? Bear fruit that befits repentance, and do not presume to say to yourselves, "We have Abraham as our Father"; for I tell you, God is able from these stones to raise up children to Abraham.*[5] So he preached a repentance that would be [a turning] from wickedness; but he, the Forerunner of Christ, did not proclaim another God apart from the one who made the promise to Abraham. Of him Matthew, and Luke too, said, *For this is he who was spoken of by the Lord through the prophet: "The voice of one crying in the wilderness, prepare the way of the Lord, make straight the paths of our God. Every valley shall be filled and every mountain and hill shall be brought low, and the crooked shall be made straight, and the rough ways shall be made smooth; and all flesh shall see the salvation of God."*[6]

There is therefore one and the same God, the Father of our Lord, who also promised through the prophets to send the Forerunner. His salvation, that is, His Word, He made visible to all flesh, Himself becoming incarnate, in order that their king might become visible in all things.[7] For it is necessary that those who are judged should see their Judge and should know Him by whom they are to be judged; and it is proper that those who obtain glory should know Him who bestows on them the gift of glory.[8]

2. Again, when Matthew spoke of the angel, he said, *An angel of the Lord appeared to Joseph in a dream.*[9] Of what Lord? He himself tells us, *This was to fulfill what the Lord had spoken by the prophet....Out of Egypt I have called my Son. Behold, a Virgin shall conceive and bear a son, and His name shall be called Emmanuel, which means, God with us.*[10] Of this

Emmanuel who was born of a Virgin, David said, *Do not turn away Your face from Your Anointed One* [*Christi*/τοῦ χριστοῦ]. *The Lord swore to David a sure oath, from which He will not turn back: "Of the fruit of your womb I will set you upon my throne."*[11] And again, *In Judah God is known...and His abode has been established in peace* [Salem], *and His dwelling in Sion.*[12] So there is one and the same God who was proclaimed by the prophets and announced by the Gospel, and there is His Son who was born *from the fruit of the womb of David,* that is, from the Virgin of David's [lineage], who is Emmanuel. About His star, Balaam prophesied thus, *A star shall come forth out of Jacob, and a leader shall rise in Israel.*[13] But Matthew says that the magi, on coming from the East, exclaimed, *For we have seen His star in the East, and have come to worship Him,*[14] and that, having been led by the star into the house of Jacob to Emmanuel, they showed, by the gifts they offered, who it was that was worshiped: *myrrh,* because it was He who would die for the mortal human race and be buried; *gold,* because He was the King *of whose kingdom there is no end;*[15] and *frankincense,* because He was God, who was also *made known in Judah*[16] and appeared to those who *did not seek Him.*[17]

3. Furthermore, in regard to His baptism Matthew said, *The heavens were opened, and he saw the Spirit of the God descending like a dove and alighting upon Him; and lo, a voice from heaven saying, "This is my beloved Son, with whom I am well pleased."*[18] For it was not then that the Christ descended into Jesus; nor is Christ one person and Jesus another.[19] The Word of God, who is the Savior of all and the Sovereign of heaven and earth, who is Jesus, as we have shown before, who also assumed flesh and was anointed by the Spirit [sent] from the Father, is become Jesus Christ. To this Isaias, on his part, testifies: *There shall come forth a shoot from the stump of Jesse, and a branch shall grow out of his roots. And the Spirit of the Lord shall rest upon Him; the Spirit of wisdom and understanding, the Spirit of counsel and might, the Spirit of knowledge and godliness; and He shall be filled with the Spirit and the fear of God. He shall not judge according to appearance, nor condemn according to hearsay; but He will render justice to the poor, and convict the haughty of the earth.*[20] Again, Isaias, pointing out beforehand His anointing and the reason for the anointing, said, *The Spirit of the Lord is upon me, because the Lord has anointed me to bring good tidings to the poor. He has sent me to bind up the brokenhearted, and to proclaim liberty to the captives,...and sight to the blind, and to proclaim the year of the Lord's favor, and the day of vengeance,...to comfort all who mourn.*[21] For the Spirit of God rested upon the Word of God, and He

[the Word] was anointed to announce the Gospel to the poor, inasmuch as He was man from the *stump of Jesse,* and the son of Abraham.[22] However, inasmuch as He was God He did *not judge according to appearance,* nor did He *judge according to hearsay,* because *He needed no one to bear witness of man, for He Himself knew what was in man.*[23] But He did console all those who were mourning, and He granted remission to those who had been led into captivity through their sins, and loosed them from their fetters. Of these Solomon said, *Each one is bound fast by the ropes of his own sins.*[24] So the Spirit of God descended upon Him, the Spirit of Him who through the prophets had promised that He would anoint Him, that we might be saved by receiving from the abundance of His anointing. Thus far Matthew.

CHAPTER 10

WITNESS FROM LUKE AND MARK

1. Luke, the follower and disciple of the apostles, related about Zacharias and Elizabeth, from whom John was born according to God's promise. He said, *They were both righteous before God, walking in all the commandments and ordinances of the Lord blameless.*[1] He also said of Zacharias, *Now while he was serving as priest before God when his division was on duty, according to the custom of the priesthood, it fell to him by lot to enter the temple of the Lord and burn incense.*[2] So he went to offer the sacrifice, entering into the temple of the Lord. Thus, standing in the presence of the Lord, he simply, absolutely, firmly and in his own name acknowledged as God and Lord Him who chose Jerusalem and gave the law of the priesthood, to whom also the angel Gabriel belongs. Really, he knew of none other besides this one. To be sure, if he had had knowledge of some more perfect God and Lord than this one, he would certainly not have acknowledged this one absolutely and entirely as the Lord and God, if he had known Him to be the fruit of Degeneracy, as we have shown before.

Moreover, speaking of John he said, *For he will be great before the Lord…and he will turn many of the sons of Israel to the Lord their God, and he will go before Him in the spirit and power of Elias, to make ready for the Lord a perfect people.*[3] For whom, then, did he make ready the people, and in the presence of what Lord was he made great? Of Him, by all means, who said John had something even *more than a prophet,* and *no one born of a woman was greater* than John the Baptist.[4] He made the people ready for the Lord's coming by announcing it beforehand to his fellow servants and preaching to them repentance, so that they might receive remission from the Lord when He would be present, upon turning to Him from whom they had been alienated because of sins and transgressions. Of this David, for his part, said, *The wicked go astray from the womb, they err from their birth.*[5] For this reason, by turning them to their Lord, he made ready for the Lord a perfect people, in the spirit and power of Elias.[6]

2. Again, speaking about the angel, [Luke] said, *At that time the angel Gabriel was sent from God...*who said *to the Virgin...Do not be afraid, Mary, for you have found favor with God.* And of the Lord he says, *He will be great, and will be called the Son of the Most High, and the Lord God will give to Him the throne of His father David, and He will reign over the house of Jacob forever; and of His kingdom there will be no end.*[7] But who else is there that *reigns over the house of Jacob* without intermission *forever,* except Christ Jesus our Lord, *the Son of* God *the Most High,* who through the Law and the Prophets promised that He would make His salvation visible to all mankind,[8] that He might become the Son of Man, in order that man in turn might become a son of God?[9] On this account Mary, too, was exultant, and she prophesied in the name of the Church as she proclaimed aloud, *My soul magnifies the Lord, and my spirit rejoices in God my Savior....For He has helped His servant Israel in remembrance of His mercy, as He spoke to our father Abraham and to his posterity forever.*[10]

By these important testimonies, therefore, the Gospel shows that the God who spoke to the fathers is the one who made the law through Moses, through which law we know that He spoke to the fathers. This same God, by virtue of His great goodness, poured out upon us His mercy: *In that mercy the Orient visited us from on high, and shone upon those who were sitting in the darkness and in the shadow of death, and He guided our feet in the way of peace.*[11] In like manner, Zacharias, when he ceased being dumb—which he had suffered on account of his unbelief—was filled with a new spirit and blessed God in a new manner.[12] Really, all things were present in a new manner when the Word arranged His coming in the flesh, so that He might make into God's possession that human nature [*hominem*/ἄνθρωπον) which had gone astray from God. For this reason [man] was likewise taught to worship God in a new manner, but not another God, since there is one God who *justifies the circumcised on the ground of their faith, and the uncircumcised because of their faith.*[13]

3. Moreover, Zacharias, prophesying, exclaimed, *Blessed be the Lord God of Israel, for He has visited and redeemed His people, and has raised up a horn of salvation for us, in the house of His servant David, as He spoke through the mouth of His holy prophets from of old, that we should be saved from our enemies, and from the hand of all who hate us; to perform the mercy promised to our fathers, and to remember His holy covenant, the oath which He swore to our father Abraham, to grant us that we, being delivered from the hand of our enemies, might serve Him without fear, in holiness and righteousness before Him in all our days.*[14] Then he addresses John: *And you, child, will be called the prophet of the Most High; for you will go before the face of the Lord to prepare His ways, to give knowledge of salvation to His people, in the forgiveness of their sins.*[15] For *the knowledge of salvation* which was wanting to them was that of God's Son, which John gave them when he said, *Behold the Lamb of God, who takes away the sin of the world. This is He of whom I said, "After me comes a man who ranks before me, for He was before me,* and *from His fullness have we all received."*[16] So this is *the knowledge of salvation.* But there is no other God, nor another Father, nor Profundity [*Bythos*], nor Fullness [*Pleroma*] of thirty Aeons, nor Mother called Ogdoad.[17] No, *the knowledge of salvation* was the knowledge of God's Son, who is truly called and is Salvation and Savior and Salutary. Salvation thus: *I await you, O Lord, for your salvation.*[18] And Savior thus: *Behold my God, my Savior, I will trust in Him.*[19] Salutary thus: *God has made known His victory* [Salutarem] *in the sight of the Gentiles.*[20] For He is Savior, because He is God's Son and Word. Salutary, because He is a spirit—for he says, *The breath [spiritus] of our face is the Lord's anointed,*[21] and Salvation, because He is flesh; for *the Word became flesh and dwelt among us.*[22] John, therefore, brought this *knowledge of salvation* to those who repented and believed in *the Lamb of God who takes away the sins of the world.*[23]

4. *And an angel of the Lord,* [Luke] says, *appeared...to the shepherds* and announced joy to them, *for...there is born...in the house of David a Savior, who is Christ the Lord....Then there was...a multitude of the heavenly host praising God and saying: "Glory to God in the highest, and on earth peace to men of* [His] *good will."*[24] The falsifying Gnostics [*falsarii Gnostici*] claim that these angels came from the Ogdoad and revealed the descent of the Christ on high. But they fall into error when they assert

that this Christ and Savior who is from on high was not born, but descended as a dove upon the Jesus of the economy after his baptism. So the angels of their Ogdoad are liars, when they say, *For there is born to you today a Savior, who is Christ the Lord, in the city of David.*[25] For according to them, neither Christ nor the Savior was born then, but Jesus of the economy, who belongs to the Demiurge of the world, upon whom they claim the Savior from on high descended after he was baptized—that is, after thirty years.[26]

But why did they [the angels] add, *in the city of David,* except to proclaim the fulfilment of the promise of the good news which had been made to David by God, namely, that *from the fruit of his womb* there would arise an eternal king?[27] It is a fact that the Maker of the entire universe made this promise to David, as David himself says, *My help is from...the Lord, who made heaven and earth.*[28] And again, *In His hand are all the ends of the earth, and the heights of the mountains are His; the sea is His, for He made it; for His hands formed dry land. O come, let us worship and bow down before Him, and weep before the Lord who made us, for He is our God.*[29] By this the Holy Spirit, through David, clearly announced to those who heard him that there would be those who would despise Him who fashioned us, who alone is God. For this reason he also spoke the words just quoted, by which he meant to say, "Do not err. Besides or above Him there is no other God to whom you should rather pay attention." He disposed us to be religious and grateful toward Him who created and formed and nourished us. What, then, will come upon those who have originated such a great blasphemy against their Creator?

This same truth the angels also [announced]. For when they said, *Glory to God in the highest, and on earth peace,*[30] they glorified by these words Him who is the Maker of the highest, that is, the supercelestial things, and also the Creator of all the things that are on the earth, who sent His blessing of salvation from heaven to His handiwork; that is, to men. For this reason also *the shepherds,* [Luke] says, *returned, glorifying...God for all they had heard and seen, as it had been told them.*[31] For the shepherds of Israel did not glorify any other God than Him who was announced by the Law and the Prophets, the Maker of all things, whom also the angels glorified. Now if the angels who came from the Ogdoad had glorified one god, and the shepherds another one, then the angels who came from the Ogdoad brought error, not the truth, to the shepherds.

5. Luke further says of the Lord, *And when the days of...purification were fulfilled...they brought Him to Jerusalem to present [Him] to the Lord, as it is written in the law of the Lord, "Every male that opens the womb shall be called holy to the Lord," and to offer a sacrifice according to what is said in the law of the Lord, "A pair of turtledoves or two young pigeons."*[32] Luke most manifestly and in his own name calls Him Lord who made the law. And he tells us, too, that Simeon *blessed God and said, Lord, now You are letting Your servant depart in peace...for my eyes have seen Your salvation, which You have prepared in the presence of all peoples, a light for revelation to the Gentiles, and glory to Your people Israel.*[33] He says, moreover, that also Anna the prophetess glorified God when she saw Christ, *and spoke of Him to all who were looking for the redemption of Jerusalem.*[34] By all of these things the one God is manifested, inaugurating for men the new economy of liberty by the new covenant of His Son's coming.

6. With this same purpose in mind, Mark too, Peter's translator and follower, began his Gospel account thus: *The beginning of the Gospel of Jesus Christ, the Son of God. As it is written in the prophets, "Behold, I send my messenger before Your face, who shall prepare Your way; the voice of one crying in the wilderness, prepare the way of the Lord, make straight the paths before our God."*[35] He says plainly that the voice of the holy prophets is the beginning of the Gospel, and he pointed out beforehand as the Father of our Lord Jesus Christ Him whom [the prophets] acknowledged to be Lord and God, who also promised to send His messenger to go before His face. This [messenger] was John, in the spirit and power of Elias,[36] who cried out *in the wilderness, "Prepare the way of the Lord, make straight the paths before our God."*[37] For the prophets did not announce different gods, but one and the same God under various expressions and by many titles. For, as we have shown in the preceding book, the Father is abundant and rich.[38] This we shall show, too, from the prophets in the course of our treatise.

Toward the end of [his] Gospel, Mark says, *So then the Lord Jesus, after He had spoken to them, was taken up to heaven, and sits at the right hand of God.*[39] Thus he confirms what the prophet has said, *The Lord said to my Lord, "Sit at my right hand, until I make Your enemies Your footstool."*[40] So it is one and the same God and Father who was announced by the prophets, handed down [*traditus*] by the Gospel, whom we Christians worship and love with our whole heart as the *Creator of heaven and earth and of all things in them.*[41]

CHAPTER 11
PROOF FROM JOHN'S GOSPEL THAT GOD IS ONE.
THERE ARE ONLY FOUR GOSPELS

1. John, the Lord's disciple, proclaimed that faith. By proclaiming the Gospel he wished to remove the error that was disseminated among people by Cerinthus, and long before by those who are called Nicolaitans, who are an offshoot of the falsely called "knowledge."[1] Thus he confounded them and persuaded them that there is one God who made all things by His Word, and not, as they allege, that the Creator differs from the Father of the Lord; that the Son of the Creator differs from Christ who is from on high and who they say remained impassible when he descended into Jesus, the Son of the Creator, and then returned again into the Fullness [*Pleroma*]; that Only-begotten [*Monogenen*] is Beginning, while Word is the Son of Only-begotten [*Unigeniti*];[2] and that our creation was not made by the first God, but by some power that was located far down and cut off from communion with the invisible and unnamable beings.[3] The Lord's disciple, therefore, wished to put an end to all such tenets, and to make firm the rule of truth in the Church, that there is one God almighty, who through His Word made all things, both the visible and the invisible. He indicated, too, that through the very Word through which God fashioned the creation, He bestowed in turn salvation on the people who are in this creation.[4] That is how he began with the doctrine according to the Gospel: *In the beginning was the Word, and the Word was with God, and the Word was God; He was in the beginning with God. All things were made through Him, and without Him was not anything made. What was made is life in Him, and the life was the light of men. The light shines in the darkness, and the darkness has not overcome it.*[5] *All things*, he said, *were made through Him.* In this *all*, therefore, is contained also this creation of ours; for we will not concede to them that the *all* was said of the beings within their Fullness. For if their Fullness contains also these things, then this vast creation of ours is not outside [the Fullness], as we have shown in the preceding book.[6] If, on the contrary, these things are outside the Fullness—which is seen as impossible—their Fullness is no longer *all things*. And so this vast creation is not outside [the Fullness].

2. John himself removed all controversy, as far as we are concerned, when he said, *He was in the world, and the world was made*

through Him, yet the world knew Him not. He came unto His own, and His own received Him not.[7] But according to Marcion and his likes, neither was the world made through Him, nor did He come unto His own, but to strangers.[8] Moreover, according to some of the Gnostics [*Gnosticorum*/γνωστικῶν], this world was made by angels, and not through the Word of God.[9] Again, according to the followers of Valentinus, it was not made by Him, but by Demiurge.[10] That one [Word], they allege, was instrumental in making likenesses in imitation of the [Aeons] on high; whereas the Demiurge completed the work of creation. For they assert that the Lord and Demiurge who belongs to the affairs of this creation—by whom they claim this world was made—was emitted by the Mother. But the Gospel plainly says that all things were made through the Word who *was with God in the beginning*; and that *Word*, it says, *became flesh and dwelt among us.*[11]

3. But according to these [heretics], neither did the Word become flesh, nor Christ, nor Savior, who was emitted from all [the Aeons]. For they hold that Word and Christ did not even come into this world, while Savior did not become incarnate, nor did he suffer. He descended as a dove upon Jesus, who was made for the economy, and when he had announced the unknown Father, he again ascended into the Fullness.[12] But some of them assert that Jesus, who exists because of the economy, passed through Mary as water through a tube, and became incarnate and suffered.[13] Others, however, assert that he is the son of Demiurge, into whom Jesus who exists because of the economy descended.[14] Still others assert that he is the Jesus who was born of Joseph and Mary, and that into him the Christ from on high descended, who is without flesh and impassible.[15] But according to the teaching of none of the heretics [*haereticorum*/τῶν αἱρετικῶν] did the *Word* of God *become flesh.* The fact is, if one examines the rules of all of them, he will find that the Word of God and the Christ who is from on high are presented by them as being without flesh and impassible. Some think that he was manifested in the form of a man, but they assert that he was neither born nor incarnate; while others assert that he did not even take the form of man, but descended as a dove upon Jesus who was born of Mary. All these, therefore, the Lord's disciple shows to be false witnesses when he says, *and the Word became flesh, and dwelt among us.*[16]

4. And so, that we might not inquire of what God the Word became flesh, He Himself teaches further, *There was a man, one sent*

from God, whose name was John. He [came] for testimony, to bear witness to the light....he was not the light, but came to bear witness to the light.[17] By what God, then, was John sent—the forerunner who bore witness concerning the light? It was indeed by that God of whom Gabriel is the messenger [*angelus*], who also announced the good news of His birth. By the God who also promised through His prophets that He would send His messenger before the face of His Son, and He would prepare His way, that is, bear witness concerning the light *in the spirit and power of Elias.*[18] And Elias, in turn, of what God was he servant and prophet? Of Him who made heaven and earth, as he himself acknowledges.[19]

Therefore, if John was sent by the Creator and Maker of this world, how could he bear witness concerning that light which descended from the beings that are unnamable and invisible? For all the heretics have given out as certain that Demiurge is ignorant of the power that is above him, of which John is recognized to be the witness and the revealer.

On this account the Lord said He considered him *more than a prophet.*[20] For all the other prophets announced the coming of the Father's light; moreover, they desired to be worthy of seeing Him whom they prophesied. But John both foretold Him, just as the others had, and saw and pointed Him out when He came, and persuaded many to believe in Him, so that he held the office [*locum*/τόπον] of both prophet and apostle. In this he is *more than a prophet,* because *first are apostles, then prophets.*[21] But all things come from one and the same God.

5. The wine that was made by God through creation in a vineyard and was drunk first was good.[22] For none of those who drank it found fault with it, and even the Lord took of it. However, that wine is better which through the Word was made from water in a summary way and in a simple manner, for the use of those who had been *invited to the marriage feast.*[23] And so, though the Lord had the power, without [using] any existing material substance, to supply wine for the guests of the banquet and to satisfy the hungry with food, nevertheless He did not do so. On the contrary, He took loaves of bread that came from the earth and, having given thanks and again made water into wine, He satisfied those who were reclining and gave drink to those who had been *invited to the marriage feast.*[24] Thus He showed that the God who made the earth and commanded it to bear fruit, and who established the waters and produced the springs,[25] this same [God]

bestows upon the human race the blessing of food and the favor of drink through His Son in these last times—the incomprehensible through the comprehensible, and the invisible through the visible, since He does not exist outside of the Father, but in His bosom.

6. He says, *No one has ever seen God, except the Only-begotten* [*Unigenitus*] *Son of God who is in the bosom of the Father, He declared* [*Him*].[26] For since the Father is invisible, the Son who is in His bosom declares Him to all. On this account, those to whom the Son has revealed Him, know Him; in turn, the Father, through the Son, gives knowledge of His Son to those who love Him.[27] From Him, Nathaniel too learned, and so acknowledged Him. The Lord Himself spoke favorably of [Nathaniel], saying, *He is a true Israelite, in whom there is no guile.* This Israelite knew his King, for he, on his part, said, *Rabbi, You are the Son of God, You are the King of Israel.*[28] Peter, too, was taught by Him and so acknowledged *Christ the Son of the living God,*[29] who said, *Behold…my beloved Son, with whom I am well pleased. I will put my Spirit upon Him, and He shall proclaim justice to the Gentiles. He will not wrangle or cry aloud; nor will anyone hear His voice in the streets. He will not break a bruised reed, or quench a smoldering wick, until He brings justice to victory; and in His name will the Gentiles hope.*[30]

7. The following are the cardinal points of the Gospel:[31] They proclaim one God, the Maker of this world—He who was announced by the prophets, and who established the economy of the law through Moses, who is the Father of our Lord Jesus Christ; and they are not aware of any other God or any other Father besides this one. Now, the authority of these Gospels is so great that the heretics themselves bear witness to them, and each one of them tries to establish his doctrine with the Gospels as a starting point.[32]

The Ebionites use only the Gospel of Matthew.[33] But by this same Gospel they are convicted of not teaching the right things about the Lord. Marcion, on the other hand, mutilated the Gospel according to Luke;[34] but by the passages he retains he is shown to be a blasphemer against the only God who exists. Those, however, who prefer the Gospel of Mark and divide Jesus from Christ, and assert that Christ remained impassible but that Jesus suffered, can be corrected if they read this Gospel with a love for the truth. Finally, the followers of Valentinus, who make very ample use of the Gospel according to John for proving their conjugal couples [of Aeons], are by this very Gospel exposed to be entirely false, as we have shown in the first book.[35]

Since, therefore, those who contradict us bear witness to and use these [Gospels], our proof drawn from them is solid and true.[36]

8. It is not possible that there be more Gospels in number than these, or fewer. By way of illustration, since there are four zones in the world in which we live, and four cardinal winds,[37] and since the Church is spread over the whole earth, and since *the pillar and bulwark* of the Church is the Gospel[38] and the Spirit of life, consequently she has four pillars, blowing imperishability from all sides and giving life [*vivificantes*] to men. From these things it is manifest that the Word, who is Artificer of all things and *is enthroned upon the Cherubim and holds together all things,* and who was manifested to men,[39] gave us the four-fold Gospel, which is held together by the one Spirit. Just as David, when petitioning His [Christ's] coming, said, *You who are enthroned upon the Cherubim, shine forth.*[40] For the Cherubim, too, had four faces, and their faces are images of the dispensation of the Son of God.[41] For the first one, he says, was like a lion, symbolizing His powerful, sovereign, and kingly nature.[42] The second was like a calf, symbolizing His ministerial and priestly rank.[43] The third animal had a face like a man, which manifestly describes His coming as man.[44] The fourth is like a flying eagle, manifesting the gift of the Spirit hovering over the Church.[45]

Now, the Gospels harmonize with these [animals] on which Christ Jesus *is enthroned.* For the Gospel according to John narrates the generation which is from the Father, sovereign, powerful, and glorious. It runs thus, *In the beginning was the Word, and the Word was with God, and the Word was God;* and *all things were made through Him, and without Him was not anything made.*[46] On this account this Gospel is full of all confidence, for such is its characteristic [*persona*]. The Gospel according to Luke, since it has a priestly character, began with Zacharias the priest as he was offering incense to God.[47] For the fatted calf which would be slaughtered when the younger son would be found was already being prepared.[48] Matthew narrates His generation inasmuch as He is man. *The book,* he writes, *of the generation of Jesus Christ, the son of David, the son of Abraham;* and again, *the birth of Christ took place in this way.*[49] This Gospel, then, belongs to the human form, and so throughout the Gospel the humble and meek man is retained.[50] Mark began with the prophetical Spirit which came down to men from on high. *The beginning,* he says, *of the Gospel...as it is written in Isaias the prophet,* pointing out the winged image [i.e., the eagle] of the Gospel.[51] For this reason he made a compendious and cursory announcement [of the Gospel], for it has a prophetic character.

Now the Word of God Himself used to speak, in virtue of His divinity and glory, with the patriarchs who lived before Moses' time. And those who lived under the law, He used to assign a priestly and ministerial function.[52] Finally, having become man for us, He sent the gift of the heavenly Spirit upon the entire earth, covering us with His pinions.[53] Therefore, such as was the economy of the Son of God, such also was the form of the living beings; and such as was the form of the living beings, such also was the character of the Gospel. And as the living creatures are fourfold, so also the Gospel is fourfold; and fourfold also is the Lord's economy. And for this reason four principal covenants were given to the human race:[54] the first, of Adam before the deluge; the second, of Noe after the deluge; the third, the law under Moses; and the fourth, which renews man and recapitulates in itself all things, that is, which through the Gospel raises up and bears men on its wings to the heavenly kingdom.

9. Since, therefore, these things are so, those are all senseless and unlearned, and more yet, even bold, who destroy the form of the Gospel by falsely introducing either more faces to the Gospel than the aforementioned, or fewer.[55] Some [do so] with the purpose of appearing to have discovered more than belongs to the truth; others with the purpose of bringing to naught God's economy.

Marcion, for example, while rejecting the entire Gospel, or rather cutting himself off from the Gospel, boasts of having part of the Gospel.[56] Still others, with the purpose of bringing to naught the gift of the Spirit, which was poured out upon the human race according to the Father's good pleasure in these last times, do not admit that form of the Gospel according to John, in which the Lord promised to send the Paraclete.[57] These in fact reject both the Gospel and the prophetic Spirit. They are wretched men indeed, who hold that there are false prophets but then reject the grace of the prophecy from the Church. They act just like those who hold themselves aloof from fellowship with the brethren because of those who come [into Church] hypocritically.[58] It is understandable, then, that these men do not accept the apostle Paul, for in his letter to the Corinthians he spoke painstakingly about the charismatic gifts, and he knows of men and women in the Church who were prophesying.[59] So these men, by sinning in all things against the Spirit of God, fall into the unpardonable sin.[60]

On the other hand, the followers of Valentinus, living without any fear whatever, put forth their own writings and boast of having more Gospels than there really are. Indeed, they have carried their boldness so far that they give the title *Gospel of Truth* to a book which they have but recently composed, and which agrees in no wise with the Gospels of the apostles.[61] The result is that among them not even the Gospel is free from blasphemy. For, if the Gospel that was composed by them is the Gospel of Truth, but differs from those handed down to us by the apostles, anyone who wishes may learn, as is proved from the Scriptures, that the Gospel handed down by the apostles is no longer the Gospel of Truth. That these alone, however, are the true and authentic Gospels, and that there cannot be more than we have predicated, nor fewer, I have proved by many and strong arguments. For since God arranged and harmonized all things well, it is necessary that also the form of the Gospel be arranged and fitted together well.

Now that we have examined, from the capital points themselves,[62] the doctrine of those who handed the Gospel down to us, let us go also to the other apostles and investigate their doctrine of God. After that we shall hear the very words of the Lord.

Chapter 12

The Doctrine of the Other Apostles,
from the Acts

1. Now after the Lord's resurrection and ascension into heaven, the apostle Peter wished to fill up the number of the twelve apostles and to elect in the place of Judas another who was chosen by God. So he addressed those present: *Brethren, this Scripture had to be fulfilled, which the Holy Spirit spoke beforehand by the mouth of David, concerning Judas who was guide of those who arrested Jesus. For he was numbered among us...:* "*Let his habitation become desolate, and let there be no one to dwell in it*"; and "*his office [episcopatum] let another take.*"[1] By the force of these words of David, he filled up the number of the apostles.

Again, when the Holy Spirit had descended upon the disciples, so that all might prophesy and speak with tongues, and when others ridiculed them as if they were drunk with new wine, Peter said that they were not drunk since it was [only] the third hour of the day, but that this event was foretold by the prophet: *And in the last days it shall be, God declares, that I will pour out my Spirit upon all flesh; and...they shall prophesy.*[2] So the God who through His prophet promised to send His Spirit upon the human race, is the one who also sent Him, and He is the same God who was announced by Peter as having fulfilled His promise.

2. Further, Peter said, *Men of Israel, hear my words: Jesus of Nazareth, a man attested to you by God with mighty works and wonders and signs which God did through Him in your midst, as you yourselves know—this Jesus, delivered up according to the definite plan and foreknowledge of God, you crucified and killed by the hands of lawless men. But God raised Him up, having loosed the pangs of death, because it was not possible for Him to be held by it. For David says concerning him: "I saw the Lord always before me, for He is at my right hand that I should not be shaken; therefore my heart was glad, and my tongue rejoiced. Moreover, my flesh will dwell in hope, for You will not abandon my soul to Hades, nor Your Holy One see corruption."*[3] He continues to speak boldly to them about the patriarch David, that he died and was buried, and that his tomb is still with them to that very day.[4] He said, *Therefore, being a prophet and knowing that God had "sworn with an oath to him that of the fruit of his womb one should sit upon his throne," he foresaw and spoke of the resurrection of the Christ, that He was not abandoned to Hades, nor did His flesh see corruption. This Jesus,* he said, *God raised up, and of that we all are witnesses. Being therefore exalted at the right hand of God, and having received from the Father the promise of the Holy Spirit, He has poured out* His gift *which you see and hear. For David did not ascend into the heavens, but he himself says, "The Lord said to my Lord, Sit at my right hand, until I make Your enemies a stool for Your feet." Let all the house of Israel therefore know assuredly that God has made Him both Lord and Christ, this Jesus whom you crucified.*[5]

Now, when the crowd had said to him, *What shall we do?*...Peter said to them, *Repent and be baptized, every one of you, in the name of Jesus for the forgiveness of your sins; and you shall receive the gift of the Holy Spirit.*[6] In this way the apostles did not preach another God, nor another Fullness, nor one Christ who suffered and then rose, and another who flew upward and remained impassible,[7] but one and the same God the Father, and Christ Jesus who rose from the dead. They also preached faith in Him to those who did not believe in the Son of God; and with the prophets as sources they exhorted them to the effect that God actually sent Jesus as the Christ He had promised, whom they crucified, but whom He raised up.[8]

3. Once more, when Peter, together with John, had looked at the man who was lame from birth as he was sitting, begging alms at the gate of the temple called Beautiful, he said to him, *Of silver and gold have I none, but I give you what I have. In the name of Jesus Christ of Nazareth arise and walk....And immediately his feet and soles were made strong...and he began to walk, and entered the temple with them, walking and leaping and praising God.*[9] Now, when the whole crowd had gathered about them on account of this unexpected event, Peter said to them, *Men of Israel, why do you wonder at this, or why do you stare at us, as though by our own power or piety we had made this man walk? The God of Abraham, the God of Isaac, the God of Jacob, the God of our fathers, glorified His Son...whom you delivered up to judgment and disowned in the presence of Pilate when he had wished to release Him. But you oppressed the Holy and Righteous One, and asked for a murderer to be granted to you; and you killed the Author of life, whom God raised from the dead. To this we are witnesses. And through faith in His name....His name has made strong this man whom you see and know; and the faith which is through [Jesus] has given the man this perfect health in the presence of you all. And now, brethren, I know that you acted wickedly in ignorance..., but what God foretold by the mouth of all the prophets, that His Christ should suffer, He thus fulfilled. Repent, therefore, and turn again, that your sins may be blotted out, that times of refreshing may come from the presence of the Lord, and that He may send the Christ prepared for you, Jesus, whom heaven must receive until the times for putting all things in order, of which God spoke by the mouth of His holy prophets from of old. Moses says to our fathers, "The Lord your God will raise up to you a prophet from your brethren as He raised me up. You shall listen to Him in whatever He tells you; and it shall be that every soul that does not listen to that prophet shall be destroyed from the people."*[10] And all the prophets who have spoken, from Samuel and those who came afterward, also proclaimed these days. You are the sons of the prophets and the covenant that God gave to your fathers, saying to Abraham, *and in your posterity shall all the families of the earth be blessed.*[11] God, having raised up His Son, sent Him to you first, to bless you in turning every one of you from your wickedness.

And thus Peter, together with John, preached to them this plain sermon, proclaiming to them the glad news that the promised blessing which God had made to the fathers was fulfilled through Jesus. He did not announce another God; but he did lead Israel to the knowledge of God's Son, who became man and suffered, and he announced the resurrection through Jesus from the dead. Thus he pointed out that God had fulfilled all the things the prophets had foretold about Christ's suffering.

4. For this reason, too, when the chief priests had gathered together, Peter courageously said to them, *Rulers of the people and elders of Israel…if we are being examined today concerning a good deed done to a cripple, by which means this man has been healed, be it known to you all and to all the people of Israel, that by the name of Jesus Christ of Nazareth, whom you crucified, whom God raised from the dead, by Him this man is standing before you well. "This is the stone which was rejected by builders, but which has become the head of the corner."…For there is no other name under heaven given among men by which we must be saved.*[12] Thus the apostles did not change God; but announced to the people that Jesus is the Christ, whom they had crucified and whom the very God who sent the prophets raised up, and through Him gave salvation to humankind.

5. They were, therefore, confounded both by the healing— Scripture says, *for the man on whom this sign of healing was performed was more than forty years old*[13]—and by the doctrine of the apostles and the explanation of the prophets. So when the chief priests had dismissed Peter and John and they had returned to their fellow apostles [*coapostolos*] and disciples of the Lord, that is, to the Church, they told them what had happened, and how they had acted courageously in the name of Jesus. *When they*—the entire Church—*heard it,* [Scripture] says, *they lifted up their voices together to God and said, Lord, who made heaven and the earth and the sea and everything in them, who by the mouth of our father David, Your servant, did say by the Holy Spirit, "Why did the Gentiles rage and the peoples plan vain things? The kings of the earth set themselves in array, and the rulers were gathered together, against the Lord and against His Anointed." For truly in this city there were gathered together against Your holy Son Jesus, whom You did anoint, Herod and Pontius Pilate with the Gentiles and the peoples of Israel, to do whatever Your hand and Your will had predestined to take place.*[14]

These are the voices of the Church, from which every Church takes its origin. These are the voices of the Mother City, of the citizens of the new covenant.[15] These are the voices of the apostles; these are the voices of the Lord's disciples, who, after the Lord's assumption, were made perfect by the Spirit and called upon the God *who made heaven and earth and sea,*[16] and who was announced by the prophets and by His Son Jesus, whom God anointed. And they knew no other.

In fact, at that time there was no Valentinus, no Marcion, nor any of these others who destroy themselves as well as those who agree with them. For this reason, God the Creator of all things also heard them [i.e., the apostles]. [Scripture] says, *For...the place in which they were gathered together was shaken; and they were all filled with the Holy Spirit, and spoke the word of God with boldness* to everyone who wished to believe.[17] Again [Scripture] says, *And with great power the apostles gave testimony to the resurrection of the Lord Jesus,*[18] saying to them, *the God of our fathers raised Jesus whom you killed by hanging Him on a tree. God exalted Him with His glory as Leader and Savior, to give repentance to Israel and forgiveness of sins. And we are witnesses to these things, and so is the Holy Spirit whom God has given to those who obey Him.*[19] *And every day in the temple and at home they did not cease teaching and proclaiming* the good news about *Christ Jesus,* the Son of God.[20] This, indeed, was *the knowledge of salvation* which renders those perfect in relation to God, who acknowledge His Son's coming.

6. Some of them [the heretics] impudently assert that the apostles, when preaching to the Jews, could not announce to them any other God than the one in whom they [already] believed. To this we answer: if the apostles spoke to men according to a notion implanted in them of old, then no one learned the truth from them, much less from the Lord, since He too, as they assert, spoke in this manner. Nor would they themselves know the truth; but since their own teaching about God was such [namely, according to precedent notions], they received the doctrine according as they were able to hear it. And so, according to this manner of speaking, no one would have the rule of truth, since all the disciples would credit their [teachers] with giving out speech according to the capacity of the one to understand and grasp it. Moreover, the Lord's coming would appear superfluous and useless if He came to permit and preserve the notion of God that each one formerly had implanted.

Furthermore, it would have been more difficult to preach Him as Christ the Son of God, their eternal King, whom the Jews saw as a man and whom they fastened to the cross. And so they did not speak to them according to their former notion. Indeed, those [apostles] who told them to their face that they were murderers of the Lord would much more boldly have announced the Father who is above

Demiurge, and not merely what each one thought. Their sin would have been much less if they had not crucified the Savior from on high, since He was impassible, to whom they must ascend. Again, just as they did not speak to the Gentiles according to their mentality but told them boldly that their gods were not gods, but idols of demons,[21] in like manner they would have announced to the Jews another greater and more perfect Father if they had known of Him, and would not have nourished and strengthened the false notion of these people about God. Moreover, by destroying the error of the Gentiles and depriving them of their gods, they assuredly did not lead them into another error; no, by depriving them of such as were not gods, they showed them Him who alone is God and true Father.

7. Furthermore, from Peter's words to Cornelius the centurion at Caesarea and to those Gentiles who were with him, to whom the word of God was declared for the first time, we can ascertain what the apostles announced, and the nature of their preaching, and what notion they had of God. For this Cornelius, the Scripture says, *a devout man, who feared God with all his household, gave alms liberally to the people and prayed constantly to God. About the ninth hour of the day he saw...an angel of God coming in and saying to him:...Your alms have ascended as a memorial before God....And now, send...Simon who is called Peter.*[22] Now Peter saw a revelation in which a heavenly voice answered him, *What God has cleansed, you must not call common.* God said this because the God who made a distinction in the law between clean and unclean, this same God—whom also Cornelius worshiped—cleansed the Gentiles through the blood of His Son.

So when Peter came to Cornelius, he said, *Truly I perceive that God shows no partiality, but in every nation anyone who fears Him and does what is right is acceptable to Him.*[23] By this Peter clearly points out that He whom Cornelius previously reverenced as God, of whom he had heard through the Law and the Prophets, for whose sake he also gave alms, this same one is in truth God. He lacked, however, the knowledge about [the Son]. And so Peter added, *You know the word which was proclaimed throughout all Judea; beginning from Galilee after the baptism which John preached, how God anointed Jesus of Nazareth with the Holy Spirit and with power; how He went about doing good and healing all who were oppressed by the devil, for God was with Him. And we are witnesses to all that He did, both in the country of the Jews and in Jerusalem. They put Him to death by hanging Him on a tree; but God raised Him on the third day and made Him manifest; not to all the people, but to us who were chosen by God as witnesses, who ate and drank with Him after He rose from the dead. And He commanded us to preach to the people, and to testify that He is the one ordained* [lit., "predestined"] *by God to be Judge of the living and the dead. To Him all the prophets bear witness that everyone who believes in Him receives forgiveness of sins through His name.*[24]

So the apostles did announce God's Son—of whom men were ignorant—and His coming, to those who before had been instructed by God; but they did not introduce another god. For if Peter had known any such thing, he would freely have preached to the Gentiles that the God of the Jews was different from the God of the Christians [*christianorum*/Χριστιανῶν]; and all of them without doubt, since they were awestruck because of the vision of the angel, would have believed whatever he would have told them.

From Peter's words, however, it is evident that he safeguarded for them the God whom they had known before, but he also testified to them that Jesus Christ is the Son of God, who is *the Judge of the living and the dead*; in Him he also commanded them to be baptized for the remission of sins. Not only that, he testified that Jesus Himself is God's Son, who even after He was anointed by the Holy Spirit is called Jesus Christ. And this same one was born of Mary, as is contained in Peter's testimony.

Or did Peter then not yet possess the perfect knowledge that these [heretics] discovered later? As such, according to them, Peter was imperfect, and the rest of the apostles were imperfect; and it will be necessary for them to come to life again and become disciples of these [heretics], so that they too may become perfect. But this is too ridiculous!

These [heretics] are exposed as disciples not of the apostles but of their own evil doctrine. For this reason they hold various opinions, each one receiving error as he is capable. The Church, however, throughout the whole world, inasmuch as it has a solid origin from the apostles, continues in one and the same doctrine about God and His Son.

8. Again, when the eunuch of the queen of the Ethiopians was returning from Jerusalem and reading the prophet Isaias, whom did Philip preach to him when they were together alone?[25] Was it not He of whom the prophet said, *As a sheep led to the slaughter, or a lamb before its shearers is dumb, so He opens not His mouth.... Who can describe His generation? For His life will be taken away from the earth.*[26] This is that Jesus, and in Him the Scripture was fulfilled. This also the eunuch said when

he had believed and asked to be baptized, *I believe that Jesus is the Son of God.*[27] He was also sent into the country of the Ethiopians to preach the very things he himself believed, namely, that one God was preached by the prophets, and that His Son has already made His appearance as man, and was led to slaughter like a sheep, and the other things that the prophets say about Him.

9. Even Paul himself, after the Lord had spoken to him from heaven and showed him that in persecuting His disciples he was persecuting his Lord, and sent Ananias to him that he might again receive his sight and be baptized, proclaimed with all boldness in the synagogues of Damascus, as [Scripture] says, *Jesus is the Christ, the Son of God.*[28] The mystery that was manifested to him in the revelation he affirms is this: that He who suffered under Pontius Pilate is the Lord of all and King and God and Judge, who received power from the God of all things, because He has been *obedient unto death, even death on a cross.*[29]

That this is true he told the Athenians when preaching the glad news in the Areopagus, where the Jews were not present and he was free to preach with boldness the true God. He said, *The God who made the world and everything in it, being Lord of heaven and earth, does not live in shrines made by hands; nor is He served by human hands, as though He needed anything, since He Himself gives to all men life and breath and everything. And He made from one blood every race of men to live on all the face of the earth, having determined allotted periods and the boundaries of their habitation; that they should seek the Deity, in the hope that they might feel after Him and find Him. Yet He is not far from each one of us. For "in Him we have our being"; even as some of your own have said, "For we are indeed His offspring." Being then God's offspring, we ought not to think that the Deity is like gold, or silver, or stone, from human art or imagination. The times of ignorance God overlooked, but now He commands all men everywhere to repent unto Him, because He fixed a day on which He will judge the world with righteousness by a man, Jesus, whom He has appointed, and of which He has given assurance...by raising Him from the dead.*[30] In this passage he not only announces to them God the Creator of the world, since the Jews were not present, but that *He made one human race to dwell on the entire earth.* Moses said the same: *When the Most High gave to the nations their inheritance, when He separated the sons of Adam, He fixed the bounds of the peoples according to the number of the angels of God; but people who believe in God are no longer under the power of the angels, but of the Lord; for the Lord's portion is His people, Jacob. Israel is His allotted heritage.*[31]

Again, *at Lystra* of Lycaonia, Paul was with Barnabas and in the name of our Lord Jesus Christ had made a man walk who *was a cripple from birth. The crowd* wished to honor them as gods on account of the wonderful deed.[32] He then said to them, *We also are human beings of like nature with you, and bring you good news of God, that you should turn from these vain things to the living God who made the heaven and the earth and the sea and all that is in them. In times past He allowed all the nations to walk in their own ways; yet He did not leave Himself without witness, for He did good and gave you from heaven rains and fruitful seasons, satisfying your hearts with good and gladness.*[33]

That all his letters agree with these sermons, we shall demonstrate, in the proper place, from the letters themselves; namely, when we come to explain the apostle. Now, while we work out these proofs from Scripture and state briefly and in a summary way the things that are said in a varied manner, please pay attention with an open mind, and do not consider it verbose. For you ought to know that scriptural proofs cannot be illustrated except from Scripture.[34]

10. Furthermore, Stephen, who was chosen by the apostles as the first deacon [*diaconus*/διάκονος], and who was the first of all men to follow in the footsteps of the Lord's martyrdom, having been the first who was put to death for professing Christ, spoke courageously to the people and taught them.[35] He said, *The God of glory appeared to our father Abraham... and said to him, "Depart from your land and from your kindred, and enter into the land which I will show you."... God removed him... to this land in which you are living; yet He gave him no inheritance in it, not even a foot of land, but He promised "to give it to him in possession and to his posterity after him." And God spoke to this effect, that his posterity would be aliens in a land belonging to others, who would enslave them and ill-treat them four hundred years. "But I will judge the nation which they serve," says the Lord. "And after that, they shall come out and worship me in this place."*[36] And He gave him the covenant of circumcision. And so he begot Isaac.[37] And the rest of his words announce the same God who was with Joseph and with the patriarchs, and who also spoke with Moses.[38]

11. That the entire doctrine of the apostles announced one and the same God, who made Abraham emigrate [*qui transtulit Abraham*], who promised him the inheritance, who in due time gave him the covenant of circumcision, who called his posterity out of Egypt, which plainly was saved by circumcision, which [itself] had been given as a sign that they might not become like the Egyptians; that this is the

Maker of all things, that this is the Father of our Lord Jesus Christ, that this is the God of glory—[this] all who are willing can learn from the very sermons and deeds of the apostles, and can discern that this is the one God above whom there is no other. Now, even if there were another god above this God, we should, by a comparison in a superlative way, say: this one is better than that one. For, a better person is manifested by his deeds, as we have said before,[39] and since these men have no work of their Father to show, this one alone is shown to be God. But if anyone *has a morbid craving for controversies*[40] and imagines what the apostles said about God should be allegorized [*allegorizanda*/ἀλληγορητέα], let him examine our previous treatises, in which we have shown that there is one God, the Creator and Maker of all things, and have overthrown and laid bare the assertions of these men; and he will find these [treatises] agreeing with the doctrine of the apostles and containing exactly what they used to teach and that of which they were themselves convinced. Namely, that there is one God, the Maker of all things. And when he has rejected so great an error from his mind, and also the blasphemy against God, he will of himself come to reason and realize that both the law of Moses and the grace of the New Covenant, each in its suitable time, were bestowed by one and the same God for the benefit of the human race.[41]

12. In fact, all those who are evil-minded, rebelling against the Mosaic Law, think it is different from, and contrary to, the doctrine of the Gospel. But they do not apply themselves to investigate the reasons for the difference between the two covenants. Since, therefore, they have been deserted by the Father's love and puffed up by Satan, and have turned to the doctrine of Simon Magus and have apostatized in their doctrines from Him who is God, they have imagined that they have found something more than the apostles did by discovering another god;[42] and that, whereas the apostles, still believing the doctrines of the Jews, proclaimed the Gospel, they [the heretics] are more sincere and wiser than the apostles.

Wherefore, Marcion, as well as his followers, have occupied themselves with cutting up the Scriptures. They disown some books entirely; [then] they mutilate the Gospel of Luke and the letters of Paul and assert that these alone, in their shortened form, are genuine.[43] I shall, however, God granting, refute them in another book by the very Scriptures which they still retain.[44] All the rest who are puffed up with a false knowledge indeed recognize the Scriptures, but they pervert their interpretation, as we have shown in the first book. Indeed, the followers of Marcion blaspheme the Creator directly, asserting He is the Maker of evil things, though they hold a more intolerable thesis in regard to His origin, saying there are by nature two gods, distinct from each other—the one good, the other evil.[45] On the other hand, the followers of Valentinus use more honorable names, and prove that He who is the Maker is Father and Lord and God. Nevertheless, they hold an even more blasphemous thesis, or heresy, by saying that He was not emitted by any of the aeons within the Fullness, but by her who because of degeneracy had been expelled outside the Fullness.[46] Now it is ignorance of the Scriptures and of God's economy that has brought all these things on them. I, however, shall in the course of my work relate the reasons, on the one hand, for the difference between the covenants; and, on the other hand, for their unity and harmony.

13. That both the apostles and their disciples thought exactly as the Church preaches, and were by this teaching made perfect and were called to perfection,[47] Stephen taught when he was still on earth. He saw God's glory and Jesus on the right hand, and said, *Behold, I see the heavens opened, and the Son of Man standing on the right of God.*[48] When he had said this, he was stoned, and thus he fulfilled the perfect doctrine, imitating in every respect the Teacher of martyrdom; he even prayed for those who killed him, and said, *Lord, do not hold this sin against them.*[49]

In this manner those were perfect who recognized one and the same God as assisting the human race from the beginning to the end by the various economies. For example, the prophet Hosea said, *It was I who multiplied visions, and through the prophets gave parables.*[50] Those, therefore, who gave up their lives for the sake of Christ's Gospel, how could they speak to people according to an implanted notion? If that is what they had done, they would not have suffered. But they preached doctrines contrary to those who did not assent to the truth, and that is why they suffered. Hence, it is manifest that they did not forsake the truth, but preached *with all boldness* to the Jews and to the Greeks: to the Jews, that Jesus who was crucified by them is *the Son of God, the Judge of the living and the dead,* who has received an eternal kingdom in Israel from the Father, as we have proved; to the Greeks, they announced one God who created all things, and His Son Jesus Christ.[51]

14. This is proved still more clearly from the letter of the apostles that they sent neither to the Jews nor to the Greeks, but to those

of the Gentiles who believed in Christ, for the sake of strengthening their faith. For some came from Judea to Antioch—where the disciples were first called Christians because of their faith in Christ[52]—and persuaded those who believed in the Lord to be circumcised and to observe the rest of the precepts of the law. When Paul and Barnabas had gone up to Jerusalem to the other apostles on account of this question,[53] and the entire Church had assembled as one, Peter addressed them: *Men, brethren, you know that in the early days God made a choice among you, that through my mouth the Gentiles should hear the word of the Gospel and believe. And God who knows the heart bore witness to them, giving them the Holy Spirit just has He did to us; and He made no distinction between us and them, but cleansed their hearts by faith. Now, therefore, why do you make trial of God by putting a yoke upon the neck of the disciples which neither our fathers nor we have been able to bear? But we believe that we can be saved through the grace of the Lord Jesus, just as they.*[54]

After that, James spoke: *Men, brethren..., Simon has related how God...thought of taking out of the Gentiles a people for His name. And with this the words of the prophets agree, as it is written, "After this I will return, and I will rebuild the dwelling of David, which has fallen; I will rebuild its ruins, and I will set it up that the rest of men may seek the Lord, and all the Gentiles who are called by my name, says the Lord, who has made these things." To the Lord His own work was known forever. Therefore my judgment is that we should not trouble those of the Gentiles who turn to God, but should write to them to abstain from the pollutions of idols and from unchastity...and from blood; and that they should not do to others what they do not wish done to themselves.*[55]

When these things had been spoken, and when all were agreed, they wrote to them as follows: *The brethren, both the apostles and the presbyters, to the brethren who are Gentiles in Antioch and Syria and Cilicia, greeting. Since we have heard that some persons from among us have troubled you with words, unsettling your minds although we gave them no such instructions, saying, "Be circumcised and observe the law," we have decided in assembly to choose men and send them to you with our beloved Barnabas and Paul, men who have risked their lives for the sake of the Lord Jesus Christ. We have therefore sent Judas and Silas, who themselves will tell you the same things by word of mouth. For it seemed good to the Holy Spirit and to us to lay upon you no greater burden than these necessary things: that you abstain from what has been sacrificed to idols and from blood,...and from unchastity; and that you should not do to others what you do not wish done to yourselves. Keep yourselves from these things, and you will get on well, walking in the Holy Spirit.*[56]

So it is clear from all these passages that they did not teach that there is another Father, but they gave the New Covenant of liberty to those who recently believed in God through the Holy Spirit. They did, moreover, clearly show that they did not envision another god by the very fact that they made an investigation whether or not the disciples still had to be circumcised.

15. Otherwise, they would not have had such a fear for the first covenant, so that they did not even wish to eat with the Gentiles. For even Peter, though he had been sent to catechize them and had been frightened by such a vision [as he had], nevertheless, spoke to them with much fear. *You yourselves know*, he said, *how unlawful it is for a Jew to associate with anyone of another nation; but God has shown me that I should not call any man common or unclean. So...I came without objection.*[57] By these words he shows that he would not have gone to them unless he had been ordered. Nor, perhaps, would he so easily have given them baptism unless the Holy Spirit had rested upon them and he had heard them prophesying. And so he said, *Can any one forbid water for baptizing these people, who have received the Holy Spirit just as we have?*[58] At the same time he convinced those who were with him. He also pointed out that if the Holy Spirit had not rested upon them, someone might have hindered them from being baptized.

Furthermore, the apostles who were with James allowed the Gentiles to act freely, while recommending us to the Spirit of God. They themselves, however, acknowledging the same God, continued in the ancient observances, so that even Peter, though earlier he had eaten with the Gentiles because of the vision and the Spirit who rested on them, still when some persons came from James, feared lest he be blamed by them [the Jews]; so he separated himself from the Gentiles and did not eat with them. And Paul said that even Barnabas did this.[59]

Thus the apostles, whom the Lord made witnesses of all His acts and His doctrine[60]—as a matter of fact, Peter and James and John were always found present with Him[61]—acted reverently toward the economy of the Law of Moses, and thus they indicated that it was from one and the same God. This they certainly would not have done, in keeping with what we have said, if they had learned from the Lord about another Father besides the one who made the economy of the law.

Chapter 13

Against Those Who Claim That, Among the Apostles, Paul Alone Had Knowledge of the Truth

1. Let Paul himself refute those who assert that he alone had knowledge of the truth, inasmuch as the mystery was manifested to him by revelation.[1] For he said that one and the same God who worked through Peter for the mission to the circumcised worked also through himself for the Gentiles.[2] Hence, Peter was the apostle of the same God as Paul; the very God and the Son of God, whom Peter announced to those in circumcision, Him Paul announced among the Gentiles. Surely, the Lord did not come to save only Paul, nor is God so poor that He would have only one apostle who would know the economy of His Son. Even Paul says, *How beautiful are the feet of those who bring good news, of those who bring good news of peace.*[3] Thus he makes clear that not one but many proclaimed the good news of the truth. Again, in his letter to the Corinthians, when he had spoken of all who saw the Lord[4] after the resurrection, he continued, *Whether then it was I, or they, so we preach and so you believed.*[5] By this he acknowledges as one and the same the preaching of all those who saw the Lord after His resurrection from the dead.

2. The Lord, too, replied to Philip who wished to see the Father, *Have I been with you so long, and yet you do not know me, Philip? He who has seen me has seen the Father; how can you say, "Show us the Father"?... For I am in the Father and the Father in me;...henceforth you know Him, and have seen Him.*[6] To these men, therefore, the Lord bore witness that they had both known and seen the Father in Himself—and the Father is the truth. To assert, then, that these did not know the truth is to play the part of false witnesses and of such as are strangers to the doctrine of Christ. Why did the Lord send the twelve apostles to the lost sheep of the house of Israel if they did not know the truth?[7] And how did the seventy preach unless they first knew the truth of the preaching?[8] Or how could Peter—to whom the Lord Himself gave testimony—have been ignorant that *flesh and blood had not revealed* to him, *but the Father who is in heaven?*[9] Thus he is, as Paul was, *an apostle, not from men, nor through man, but through Jesus Christ and God the Father.*[10] The Son led them to the Father and the Father revealed the Son to them.

3. But Paul himself relates that he acceded to those who summoned him to the apostles in regard to the dispute, and that with Barnabas he went up to them at Jerusalem, not without a purpose; rather, that the liberty of the Gentiles might be established by them. Thus he writes in his letter to the Galatians, *Then after fourteen years I went up to Jerusalem with Barnabas, taking Titus along with me. I went up by revelation; and I laid before them...the Gospel which I preached among the Gentiles.*[11] And again he says, *For we did...yield submission, even for a moment, that the truth of the Gospel might be preserved for you.*[12] Now if anyone diligently examines the Acts of the Apostles about the period under discussion, when he went up to Jerusalem on account of the aforementioned dispute, he will find that the years that Paul mentioned agree. Thus, the preaching of Paul agrees with and is the same as the testimony of Luke [in Acts] in regard to the apostles.

CHAPTER 14

NARRATIVES WE KNOW ONLY THROUGH LUKE

1. This Luke was Paul's inseparable companion and his fellow worker in the Gospel. Paul himself makes this clear, not by way of boasting but compelled by truth itself. When both Barnabas and John—who was called Mark—had been separated from Paul, and had sailed to Cyprus, he said, *We came to Troas.*[1] Now when in a dream Paul had seen a Macedonian saying to him, *Come over to Macedonia and help us, Paul,*[2] he says, *immediately we sought to go to Macedonia, concluding that God had called us to preach the Gospel to them. Setting sail, therefore, from Troas, we made a direct voyage to Samothrace.*[3] And so from there on Luke carefully points out all the rest of the journey to Philippi, and how they first proclaimed the word: *And we sat down,* he says, *and spoke to the women who had come together.*[4] He points out who they were that believed, and how many. And again he says, *But we sailed from Philippi after the days of the unleavened bread...and we came to them at Troas, where we stayed for seven days.*[5] Then he related in order the remaining details [of the journey] with Paul, pointing out with all care both the places and the cities and the number of days until they went up to Jerusalem;[6] also what happened to Paul there, and how he was bound and sent to Rome,[7] and the name of the centurion who took him in

charge,[8] and the signs of the ships, and how they suffered shipwreck, and on what island they were saved, and how they were received with kindness there when Paul healed the ruler of that island; and how they sailed from there to Puteoli; and how from there they arrived at Rome; and how long a time they stayed at Rome.

Since Luke was present for all these events, he wrote them down carefully and so cannot be reproved as a liar or one who is puffed up,[9] because all these things make it clear both that he is older than all those who now teach something different, and that he was not ignorant of the truth. That he was not merely a follower of the apostles but also a fellow worker, especially of Paul, Paul himself declared in his letters. *Demas...has deserted me,* he said, *and gone to Thessalonica; Crescens has gone to Galatia, Titus to Salmatia. Luke alone is with me.*[10] By that he shows that Luke was always associated with him, and inseparable from him. Again, in his letter to the Colossians he writes, *Luke, the beloved physician...greets you.*[11] Now if Luke, who always preached with Paul and was called "beloved," and together with him proclaimed the good news and was entrusted with recording the Gospel for us, never learned anything else—as we have shown from his own words—how can these men who were never associated with Paul boast that they have learned hidden and ineffable mysteries?

2. Paul himself makes clear that what he knew he taught with simplicity, not only to his companions but to all his hearers. For example, when the bishops and presbyters of Ephesus and of other neighboring cities had been called together at Miletus, since he was hastening to Jerusalem to observe Pentecost, he bore witness in regard to many things, and he spoke of the things that would happen to him in Jerusalem. He added, *I know that...you will see my face no longer. Therefore I testify to you this day that I am innocent of the blood of all...; for I did not shrink from declaring to you the whole counsel of God. Take heed to yourselves and to all the flock in which the Holy Spirit has made you overseers, to rule the church of the Lord, which He obtained for Himself with His own blood.*[12] Then, pointing to wicked teachers of the future, he said, *I know that after my departure fierce wolves will come in among you, not sparing the flock; and from among your own selves will arise men speaking perverse things, to draw away the disciples after them.*[13] He said, *I did not shrink from declaring to you the whole counsel of God.* Thus did the apostles, with simplicity and with envy toward no one, hand down to all whatever they had learned from the Lord. Luke, likewise, with envy toward no

one, handed down to us what he had learned from them, as he himself testifies: *Just as they who from the beginning were eyewitnesses and ministers of the word have handed them down to us.*[14]

3. Now if any one would discard Luke, as if he did not know the
truth, he would manifestly be cast out of the Gospel of which he pre-
tends to be a disciple.[15] For through him [Luke] we have knowledge
of a number of rather necessary parts of the Gospel, such as the birth
of John, the story of Zacharias, the coming of the angel to Mary, the
exclamation of Elizabeth, the descent of the angels to the shepherds
and the things which were said by them, the testimony of Anna and
Simeon concerning Christ, and that at the age of twelve He was left at
Jerusalem;[16] also John's baptism, and at what age the Lord was baptized, and that this took place in the fifteenth year of Tiberius
Caesar.[17] Likewise, what He said in His teaching to the rich, *Woe to you
that are rich, for you have received your consolation!* And, *Woe to you who are
full now, for you shall hunger!* And, *Woe to you who laugh now, for you shall
mourn and weep.* And, *Woe to you when all men shall speak well of you, for
so your fathers did to the false prophets.*[18] All such things we know solely
through Luke. Many of the Lord's deeds, too, which all [the heretics]
use, we learn through him. For instance, the multitudes of fish that
Peter and his companions caught when the Lord commanded them
to cast out their nets;[19] the woman who had suffered for eighteen years
and was cured on the Sabbath;[20] the man with dropsy whom the Lord
healed on the Sabbath, and how He disputed about healing on that
day;[21] and how He taught the disciples not to seek the first places at
the table;[22] and that they ought to invite the poor and the lame who
are unable to repay;[23] and of the one who knocked at the door during
the night to get bread, and received some because of his urgent insistence;[24] and that while He was dining with a Pharisee, a sinful woman
kissed His feet and anointed them with ointment, and what He then
said on her account to Simon about the two debtors;[25] and the para-
ble of the rich man who stored up his crops, to whom it was also said,
This [very] *night do they demand your soul of you; and the things you have
prepared, whose will they be?*[26] Likewise, about the rich man who was
clothed in purple and banqueted sumptuously, and about poor
Lazarus;[27] and His answer to the disciples when they said to Him,
Increase our faith;[28] also His conversation with Zaccheus the publican;[29]
and about the Pharisee and the publican who were praying in the
temple at the same time;[30] and about the ten lepers whom He healed

simultaneously on the way;[31] also how He ordered the lame and the blind to be gathered from the lanes and streets to the wedding feast;[32] and about the judge who did not fear God, whom the widow's insistence led to vindicate her cause;[33] and about the fig tree in the vineyard which did not bear fruit.[34] There are many other things that one will find narrated only by Luke, which Marcion and Valentinus yet use. And besides all these, there are all the things He spoke to the disciples on the way [to Emmaus] after the resurrection, and how they recognized Him in the breaking of the bread.[35]

4. It is necessary, therefore, that these men accept the rest of Luke's narrative or discard also these parts; for no person with intelligence will permit them to accept some of the things Luke narrated, as if they belonged to the truth, and to discard the others, as if he had not known the truth. And if Marcion's followers discard them, they will have no Gospel at all! For, as we have said, they mutilate the Gospel of Luke and then boast that they have a Gospel.[36] And let the followers of Valentinus stop their senseless talk; for from Luke they got many of the pretexts for their subtleties, daring to give a bad interpretation to things he has said well. If, however, they are compelled to accept also the rest, they must give heed to the complete [*perfecto*] Gospel, and to the doctrine of the apostles, and so repent that they may be saved from danger and ruin.[37]

CHAPTER 15
AGAINST THOSE WHO MUTILATE THE WRITINGS OF THE APOSTLE PAUL

1. The same things we will allege also against those who do not acknowledge the apostle Paul. Either they will have to reject the rest of the words of the Gospel, namely, those which we know only through Luke, and not use them, or if they receive all of them, they must also accept the testimony that Luke gives concerning Paul. For Luke said that the Lord first spoke to him [Paul] from heaven: *Saul, Saul, why do you persecute me?... I am Jesus* Christ *whom you are persecuting;* and then to Ananias, saying concerning him [Paul], *Go, for he is a chosen instrument of mine to carry my name before the Gentiles and kings and the sons of Israel; for I will show him how much he must suffer for the sake of*

my name.[1] So those who do not receive him who was chosen by God for
the very purpose of boldly carrying His name, [and] that he was sent
to the aforementioned Gentiles, despise God's election and segregate
themselves from the assembly [*conventu*/συνοδίας] of the apostles.
They can indeed not contend that Paul is not an apostle, since he was
chosen for that purpose. Nor can they show that Luke is a liar, since
he announces to us the truth with all care. Indeed, it might be that
God saw to it that many passages of the Gospel be made known [only]
to Luke, which all would have to use, so that all would follow his subsequent testimony concerning the deeds and the doctrine of the apostles, and retain the rule of truth unadulterated, and thus could be
saved.[2] His testimony, therefore, is true, and the doctrine of the apostles is open and firm, subtracting nothing;[3] nor did they teach some
things secretly and other things openly.

2. Such a manner of acting is the subterfuge of liars, evil seduc-
ers, and hypocrites; indeed, the followers of Valentinus act this way.
These address words to the crowd for the purpose of [attracting]
those who belong to the Church, whom they call "catholic" and
"ecclesiastic."[4] Through these [words] they trap the simpler folk and
entice them. Further, they mimic our manner of treating a subject, so
that these might listen more often. Moreover, they [the deceivers]
complain that, since they hold beliefs similar to ours, we unreasonably
keep ourselves aloof from their fellowship; and that though they say
the same things and have the same doctrines [as we], we call them
"heretics" [*haereticos*/αἱρετικούς]. And, when they have driven some
[faithful] from the faith by the questions they put, and have made
them their own hearers when they made no opposition, they tell them
in private about the unspeakable mystery of their Fullness. But they
are all deceived who think they can discern in their words what is specious from the truth.[5] For error is plausible and specious and dissim-
ulates; but the truth is without dissimulation, and consequently has
been entrusted to children.[6]

Now, if any one of their hearers asks for answers or opposes
them, they assert that he does not grasp the truth and does not possess the seed of their Mother from on high. They tell him absolutely
nothing and say that he belongs to the "intermediate region," that is,
to the ensouled [*psychicorum*/τῶν ψυχικῶν].

But if anyone yields himself up to them like a little sheep and
has, by imitating them, attained even their "redemption," he is puffed

up to such an extent that he thinks he is neither in heaven nor on the earth, but has entered the Fullness and is already in the embrace of his angel.[7] He struts about with arrogance and pride and has the air of a proud cock. There are those among them who assert that good conduct is necessary for them to receive the Man who descends from on high; and because of this, with a certain pride, they feign dignity. But many of them, having become scoffers, as if they are already perfect, live irreverently and contemptuously. They call themselves "spiritual" [*spiritales*/πνευματικούς] and assert that they already know the place of refreshment, which is in their Fullness.[8]

3. But let us return to the treatise at hand. For, when it has been clearly stated that those who were the preachers of the truth and the apostles of liberty, styled no one else God or named Him Lord except the only true God the Father and His Word, who has sovereign power in all things,[9] it will then have been clearly proved that they [the apostles] acknowledged the Creator of heaven and earth as the Lord God, who also spoke with Moses and gave to him the economy of the law, and who called the fathers; and that they know of no other. The doctrine, therefore, both of the apostles and of their disciples concerning God, has been made manifest.

CHAPTER 16
PROOF THAT CHRIST HIMSELF IS GOD'S WORD

1. There are, however, those who say that Jesus was the vessel of Christ, upon whom Christ descended as a dove from on high, and when he had pointed out the unnamable Father, he entered the Fullness in an incomprehensible and invisible manner. For he was not only not comprehended by men, but not even by the powers and virtues that are in heaven. [They also assert] that Jesus is a son, but Christ is a father, and Christ's father is God.[1] Others, however, [say] he suffered only in appearance, being naturally impassible.[2]

The followers of Valentinus claim that the Jesus of the economy [*Iesum...qui sit ex dispositione*] is the one who passed through Mary, and upon Him descended the Savior from on high, who is also called the All,[3] because he possesses the names of all who produced him; but that this [Savior] shared with [Jesus] of the economy his power and his name, that death might be abolished through him, and that Father might be known through that Savior who descended from on high. Him, too, they call the vessel of Christ and of the entire Fullness. So in words they profess one Christ Jesus, but in doctrine they reveal a division. For this is their rule, as we have said before: They assert that Christ who was sent forth by Only-begotten for the correction of the Fullness is one being, but that Savior who was sent for the glorification of Father is another being; still another being, moreover, is Savior who was made for the economy, who gave support to Christ, who, they say, also suffered and returned to the Fullness. Consequently, we consider it necessary to make use of the entire doctrine of the apostles concerning our Lord Jesus Christ, and to show that they not only did not think anything of the kind about Him, but more yet, that through the Holy Spirit they even pointed out the ones who would in the future teach such things, instigated by Satan to overthrow the faith of some and draw them away from life.

2. That John knew one and the same Word of God, and that this was the Only-begotten, and that He was the one who became incarnate for our salvation, [namely,] Jesus Christ our Lord, we have sufficiently demonstrated from John's own words.[4]

But Matthew, too, knew of one and the same Christ Jesus, and he explained His generation from the Virgin according to His human nature [*secundum hominem*]—just as God promised to David that He would raise up the eternal King *from the fruit of his womb*,[5] and just as, long before that, He made the same promise to Abraham.[6] [Matthew] said, *The book of the generation of Jesus Christ, the Son of David, the Son of Abraham.*[7] Then in order to free our mind from any suspicion regarding Joseph, he wrote, *Now the generation of Christ was in this wise. When His mother had been betrothed to Joseph, before they came together, she was found to be with child of the Holy Spirit.*[8] Then when Joseph thought of dismissing Mary because she was with child, an angel of God appeared to him, saying, *Joseph, son of David, do not fear to take Mary for your wife, for that which she has in her womb is of the Holy Spirit; she will bear a Son and you shall call His name Jesus, for He will save His people from their sins. All this took place to fulfill what the Lord had spoken by the prophet, saying, Behold, a virgin shall be with child, and bear a Son, and they will call His name Emmanuel, which means God with us.*[9] Thus he clearly indicates that the promise that had been made to the fathers was fulfilled, namely, that the Son of God was born of the Virgin, and that this one is Himself the Savior Christ whom the prophets foretold. It is not, as these heretics assert, that Jesus indeed is the one who was born of Mary, but that Christ is the one who descended from on high. In that case, Matthew would have said, *The generation of* Jesus *was in this wise.* But since the Holy Spirit foresaw the perverters, He fortified against their fraud beforehand by saying through Matthew, *The generation of Christ was in this wise,* and also that this one is *Emmanuel,* so that we would not consider Him merely a man—for *the Word became flesh...not of the will of flesh, nor of the will of man, but of the will of God;*[10] and that we would not think that Jesus was one being while Christ was another, but that we would know that He is one and the same.[11]

3. Paul, when writing to the Romans, explained this very thing: *Paul...an apostle...of Christ Jesus...set apart for the Gospel of God which He promised beforehand through His prophets in the holy Scriptures, concerning His Son who was descended from David according to the flesh, and designated Son of God in power according to the Spirit of holiness, by resurrection from the dead, of Jesus Christ our Lord.*[12] Again, writing to the Romans about Israel, he said, *To them belong the patriarchs* [lit., "fathers"], *and of their race, according to the flesh, is the Christ, who is over all, God blessed forever.*[13]

Once more, in his letter to the Galatians he says, *But when the fullness of time had come, God sent forth His Son, made of a woman, made under the law, to redeem those who were under the law, so that we might receive adoption as sons.*[14] He clearly points out one God who, through the prophets, made the promise regarding His Son; and that there is one Jesus Christ our Lord, who belongs to David's offspring by virtue of the generation from Mary;[15] that this Jesus Christ was designated Son of God in power, according to the Spirit of holiness, by resurrection from the dead,[16] that He might be *the firstborn of the dead,* just as He is the firstborn of all creation.[17] The Son of God was made the Son of Man, that through Him we might receive adoption, since human nature bore and contained and embraced the Son of God.[18]

For the same reason Mark says, *The beginning of the Gospel of Jesus Christ, the Son of God. As it is written in the prophets.*[19] He knows of the one and same Son of God, Jesus Christ, who was announced by the prophets, who is the Emmanuel from the fruit of the womb of David, *the messenger of the great counsel of the Father,*[20] by means of whom God made the Orient and the Just One arise for the house of David, and *raised up for it a horn of salvation,*[21] and *established a testimony in Jacob.*[22] David, likewise, when relating the reasons for His generation, said,

And He appointed a law in Israel...that the next generation might know them,
the children yet unborn, and arise and tell them to their children, so that they
should set their hope in God...and may keep His commandments.[23]

Again, when the angel proclaimed the good news to Mary, he
said, *He will be great, and will be called the Son of the Most High; and the*
Lord...shall give to Him the throne of His father (David).[24] Thus he con-
fessed that the same one who is the Son of the Most High is also the
Son of David. David, too, knowing through the Spirit the economy of
His coming—by which He has dominion over the living and the
dead[25]—confessed Him to be the Lord sitting at the right hand of the
Most High Father.[26]

4. Also Simeon—he to whom it had been revealed by the Holy
Spirit that he should not see death until he had seen Christ Jesus—
received this Firstborn of the Virgin in his arms and blessed God.[27] He
said, *Now You are dismissing Your servant, O Lord, according to Your word,*
in peace; because my eyes have seen Your salvation, which You have prepared
before the face of all peoples, a light of revelation to the Gentiles, and a glory
for Your people Israel.[28] He thus confessed that the infant Jesus whom he
was holding in his arms, who was born of Mary, was Christ the Son of
God,[29] the light of the human race and the glory of Israel itself, and
the peace and refreshment of those who had fallen asleep. Indeed,
He was already despoiling men, by removing their ignorance and giving them His knowledge, and making a division of those who acknowledged Him, as Isaias said, *Call His name, Quickly-spoil, Speedily-divide.*[30]
These indeed are the works of Christ. So that was the Christ whom
Simeon, when he carried Him, blessed Him as the Most High;[31] whom
the shepherds, when they saw Him, glorified God;[32] whom John, when
he was still in his mother's womb, and He in Mary's, acknowledged as
the Lord and, rejoicing, saluted Him;[33] whom the Magi saw and
adored, and to whom they offered gifts, which we mentioned before,[34]
and, having prostrated themselves before the Eternal King, they
returned by another way, and no longer returned by the way of the
Assyrians[35]—*for before the child knows how to call His father and His mother,*
He will take the wealth of Damascus and the spoil of the Assyrians.[36] By all
this he declared in a mysterious but effective manner that the Lord
overcame Amalech with a hidden hand.[37] On this account, too, He
snatched away those boys of the house of David who had the happy lot
of being born at that time, that He might send them on ahead into
His kingdom. For, when He Himself was yet an infant, He prepared

the infants of human parents as witnesses [*martyras*] who, according to the Scriptures, were slain for the sake of Christ who was born in Bethlehem of Judah, in the city of David.[38]

5. For this reason, the Lord, too, said to the disciples after the resurrection, *O foolish ones and slow of heart to believe in all that the prophets have spoken! Did not the Christ have to suffer these things and so enter into His glory?*[39] Again, He said to them, *These are the words which I spoke to you while I was still with you, that everything written about me in the Law of Moses and the Prophets and the Psalms must be fulfilled. Then He opened their minds to understand the Scriptures. He said to them, Thus it is written, that the Christ should suffer and rise from the dead, and that repentance and forgiveness of sins should be preached in His name to all nations.*[40] And this is the one who was born of Mary. It says, *For the Son of Man must suffer many things and be rejected...and be crucified, and on the third day rise.*[41] Therefore, the Gospel knows no other Son of Man except this one who was born of Mary, who also suffered; nor of another Christ who flew upwards from Jesus before the passion. But it recognizes as the Son of God this Jesus Christ who was born, this same one who suffered and rose again, as John the disciple of the Lord confirms. *But these are written,* he says, *that you may believe that Jesus is the Christ, the Son of God, and that, believing, you may have eternal life in His name.*[42] [John] foresaw these blasphemous rules that divide the Lord, as far as is in their power, saying that He was made from two different substances [*substantia*].[43] On that account he has borne witness for us also in his letter as follows: *Dear children, it is the last hour; and as you have heard that Antichrist is coming, so now many have become antichrists; whence we know it is the last hour. They have gone forth from us, but they were not of us. For if they had been of us, they would surely have continued with us; but they were made to be manifest, that they were not...of us....Know therefore that every lie is from without and is not of the truth. Who is the liar but he who denies that Jesus is the Christ? He is the Antichrist.*[44]

6. Now, all those mentioned before, even though in speech they confess one Jesus Christ, make fools of themselves by thinking one thing and saying another. For they have various systems [*argumenta*], as we have shown. They proclaim the one suffered and was born, and that this is Jesus; and there was another who descended to him who also ascended again, and that this is Christ.[45] And they claim one of theirs is from Demiurge, either[46] the one from the economy or the one who is from Joseph, who suffered; but they maintain that the

other of theirs descended from the invisible and unspeakable regions, who, they state, is invisible and incomprehensible and impassible. But in this they stray from the truth, because their doctrine forsakes Him who is truly God. They are ignorant that His Only-begotten Word, who is always present with the human race, was united and closely grafted[47] to His handiwork according to the Father's good pleasure, and who *became flesh*, is Himself Jesus Christ our Lord, who in turn suffered for us and rose for our sakes, and will come again in the Father's glory to raise up all flesh, to manifest salvation, and to reveal the standard of just judgment to all who were made subject to Him.[48] There is, therefore, as we have shown, one God the Father and one Christ Jesus our Lord, who comes through every economy and *recapitulates in Himself all things*.[49] Now, man too, God's handiwork, is contained in this "all." So He also recapitulated in Himself humanity; the invisible becoming visible; the incomprehensible, comprehensible; the impassible, passible; the Word, man.[50] Thus He *recapitulated in Himself all things*, so that, just as the Word of God is the sovereign Ruler over supercelestial, spiritual, and invisible beings, so too He might possess sovereign rule over visible and corporeal things; and thus, by taking to Himself the primacy, and constituting Himself the Head of the Church,[51] He might draw all things to Himself at the proper time.[52]

7. In fact, with Him [the Word] there is nothing unplanned or untimed, just as there is nothing out of harmony with the Father.[53] To be sure, all things have been foreknown by the Father; they are, however, wrought by the Son at the right time, with due harmony and sequence. For this reason, when Mary hastened to the wondrous miracle [*signum*] of the wine, and wished to partake of the compendious cup before the time, the Lord repelled her untimely haste.[54] *Woman, He said, what is this to me and to you? My hour has not yet come.*[55] He was waiting for the hour that was foreknown by His Father. Because of that, when often the people wanted to capture Him, Scripture states, *No one laid hands on Him, because the hour* of His capture *had not yet come;*[56] nor the time of His passion, which was foreknown by the Father, as also the prophet Habakkuk says, *When the years will draw nigh, you will be known; when the time comes, you will be manifested; when my soul will be troubled in anger, you will remember your mercy.*[57]

Paul, too, says, *When however the fullness of time had come, God sent His Son.*[58] This makes it clear that our Lord, being one and the same, nevertheless rich and abundant, brought all things to fulfillment in the order and the time and at the suitable hour, as foreknown. For He ministers to the Father's rich and abundant will, since He is the Savior of those who are saved, and the Lord of those who are under dominion, and the God of all the things that have been created, and the Only-begotten of the Father, and the Christ who had been heralded, and the Word of God who became incarnate *when the fullness of time had come*, in which it behooved the Son of God to become the Son of Man.[59]

8. All, therefore, are outside of the economy who, under pretext of knowledge, understand Jesus as one person and Christ as another, and Only-begotten as still another, the Word as yet another, and Savior as another too, whom these disciples of error assert to be the emission of the Aeons who were made in degeneracy.[60] These men are outwardly sheep, because they employ language similar to ours, and so seem to be like us, saying the same things as we; but inwardly they are wolves.[61] Indeed, their doctrine is homicidal, since it invents many gods and counterfeits many fathers, but it breaks up and divides the Son of God into many beings.[62] The Lord Himself forewarned us to avoid such men, and His disciple John, in the above mentioned letter,[63] commanded us to flee from them: *For many deceivers have gone out into the world, men who do not confess the coming of Jesus Christ in the flesh; such a one is a deceiver and the Antichrist. Look to yourselves, that you may not lose what you have worked for.*[64] Again, he writes in this letter, *Many false prophets have gone out into the world. By this you know the Spirit of God; every spirit which confesses that Jesus Christ has come in the flesh is of God, and every spirit which severs Jesus Christ...is not of God, but is of the Antichrist.*[65] These words are similar to what he said in the Gospel, namely, that the *Word became flesh and dwelt among us.*[66] For this reason he again explains in his letter, *everyone who believes that Jesus is the Christ is a child of God.*[67] He knows one and the same Jesus Christ, to whom the gates of heaven were opened because of His bodily assumption. He will also come in the same flesh in which He suffered, in order to reveal the glory of the Father.[68]

9. Paul, on his part, agrees with these statements when addressing the Romans. He says, *Much more will those who receive the abundance of the grace and...of righteousness reign in life through the one man Jesus Christ.*[69] So he knows nothing of a Christ who flew away from Jesus; nor does he know anything of a Savior who is on high, whom they assert is impassible. For, if the one suffered and the other remained impassible, and if the one was born whereas the other descended on him

who was born and afterward left him again, not one but two are mani-fested. That the apostle, however, knew of one Christ Jesus who was born and who suffered, he tells us in the same letter: *Do you not know that all of us who have been baptized into Christ Jesus were baptized into His death?...so that, as Christ was raised from the dead...we too may walk in the newness of life.*[70] Again, he pointed out that it was Christ who suffered, and that He is the Son of God who died for us and redeemed us by His blood at the time that had been set beforehand. He says, *For why did Christ at the set time die for the ungodly, when as yet we were weak?...But God shows His love for us, in that while we were yet sinners, Christ died for us. Since, therefore, we are now justified by His blood, much more shall we be saved by Him from the wrath....For if while we were enemies we were reconciled to God by the death of His Son, much more, now that we are reconciled, shall we be saved by His life.*[71] And so, he most clearly announces that the same one who was captured and suffered and shed His blood for us was Christ, the Son of God, who also rose and was taken up into heaven,[72] just as Paul himself said, *At the same time Christ who died, yes, who was raised...He who is at the right hand of God;*[73] and, *For we know that Christ, being raised from the dead, will never die again.*[74] Indeed, foreknowing through the Spirit the subdi-visions of these evil teachers, and wishing to cut off from them every occasion for contention, he expressed what has been mentioned. [Again he said,] *But if the Spirit of Him who raised Jesus from the dead dwells in you, He who raised Christ...from the dead will give life to your mortal bodies also.*[75] He all but cries out to those who wish to listen,[76] "Do not err; Christ Jesus, the Son of God, is one and the same, who reconciled us with God through the passion and rose from the dead, and is at the right hand of the Father, having been perfected in all respects; who when He was reviled, did not revile in return; *when He suffered, He did not threaten,*[77] and when He endured tyranny, He asked the Father to forgive them who had crucified Him.[78] He truly saved us, for He is the Word of God, the Only-begotten of the Father, Christ Jesus our Lord."

CHAPTER 17

THE SPIRIT WHO DESCENDED ON JESUS CHRIST

1. The apostles, to be sure, had it in their power to declare that Christ descended on Jesus, or that Savior from on high descended on

the one of the economy, or that he who is from the invisible regions descended on him who is from Demiurge; however, they neither knew nor said anything of the kind. For if they had known [any such thing], they would certainly also have spoken of it. On the contrary, they told us what actually happened; namely, the Spirit of God descended on Him as a dove.[1] This is the Spirit of whom Isaias said, *And the Spirit of God shall rest upon Him,*[2] as we have mentioned. Again, *The Spirit of the Lord...is upon me, because the Lord has anointed me.*[3] This is the Spirit of whom the Lord said, *For it is not you who speak, but the Spirit of your Father speaking in you.*[4] Again, when He gave to the disciples the power of regeneration unto God, He said to them, *Go therefore and make disciples of all nations, baptizing them in the name of the Father, and of the Son, and of the Holy Spirit.*[5] For this is the one whom He promised through the prophets, to pour out even upon menservants and maidservants in those days, that they might prophesy.[6] And for that purpose He [the Spirit] descended on the Son of God, when He had been made the Son of Man, becoming accustomed with Him [Christ] to dwell in the human race, and to rest among human beings, and to dwell in God's handiwork, thus fulfilling the Father's will in them, and renewing them from their old selves for the newness of Christ.[7]

2. This is the Spirit whom David petitioned for the human race, saying, *And strengthen me with Your sovereign Spirit.*[8] Luke tells us that this Spirit descended on the disciples after the Lord's ascension, at the Pentecost,[9] since He possessed the power over all nations for admitting them to life and for opening the New Covenant. Wherefore, with one accord in all languages they sang a hymn to God, while the Spirit brought together in unity distant tribes and offered the firstfruits of the Gentiles to the Father.[10] Wherefore, the Lord too promised to send the Paraclete, who would prepare us for God.[11] For just as out of dry wheat without some moisture one cannot make dough or bread, so neither could we, the many, have become one in Christ Jesus, without the water that is from heaven.[12] And just as dry earth, if it does not receive moisture, does not produce fruit, so also we, since we were first dry wood, would never produce the fruit that is life without the gratuitous heavenly rain. For our bodies were united to imperishability by means of the bath; but our souls, by means of the Spirit.[13] And so both are necessary, since both prepare [us] for life with God. Our Lord pitied the Samaritan woman, that sinner, who did not remain with the one husband but committed immorality [*forni-*

cata est] in many marriages, and He pointed out and promised her the living water, so that she would no longer thirst, and would not be occupied with refreshing herself with water gotten laboriously; for she would have within herself a drink welling up to eternal life.[14] The Lord received this life as a gift from the Father, and He, by sending the Holy Spirit into the whole world, bestows it upon those who partake of Him [*participantur ex ipso*].[15]

3. Gideon—an Israelite—whom God chose to liberate the people from the power of foreigners, foresaw this grace as a gift and changed his petition, and prophesied that the dryness would come upon the fleece of wool—a type of the people [*typus populi*]—on which there had first been only dew.[16] This signified that they would no longer possess the Holy Spirit from God, as Isaias said, *I will also command the clouds that they rain no rain upon it,*[17] and that, on the contrary, on the entire earth there would be dew, which is the Spirit of God, who descended on the Lord, *the Spirit of wisdom and understanding, the Spirit of counsel and might, the Spirit of knowledge and piety, the Spirit of the fear of God.*[18] The Lord Himself in turn gave Him to the Church, when He sent upon the entire earth the Paraclete from heaven, from where the Lord said the devil, too, was cast like a bolt of lightning.[19] Wherefore, we have need of God's dew, that we might not be burned up or become unfruitful; and that where we have an Accuser, we would have also the Advocate [*Paraclete*].[20] And so the Lord entrusted His human nature to the Holy Spirit.[21] It had fallen in with robbers, but He had pity on it and bound its wounds, giving it also two royal denarii,[22] that having received through the Spirit the image and inscription of the Father and the Son, we might make the denarius entrusted to us productive, thereby returning to the Lord the increase in denarii.[23]

4. And so the Spirit descended because of the preordained economy; and the Only-begotten Son of God, who is also the Word of the Father, *when the fullness of time had come,*[24] became incarnate in humanity for the sake of humanity, and fulfilled the entire economy concerning humanity. Nevertheless, Jesus Christ our Lord is one and the same, as even the Lord Himself testifies, and as the apostles profess and the prophets announce. Consequently, all the teachings of those who have excogitated Ogdoads and Tetrads and <Dodecads>[25] and have thought up subdivisions have proved false. These men get the Spirit out of the way altogether and understand Christ as one

being and Jesus as another; indeed, they teach that there was not one Christ but many. Even if they might say these are united, they follow this by showing that the one partook of sufferings while the other remained impassible; the one remained in the intermediate region while the other ascended into the Fullness; the one banquets and enjoys himself in the invisible and unnamable regions, while the other sits beside Demiurge, depriving him of power.

Consequently, it will be incumbent on you, in fact, on all who read this writing [*scripturae*/ταύτῃ τῇ γραφῇ] and are solicitous about their salvation, not to succumb readily to the discourses of these men, which they hear in public. Because, as we have said, though they speak words that sound like those of the believers, they understand not only different doctrines but even contrary ones, and such as are made up wholly of blasphemies. And by these doctrines they kill those who because of the similarity of words take to themselves a poison that disagrees with their constitution. It is as if one would mix gypsum with water and give it as milk, thus deceiving others by the similarity of color.[26] One superior to us, referring to everything that in any way corrupts the things of God and adulterates the truth, put it this way: "Gypsum is wickedly mixed with the milk of God."[27]

CHAPTER 18

WHAT WAS THE REASON FOR THE WORD OF GOD TO BECOME MAN?

1. We have clearly shown that *in the beginning the Word was with God*, and that *through Him all things were made*,[1] that He was also always with the human race, and that, according to the time preordained by the Father, even in these latter days, this same one was united with His handiwork and became man, capable of suffering. Consequently, every objection of those who say, "If therefore Christ was born, then He did not exist before," is rejected. For we have shown that the Son of God did not begin to exist then, having been always with the Father; but when He became incarnate and was made man, He recapitulated in Himself the long unfolding of humankind, granting salvation by way of compendium,[2] that in Christ Jesus we might receive

what we had lost in Adam, namely, to be according to the image and likeness of God.[3]

2. In fact, it was not possible for humankind, which had once been conquered and had been dashed to pieces by its disobedience, to refashion itself and obtain the prize of victory.[4] Again, it was not possible for the human race, which had fallen under sin, to receive salvation. And so the Son, Word of God that He is, accomplished both, by coming down from the Father and becoming incarnate, and descending even to death, and bringing the economy of our salvation to completion.

Paul, while undoubtedly exhorting us to believe this, says, *Do not say in your heart, "Who will ascend into heaven?" (that is, to bring Christ down); or, "Who will descend into the abyss?" (that is, to bring Christ up from the dead).*[5] Then he continues, *For if you confess with your mouth that Jesus is the Lord, and believe in your heart that God has raised Him up from the dead, you will be saved.*[6] And he gave the reason why the Word of God did these things when he said, *For to this end Christ lived and died and rose again, that He might be Lord both of the dead and the living.*[7] Again, when writing to the Corinthians, he said, *But we preach Christ Jesus crucified;*[8] and later he says, *The cup of the blessing which we bless, is it not a participation in the blood of Christ?*[9]

3. Now, who is it that has shared food with us? Is it the Christ from on high who is imagined by these [heretics], who has extended himself across Limit and has given form to their Mother?[10] Or is it *Emmanuel* who was born of *the Virgin, who ate butter and honey,*[11] of whom the prophet said, *And He is a man, and who will recognize Him?*[12] This same one was announced by Paul: *For I delivered to you,* he said, *as of first importance, that Christ died for our sins in accordance with the Scriptures, that He was buried, that He was raised on the third day, in accordance with the Scriptures.*[13] So it is evident that Paul did not know another Christ besides Him alone who suffered and was buried and rose again, who was also born, whom he also called man. For, when he had said, *Now if Christ is preached as raised from the dead,*[14] he continued, giving the reason for His incarnation, *For as by man came death, by a man has come also resurrection from the dead.*[15] And whenever he speaks of the passion of our Lord, and of His human nature and death, he uses the name of Christ. For example, *Do not let what you eat cause the ruin of one for whom Christ died;*[16] again, *But now in Christ...you, who were once afar off, have been brought near through the blood of Christ;*[17] once again, *Christ*

redeemed us from the curse of the law, having become a curse for us—for it is written, Cursed be everyone who hangs on a tree,[18] once more, *And so by your knowledge this weak man is destroyed, the brother for whom Christ died.*[19] Thus he points out that it was not an impassible Christ who descended on Jesus, but, since He was Jesus Christ, He Himself suffered for us; He who lay in the tomb also rose again; He who descended also ascended, the Son of God having been made man, as the very name indicates. Indeed, in the name of Christ is implied He who anoints, and He who is anointed, and the ointment with which He is anointed. And so it is the Father who anoints, and the Son is anointed in the Spirit, who is the Ointment.[20] This the Word says through Isaias, *The Spirit of... God is upon me, because He has anointed me,*[21] by which he points out the Father who anoints, and the Son who is anointed, and the Ointment, which is the Spirit.

4. The Lord Himself makes it plain who suffered. When He asked the disciples, *Who do men say that the Son of Man is?*[22] and when Peter answered, *You are the Christ, the Son of the living God,*[23] and when he was praised by Him, *for flesh and blood has not revealed this to* him, *but* the *Father who is in heaven,* then He made it plain that this Son of Man is *Christ the Son of the living God. For from that time He began to show His disciples that He must go to Jerusalem and suffer many things from the...priests...and be rejected...and crucified, and on the third day be raised.*[24] The very one who was recognized by Peter as Christ, who pronounced him blessed because the Father revealed to him the Son of the living God, said that He Himself would have to suffer many things and be crucified. Then He reproved Peter who thought He was Christ according to the view of men, and so he was opposed to His sufferings.[25] Then He told His disciples, *If any man would come after me, let him deny himself, and take up his cross, and follow me. For whoever would save his life, will lose it; and whoever loses his life for my sake, will save it.*[26] Christ spoke these things openly, for He Himself was the Savior of those who would be handed over to death and would lose their lives because of their confession of Him.[27]

5. Now, if He Himself was not to suffer, but should fly away from Jesus,[28] why did He exhort the disciples to take up the cross and follow Him, if, according to them, He did not take up the cross, but forsook the economy of suffering? To be sure, He did not say this with reference to the knowledge about the Stake [i.e., aeonic Cross] who is above, as some of them make bold to explain,[29] but of His passion

which He had to suffer, and which His disciples themselves would have to suffer. [So] He added, *For whoever would save his life, will lose it; and whoever loses [it] will find it.*[30] To the Jews He was wont to say that His disciples would suffer for His sake. *Behold I send you prophets and wise men and scribes, some of whom you will kill and crucify.*[31] He also used to say to the disciples, *And you will be brought before governors and kings for my sake..., and some of you they will scourge and put to death and persecute you from town to town.*[32] He knew therefore who would suffer persecution, and who would be scourged and put to death for His sake. And He did not [say this] of the other Cross [Stake], but of the passion which He Himself would endure first, and then afterward His disciples. So He gave an exhortation to them, too: *And do not fear those who kill the body but cannot kill the soul; rather fear Him who has the power to send both soul and body into hell,*[33] and saved those who would acknowledge Him. For He promised to acknowledge those before the Father who would acknowledge His name before others; whereas He would deny those who would deny Him, and He would be ashamed of those who would be ashamed of acknowledging Him.[34]

And even though these things are so, certain ones have advanced to such a pitch of boldness that they even hold the martyrs in contempt, and reproach those who are killed because they acknowledge the Lord and endure all things the Lord predicted, and by virtue of this strive to follow in the footsteps of the Lord's suffering, having become witnesses [lit., "martyrs"] to the suffering [Lord]. Such, too, we commend to the martyrs. For when their blood will be sought out,[35] and they will attain glory, then all who held their martyrdom in dishonor shall be put to shame by Christ.

Now, by the fact that the Lord said on the cross, *Father, forgive them, for they know not what they do,*[36] Christ's long-suffering, patience, compassion, and goodness are shown forth, inasmuch as He Himself who suffered also excused those who had treated Him wickedly. For the Word of God who told us, *love your enemies and pray for those who hate you,*[37] did just that on the cross, loving the human race so much that He prayed even for those who put Him to death.

But if anyone would pass judgment on these things under the supposition that there are two [Christs], he would find that the one who is kind amid the very wounds and stripes and the other things done to Him, and is unmindful of the evil done against Him, will be recognized as much better, more patient, and truly good, rather than the one who flew away and did not suffer any injury or reproach.[38]

6. This same objection is against those who claim that He suffered [only] apparently. Indeed, if He did not suffer in reality, He deserves no thanks since He did not suffer at all. And when we would suffer in reality, He would be considered a seducer, because He exhorted us to endure being reviled and to offer the other cheek, though He did not suffer that first in reality.[39] Just as He deceived those by seeming to them to be what He was not, so he deceives us by exhorting us to suffer what He Himself did not suffer. But then we would be above even the Teacher while we suffer and endure what the Teacher neither suffered nor endured. But since our Lord is the only true Teacher, the true Son of God is both good and patient, inasmuch as the Word of God the Father became the Son of Man. He fought, indeed, and conquered; for He was a man fighting for the fathers,[40] and by obedience He destroyed disobedience, because He bound the strong one and loosed the weak ones and gave salvation to His handiwork by destroying sin.[41] For the Lord is most kind and merciful and loves humankind.

7. Therefore, as we have said, He caused humanity to adhere to and be united with God. For if humankind had not overcome the enemy of humankind, the enemy would not justly have been overcome.[42] Again, unless God had given salvation, we would not possess it securely; and unless the human race had been united with God, it would not be partaker of imperishability. For it behooved *the Mediator of God and humanity*, by His kinship to both, to lead them back to friendship and concord, and to bring it about that God would take humankind to Himself, and that humankind would give itself to God.[43]

Really, in what way could we be partakers of filial adoption, unless we had received through the Son participation in Himself; unless His Word, having become flesh, had granted us communion in God? For that reason He also came [that is, lived] through every age, restoring to all the participation in God.[44] Those, then, who assert that He was manifested putatively and was not born in the flesh and was not made man are still under the ancient condemnation; they extend patronage to sin,[45] since according to them death has not been overcome, which *reigned from Adam to Moses, even over those whose sins were not like the transgression of Adam.*[46] But when the law which was given by Moses came and bore witness to sin, that it [sin] is a transgressor, the law took away its kingdom by exposing it to be a robber and not a king, and by showing it to be a homicide.[47] On the other hand, it put a burden on humankind, which had sin in itself, and showed humans to be deserving of death. For since the law was spiritual, it merely manifested sin, but it did not get it out of the way; for sin did not have dominion over the Spirit, only over humanity.

Certainly, it behooved him who could put sin to death and redeem humanity who was liable to death, to become what [this latter] was, namely, humanity—humanity which had been drawn into slavery by sin, but was held bound by death. The result would be that sin would be put to death by humanity, and humanity would escape from death. For, just as through the disobedience of one man who was fashioned first from untilled earth many were made sinners and lost life, so it was fitting also through the obedience of the one man, who was born first of the Virgin, that many be made just and receive salvation.[48] Thus, then, the Word of God was made Man, as also Moses said, *God, true are His works.*[49] But if He seemed to be flesh without becoming flesh, His work was not true. On the contrary, what He seemed to be, that He also was, namely, God, who recapitulated in Himself the ancient handiwork of man [Adam], that He might kill sin and destroy death and give life to humankind. And for this reason His works are true.

Chapter 19
Against Those Who Say Jesus Was Begotten by Joseph

1. Furthermore, those are liable to death who bluntly assert that He is a mere man, begotten of Joseph, since they remain in the slavery of the former disobedience;[1] for they have not yet been united with the Word of God the Father,[2] nor have they received liberty through the Son, as He Himself said, *If therefore the Son makes you free, you will be free indeed.*[3] But since they are ignorant of the Emmanuel who was born of the Virgin,[4] they are deprived of His gift, which is eternal life.[5] And since they do not receive the Word of imperishability, they continue in the mortal flesh and are debtors to death, because they do not accept the antidote to life.[6] In reference to them the Word, speaking of His gift of grace, said, *I have said, "You are gods, sons of the Most High, all of you; nev-*

ertheless, you shall die like men."[7] Doubtless He speaks these words to those who have not received the gift of adoption, but who despise the incarnation of the pure generation of the Word of God, defraud humankind of its ascent to God, and are ungrateful to the Word of God who was incarnate for their sakes.[8] For the Word of God became man, and He who is God's Son became the Son of man to this end, [that man,] having been united with the Word of God and receiving adoption, might become a son of God. Certainly, in no other way could we have received imperishability and immortality unless we had been united with imperishability and immortality. But how could we be united with imperishability and immortality unless imperishability and immortality had first become what we are, in order that the perishable might be swallowed up by imperishability, and the mortal by immortality,[9] that *we might receive the adoption of sons?*[10]

2. On that account, *Who shall declare his generation?*[11] since *He is a man, and who shall recognize Him?*[12] He, however, knows Him [the Son] to whom the Father in heaven has revealed Him, in order that he might understand that He [the Son] *who was born not of the will of flesh nor the will of man*, is the Son of man; He is Christ, the Son of the living God.[13] For we have demonstrated from the Scriptures that none of Adam's sons is in view of himself absolutely called God or named Lord. On the other hand, that He [Christ] is God[14] in a more proper sense than all people who then existed, and is proclaimed as Lord and eternal King, Only-begotten Son and incarnate Word, by all the prophets and apostles, and by the Spirit Himself, can be seen by everyone who has attained to even a modicum of the truth. Now the Scriptures would not have testified these things of Him if, like all others, He had been only man.[15] However, the divine Scriptures do testify concerning Him that He possessed in Himself the generation from the most high Father which is more noble than that of all others,[16] and that He experienced the noble birth from the Virgin[17]—all these things the Scriptures prophesied about Him: both that He was a man of suffering and without beauty,[18] that He sat upon a foal of an ass,[19] that He was given vinegar and gall to drink,[20] that He was despised by the people[21] and descended even to death;[22] and [second] that He is the Holy Lord and the Wonderful Counselor, and the Beautiful in appearance, and the Mighty God,[23] coming on the clouds as Judge of all people.[24]

3. Indeed, just as He was man that He might undergo temptation, so He was the Word that He might be glorified. The Word, on

the one hand, remained quiescent [*requiescente*/ἡσυχάζοντος], that He could be tempted and dishonored and crucified and die; on the other hand, the man was absorbed [*absorto*], that He might conquer and endure and show Himself kind, and rise again and be taken up [into heaven].[25] So this Son of God, our Lord, was both the Word of the Father and the Son of Man. Since He had a human generation from Mary, who was of the human race and was herself a human being, He became the Son of Man. For this reason the Lord Himself gave us a sign in the depths below and in the heights above.[26] Man [Ahaz] did not ask for that [sign], because he did not hope that a virgin, as a virgin, could become pregnant, and that she [could] also give birth to a son, and that this child [could] be "God with us,"[27] and that He [could] descend into the lower parts of the earth, searching for the sheep that was lost—which really was His own handiwork—and ascend to the heights above, there offering and recommending to the Father humanity who was found.[28] Thus He, in Himself, offered the firstfruits of the resurrection of humankind,[29] that, as the Head rose from the dead, so also, when the time of his condemnation has been fulfilled, which was merited by the disobedience, the rest of the body [made up] of every human being who is found in life might rise,[30] having been nourished through its joints and ligaments, and having grown with the growth that is from God,[31] since each member has its proper and apt position in the body.[32] For in my Father's house are many rooms,[33] since there are also many members in the body.[34]

CHAPTER 20
WHY GOD WAS MERCIFUL TOWARD
DISOBEDIENT HUMANITY

1. God, therefore, was long-suffering when, upon the default of the human race, He foresaw the victory to be granted through His Word. In truth, when power was made perfect in weakness, [the Word] showed forth God's kindness and His most magnificent power.[1]

To illustrate, He patiently endured that Jonas be swallowed [*absorbi*] by the whale,[2] not that he be swallowed up and perish altogether, but that when he had been vomited up again, he might be more submissive to God, and might the more glorify Him who granted him a salvation he could not have hoped for; and he made for the Ninevites a secure repentance, that they might return to the Lord who liberated them from death when they were frightened by the miracle [*signum*] that had been worked on Jonas. This is what the Scripture says of them: *And every one of them turned from his evil way and from the injustice which was in his hands, saying, "Who knows, God may yet repent and turn away from us His anger, and we will not perish."*[3]

In the same way, from the beginning God permitted humanity to be swallowed up by the great whale who was the author of the transgression, not that he be swallowed up and perish altogether; no, God, through the miracle of Jonas, planned the method of salvation that was effected by the Word for those who possessed the same teaching about the Lord as Jonas, and confessed and said, *I am a servant of the Lord, and I fear the Lord, the God of heaven, who made the sea and the dry land.*[4] Thus humankind, receiving from God the salvation it could not have hoped for, might rise from the dead, glorify God, and utter the cry that was prophesied by Jonas, *I called out to the Lord from my distress and He answered me from the belly of hell.*[5] Thus he might also always continue [to live], glorifying God and rendering thanks to Him unceasingly for the salvation he has received from Him. The result was to be *that no human being might boast in the presence of the Lord,*[6] and humans might never accept a contrary opinion in regard to God, thinking that the imperishability that they have is their own naturally, and, not holding fast to the truth, might boast with a vain pride as if they were naturally like unto God. In point of fact, by this humans made themselves more ungrateful toward Him who created them: they both obscured the love that God was wont to have toward them, and blinded their minds so that they could not have thoughts about God worthy of Him, comparing themselves to and judging themselves equal to God.

2. Such, therefore, was the long-suffering of God, that humans might pass through all things and might experience the knowledge of death[7] and arrive at the resurrection from the dead, and learn by experience from what they were freed. Thus humankind might always continue to be grateful to God, since it was from God that the human race received the gift of imperishability, in order that it might love Him the more. Surely those love more to whom more has been forgiven.[8] Moreover, as a result humans would know themselves, that they are mortal and weak; they would understand God, too, that He is immortal and powerful to such an extent that He grants immortality

to the mortal, and eternity to the temporal. They would understand the rest of God's powers that were shown toward themselves, and, having been taught through these, they would understand about God, how great God is.

In truth, God is the glory of humanity, but humanity is the vessel of God's working, of all His wisdom and power.[9] Just as a physician proves himself among the sick, so God is manifested among human persons. For this reason, Paul said, *For God has consigned all things to disobedience, that He may have mercy on all.*[10] And this he did not say of the spiritual Aeons but of humanity who had been disobedient to God and had been cast out from immortality, but then attained mercy inasmuch as humans received the adoption that is through God's Son Himself. For they who, without being puffed up and boasting, hold fast the true opinion about the creatures and their Creator[11]—who is the most powerful God of all things and grants existence to all things—and by continuing to love Him and to be submissive to Him and to render thanks to Him, will receive the greater glory from Him, making such progress as to become wholly like Him who died for them. For He was made *in the likeness of sinful flesh* that He might condemn sin, and then cast it out of the flesh as condemned;[12] and also, that He might invite humankind to His own likeness, inasmuch as He designated humans as imitators of God, led them to the Father's law that they might see God, and granted them the power of receiving the Father. He was the Word of God who dwelt in humanity, and was made the Son of Man in order that He might accustom humankind to receive God, and accustom God to dwell in humanity according to the Father's good pleasure.[13]

3. So it was on this account that the Lord Himself [gave] the sign of our salvation, namely, Him who is Emmanuel, born of the Virgin,[14] because the Lord Himself saved them who were not able to save themselves.[15] On this account Paul, preaching on human weakness, said, *I know that nothing good dwells in my flesh,*[16] thereby pointing out that the good of our salvation is not from ourselves but from God. Again, *Unhappy man that I am! Who will deliver me from the body of this death?*— then he adds the Liberator—*The grace of Jesus Christ our Lord.*[17] Isaias too spoke of this: *Strengthen the weak hands, and make firm the feeble knees. Say to those who are of a fearful heart, "Be strong and fear not. Behold, our God will come and save us."*[18] This [he said] because we were able to be saved not by ourselves but by God's help.

4. Again, [the same prophet] foretold that the one who would save us would not be a mere man, nor without flesh—for the angels are without flesh. He said, *Neither an elder, nor an angel, but the Lord Himself will save them, because He loves them, and has mercy on them; He Himself will liberate them.*[19] And that this very one would be a true and visible man, though He is the salutary Word, Isaias again informs us: *Look upon Sion the city, your eyes will see…our Savior.*[20] And that He who died for us was not a mere man, [Jeremias] tells us, *And the Lord, the Holy One of Israel, was mindful of the dead who had slept in the land of burial; and He came down to them to announce to them the good news of salvation that comes from Him, in order to save them.*[21] The same thing was spoken of by the prophet [Micah], *He will turn again and have mercy on us; He will put away our iniquities, and He will cast all our sins into the bottom of the sea.*[22] And again, indicating the place of His coming, he says, *The Lord has spoken from Sion, and from Jerusalem He has uttered His voice.*[23] The prophet Habakkuk, too, said that it is from the south section of Judah's inheritance that God's Son will come, who is God—to that part belongs Bethlehem, where the Lord was born[24]—and will send forth His praises over the whole earth. He said, *God will come forth from the south, and the Holy One from the mount of Ephrem. His power covered the heavens, and the earth is full of His praise.…The Word shall go before His face, and His feet shall go forth in the fields.*[25] He plainly points out that He is God, that His coming is at Bethlehem and from Mount Ephrem, which is to the south of the inheritance, and that He is a man. *For His feet,* he said, *shall go forth in the fields,* which is a characteristic peculiar to humanity.

Chapter 21

Proof That a Virgin Will Conceive, and Not a Young Girl, as Some Explain

1. So God became man, and the Lord Himself saved us, having Himself given the sign of the Virgin.[1] Consequently, the interpretation of certain ones who dare to explain the Scripture thus: *Behold, a* young girl *will conceive and bear a son,* is not true.[2] Among these are Theodotion of Ephesus and Aquila of Pontus, both of them Jewish proselytes. These were followed by the Ebionites, who assert that He

was born of Joseph, thus, as far as in them lies, destroying so great an
economy of God[3] and making void the prophets' testimony, which is
the work of God. This was indeed prophesied before the transmigra-
tion of the people into Babylon took place, that is, before the Medes
and the Persians acquired dominion. It was, however, translated into
Greek by the Jews themselves a long time before our Lord's coming,
so that there is no room for suspicion that the Jews did so to accommodate themselves to us. For if they had known that we would ever
exist and could use the testimonies of the Scriptures, they would
never have hesitated to burn the Scriptures that make it clear that the
rest of the nations all have a share in life, and that show that those
who boast that they are the house of Jacob and the people of Israel
are disinherited from the grace of God.

2. In explanation, before the Romans held supreme power and
the Macedonians still occupied Asia, Ptolemy the son of Lagus desired
to adorn the library, which was built in Alexandria, with the worth-
while books of all peoples. So he asked the people of Jerusalem to
have their Scriptures translated into the Greek language. For, at that
time the Jews were still under the Macedonians. So they sent seventy
elders—their most accomplished scholars of the Scriptures, who also
knew both languages—to Ptolemy to carry out his wishes. But he
wished to put them to the test, for he feared lest they should confer
among themselves and in the translation hide the truth that is in the
Scriptures. So he separated them all and ordered each one to make a
translation of the same Scripture. This was done with all the books.
Afterwards they gathered in assembly with Ptolemy and compared
their translations. God was glorified and the Scriptures were recognized to be truly divine, for all of them read exactly the same things
with the same words and names from beginning to end, so that even
the Gentiles who were present acknowledged that the Scriptures were
translated through the inspiration of God.[4] That God did this for
them is not surprising, because during the captivity of the people
under Nebuchadnezzar the Scriptures had been ruined, so when after
seventy years the Jews had returned to their own land and Artaxerxes
was king of the Persians, God inspired Esdras, a priest of the tribe of
Levi, to restore all the discourses of the ancient prophets and to
restore to the people the law given by Moses.[5]

3. The Scriptures, then, have been translated with such fidelity
by God's grace, and from these God has prepared and prefashioned

our faith in His Son. For He has preserved the Scriptures unadulterated for us in Egypt—the place where the house of Jacob flourished
after escaping the famine in Canaan,[6] where also our Lord was saved
when He fled from Herod's persecution.[7] Moreover, this translation of
these Scriptures [was made] before our Lord descended [to earth],
and before the Christians appeared. In point of fact, the Lord was
born about the forty-first year of the reign of Augustus;[8] but Ptolemy,
under whom the Scriptures were translated, lived much earlier. In
view of this, truly impudent and bold do those show themselves who
wish at present to make other translations when they are refuted by us
from the Scriptures themselves and are obliged to believe in the coming of God's Son.

But our faith is firm and not fictitious, and alone true. This can
be proved clearly from these Scriptures, which were translated in the
manner we described. Furthermore, the preaching of the Church is
without additions [*interpolatione*]. For since the apostles are much earlier than all of these [heretics], they agree with the above mentioned
translation, and the translation agrees with the tradition of the apostles [*apostolorum traditioni*]. For Peter and John and Matthew and Paul,
and the rest after them, and also the followers of these, preached all
the prophetical writings, just as they are contained in the translation
of the elders.[9]

4. In truth, one and the same Spirit of God, who through the
prophets foretold how and in what manner the Lord would come,
and who through the elders translated well the things that had been
prophesied well, preached in turn through the apostles that the fullness of the times of the adoption had come,[10] and that *the kingdom of
the heavens was near*,[11] and that it dwells within those who believe in *the
Emmanuel* who was born of *the Virgin*.[12] They testify that *before Joseph had
come together with Mary*—so while she was still in virginity—*she was found
to be with child of the Holy Spirit*;[13] and that the angel Gabriel said to her,
*The Holy Spirit will come upon you, and the power of the Most High will over-
shadow you; and therefore the Holy One to be born of you will be called the Son
of God*;[14] and that the angel said to Joseph in a dream, *Now all this took
place to fulfill what was spoken by…the prophet Isaias: Behold, the Virgin shall
be with child*.[15]

Now the elders gave this translation of what Isaias said: *Again the
Lord spoke to Ahaz, Ask a sign of the Lord your God; let it be to the depth below
or to the heights above. But Ahaz said, I will not ask, and I will not put the*

*Lord to the test. And he said: Hear then, O house of David: Is it not a small
thing for you to put men to the test, the way the Lord puts to the test? Therefore
the Lord Himself will give you a sign: Behold, the Virgin shall be with child
and bear a Son, and you will call His name Emmanuel. He shall eat curds
and honey;... before He knows or chooses evils, He will choose the good. For
before the child knows evil or good, He will not consent to wickedness, in order
that He may choose the good.*[16]

So by these words the Holy Spirit carefully pointed out His birth
from the Virgin, and also His nature [*substantia*], namely, that He is
God (for the name Emmanuel signifies this); and that He is a man,
when He[17] says, He shall eat curds and honey, and when He calls Him
an infant, before he knows the good and evil; for all these things are
characteristic of a human infant. But the fact that He will not consent
to wickedness, in order that He may choose the good, is peculiar to
God. [This was said] so that by the fact that He will eat curds and
honey, we might not understand Him to be a mere man; and, on the
other hand, that we might not suspect Him to be God without flesh
because of the name Emmanuel.[18]

5. And when he says, *Hear, O house of David*, he indicated that the
eternal King, whom God promised David that He would raise up *from
the fruit of his womb*, is the one who was born of the Virgin who was of
David's line.[19] In fact, for this reason He promised the King from the
fruit of David's womb, which is proper to a pregnant virgin; and not
from the fruit of his loins or from the fruit of his reins, which is proper
to a man who begets and of a woman who conceives by the aid of a
man. Scripture, therefore, in the promise excluded the generative
powers of a man. Why, he [Joseph] is not even mentioned, since the
one who was born was not of the will of man.[20] But Scripture mentioned and emphasized *the fruit of the womb*, that it might declare the
generation of Him who was to come from the Virgin. For example,
Elizabeth, *filled with the Holy Spirit*, bore witness [to this] when she said
to Mary, *Blessed are you among women, and blessed is the fruit of your
womb.*[21] By this the Holy Spirit pointed out, to all who wish to hear, that
the promise that God had made, namely, that He would raise up the
King *from the fruit of the womb*, was fulfilled in the birth-giving of the
Virgin, that is, of Mary. Consequently, those who change the passage
of Isaias into *Behold, a* young girl *will be with child* and hold that He is
Joseph's son should change also the promise that was made to David,
where God promised him that He would raise up from the fruit of his

womb the horn of Christ the King.[22] But this they did not understand, otherwise they would have made bold to change it, too.

6. Again, when Isaias said, *to the depths below, or to the heights above,*[23] he pointed out that He *who descended* is the one *who ascended.*[24] And when he said, *The Lord Himself will give you a sign,*[25] he indicated something unexpected about His birth, which would never have taken place unless the Lord God, the God of all things, *had Himself given a sign in the house of David.* Indeed, what would there have been great about, or what kind of a sign would there have been in, the fact that a young girl would have conceived by a man and given birth, which happens to all women who bear children? But since an unexpected salvation of humanity was to take place with God's aid, so also an unexpected birth from the Virgin took place—God giving the sign, without a man producing it.[26]

7. With that in mind, Daniel, in turn, foreseeing His coming, said that *a stone cut out by no hands* had come into this world.[27] For this is what *by no hands* meant, that His coming into the world was not by the operation of human hands, that is, of men who usually cut stones. In other words, Joseph took no part in [producing] Him; Mary alone cooperated in the economy. For this stone which is from the earth gets its existence by both the power and the skill of God. For this reason Isaias said, *Thus says the Lord, Behold I am laying in Sion for a foundation a stone, a precious stone, chosen, the chief cornerstone, one to be held in honor,*[28] that we might understand that His coming as man was *not of the will of man, but of the will of God.*[29]

8. On this account also Moses, manifesting a type, threw a rod to the ground, that when it had become enfleshed [*incarnata*] it might expose and swallow up all the sinfulness of the Egyptians that was rising up against God's economy, that even the Egyptians might bear witness that it was God's finger that wrought salvation for the people, and not Joseph's son.[30] For if it had been Joseph's son, how could he have had more power than Solomon, or than Jonas,[31] or how could he have been greater than David, since he was born of the same seed and was their offspring?[32] How, moreover, could He [the true Jesus] pronounce Peter blessed for acknowledging Him as *the Son of the Living God?*[33]

9. But above all, according to Jeremias, neither could He have been king if He had been Joseph's son, nor heir. For Joseph is seen to be the son of Joachim and Jechonias, as also Matthew explains His origin.[34] Now Jechonias and all his descendants were disinherited from

the kingdom. So says Jeremias, *As I live, says the Lord, though Jechonias, the son of Joachim, the king of Judah, were the signet ring on my right hand, yet would I tear him off and give him into the hands of those who seek your life.*[35] Again, *Jechonias was despised as a pot which no one cares for..., because it is cast into a land which he did not know. O land,...hear the word of the Lord!...Write that this man is disinherited;...for none of his offspring shall succeed in sitting on the throne of David, and ruling in Judah.*[36] Again, God says in regard to Joachim his father, *Therefore thus says the Lord concerning Joachim the king of Judah: He shall have none to sit upon the throne of David, and his dead body shall be cast out to the heat by day and to the frost by night. And I will look upon him and his sons, and I will bring upon them and upon the inhabitants of Jerusalem, upon the land of Judah, all the evils that I have pronounced against them.*[37]

Those therefore who assert that He was generated from Joseph and place their hope in Him have disinherited themselves [*abdicatos se faciunt*] from the kingdom, thus falling under the curse and rebuke which is against Jechonias and his posterity. For on this account were these things said about Jechonias—since the Spirit foreknew the assertions of evil teachers—that they might learn that, according to the promise of God, the eternal King who recapitulates in Himself all things, would not be born from the offspring of Jechonias, that is, from Joseph, but from David's loins.[38]

10. He has recapitulated in Himself even the ancient first-fashioned man. To explain, *just as by one man's disobedience...sin came...and death through sin...reigned...*, *so by one man's obedience, justice was brought* and produces the fruit of life for those who in times past were dead.[39] First, just as the first-fashioned Adam got his substance from untilled and as yet virgin soil—*for God had not yet caused it to rain...and man had not tilled* the ground[40]—and was formed by God's hand, that is, the Word of God—for *all things were made through Him*[41]—and the Lord took *mud from the earth and fashioned man.*[42] In like manner, since He is the Word recapitulating Adam in Himself, He rightly took from Mary, who was yet a virgin, His birth that would be a recapitulation of Adam.[43] If then the first Adam would have had a human father and had been born of a man's seed, rightly would they assert that the second Adam too was born from Joseph. But if the former was from the earth and fashioned by the Word of God, it was necessary that the same Word, since He was recapitulating Adam in Himself, have the same kind of birth. Why, then, did God not take earth a second time, instead of making the handi-

work from Mary? In order that no different handiwork might be made, and that it might not be a different handiwork that would be saved; but that the same might be recapitulated, the likeness having been preserved.[44]

Chapter 22
Against Those Who Say Jesus Received Nothing from the Virgin

1. They, therefore, err who, to cast out the inheritance of the flesh, assert that He received nothing from the Virgin; and they also reject the likeness. For if the former [Adam] had a formation and substance from the earth by both God's hand and skill, whereas the latter [Christ] was not made by God's hand and skill, then He did not preserve the likeness of man, who *was made according to His image and likeness,* and He will appear to be an inconsistent artificer, since He has nothing on which to manifest His wisdom.[1]

Moreover, that would be saying that He appeared putatively as man, when He was not a man; and that He was made a man though He received nothing from humanity. For if He did not receive the substance of [His] flesh from a human being, neither was He made man, nor the Son of Man. And if He was not made what we are, He did nothing great when He suffered and endured. That we, however, are a body taken from the earth and a soul that receives the Spirit of God, everyone will acknowledge. This, then, is what the Word of God became, since He recapitulated in Himself His own handiwork. For this reason, too, He professes to be the Son of Man and blesses *the meek, for they shall inherit the earth.*[2]

The apostle Paul, too, in his letter to the Galatians, says plainly, *God sent His Son, made from a woman.*[3] And again in the letter to the Romans, *concerning His Son, who was descended from David according to the flesh and designated Son of God in power according to the Spirit of holiness by His resurrection from the dead, Jesus Christ our Lord.*[4]

2. On the other hand, His [supposed] "descent into Mary" would be useless. For why would He descend into her if He were to receive nothing from her? And, if He received nothing from Mary, He would never have taken of the foods got from the earth, by which the

body that was taken from the earth is nourished; nor would His body have hungered and sought its food after the fast of forty days, in imitation of Moses and Elias.[5] Neither would His disciple John, when writing of Him, have said, *So Jesus, wearied as He was with the journey, sat down.*[6] Nor would David have exclaimed of Him in prophecy, *And they had added to the grief of my wounds;*[7] nor would Jesus have wept over Lazarus;[8] nor would He have sweat drops of blood;[9] nor would He have said, *My soul is very sorrowful;*[10] nor would blood and water have flowed from His side when it was pierced.[11] For all these things are indications of the flesh that was taken from the earth, which He recapitulated in Himself, thus saving His handiwork.

3. To prove this, Luke shows that the genealogy of our Lord, which extends to Adam, contains seventy-two generations,[12] and so he joins the end to the beginning and points out that He [Christ] it is who recapitulates in Himself all the nations that had been dispersed from Adam onward, and all the tongues, and the human race, including Adam himself. Hence Paul, too, styled Adam *a type of the one who was to come,*[13] because the Word as Artisan of all things had designed beforehand, with a view to Himself, the future economy relating to the Son of God on behalf of the human race;[14] namely, God destined the first, the ensouled man [Adam], that he might be saved by the spiritual man [Christ]. For inasmuch as the Savior existed beforehand, it was necessary that what was to be saved should also exist, so that the Savior would not be something without a purpose.[15]

4. Consistently,[16] then, also the Virgin Mary was found to be obedient when she said, *Behold I am the handmaid of the Lord, let it be done to me according to Your word;*[17] but Eve was disobedient, for she did not obey when she was yet a virgin (*for they...were both naked* in paradise, *and were not ashamed,* because they had recently been made and had no knowledge about generating children; for they had first to grow up, and then multiply[18]). She was disobedient, and became the cause of death for herself and for the entire human race. In the same way, Mary, though she had a man destined for her beforehand, yet nevertheless a virgin, was obedient and was made the cause of salvation for herself and the entire human race.[19] For this reason, the law calls her who is espoused to a man, though she is still a virgin, the wife of him who espoused her,[20] pointing out thereby the return-circuit from Mary to Eve.[21] For in no other way is that which is tied together loosed, except that the cords of the tying are untied in the reverse order, so

that the first cords are loosed by [loosing] the second; in other words, the second cords release the first. And so it happens that the first cord is untied by the second cord, and the second cord serves as the first's untying.[22] With this in view the Lord said, the first will be last, and the last first.[23] The prophet, too, pointed out the same thing: *in place of your fathers, sons were born to you*, he said.[24] For the Lord, who was born *the firstborn of the dead*,[25] receiving the ancient fathers into His bosom, regenerated them to the life of God, having become the beginning of living beings, since Adam had become the beginning of the dying.[26] For this reason Luke, when he began the genealogy of the Lord, carried it back to Adam, pointing out that they did not regenerate Him for the Gospel of life, but He them. In like manner, the knot of Eve's disobedience was untied by Mary's obedience. For what the virgin Eve tied by her unbelief, this Mary untied by her belief.[27]

CHAPTER 23

THE FIRST ADAM SHOULD HAVE BEEN THE FIRST TO PARTAKE OF THE SECOND ADAM'S SALVATION

1. It was necessary, therefore, that the Lord, when coming to the lost sheep[1] and making a recapitulation of so great an economy, and seeking out His handiwork, should save the very man who was made according to His image and likeness,[2] that is, Adam, who was filling out the time of his punishment, which was imposed because of his disobedience. These times *the Father has fixed by His own authority*.[3] In point of fact, every economy of salvation that concerned humanity took place according to the Father's good pleasure, that God might not be overcome nor His skill be powerless. For if humankind, which was made by God that it might live, but which lost that life when it was injured by the serpent who corrupted it,[4] would no longer return to life but would be altogether abandoned to death, God would be overcome and the serpent's wickedness would thus prevail over God's will.[5]

But since God is unconquerable and long-suffering, He showed Himself long-suffering in the correction of humanity and put all under probation, as we have said. He bound the strong one by the second Man, and plundered his vessels, and abolished death by vivifying the man who had been killed.[6] For Adam was made the first vessel of his [Satan's] possession, whom he [Satan] had also held in his power; that is, he wickedly brought transgression on him, and under pretext of immortality wrought death in him. For though he promised that they would be like gods[7]—a thing in no way possible for him—he wrought death in them. And so he who had led humanity into captivity was justly recaptured by God. Moreover, the human race, which had been led captive, was loosed from the bonds of punishment.

2. So, then, since it behooves us to speak the truth, this is Adam, the first-fashioned, concerning whom Scripture affirms that God said, *Let us make man in our image and likeness.*[8] We, moreover, all take our origin from him [Adam], and since we are from him, therefore we also inherit his name. Now since humanity is saved, it is proper that that man be saved who was created first. For it would be quite irrational to say that he who suffered severe injuries from the enemy, and first endured captivity, is not freed by Him who overcame the enemy, though his children whom he begot in captivity were freed. The enemy would still not seem to be conquered, if the ancient spoils were still to remain in his power. By way of illustration, suppose an enemy people overcomes certain people and takes these conquered ones captive, holding them a long time in slavery, so that they would beget children among them; and suppose someone would have pity on those who had been made slaves, and would overcome those same enemies. Now, he would not act justly if he would free the children of the captives from the power of those who had led their fathers into slavery, but those who had endured the captivity he would leave subject to the enemies on account of whom he had his revenge—namely, if the children would attain freedom in vindication of the cause of the fathers, but the fathers themselves who endured captivity would be left behind. But God, who has given aid to humanity and restored humans to their freedom, is not devoid of power, nor is He unjust.[9]

3. In keeping with this idea, immediately after Adam had transgressed, as the Scripture relates, God uttered no curse against Adam himself, but against the earth on account of his deeds;[10] as a certain of the elders has said, "God transferred the curse to the earth, that it might not remain in man."[11] But as punishment for his transgression, the man received weariness and earthly labor, and to eat his bread in the sweat of his face, and to return to the ground from which he was taken.[12] In like manner, the woman [received] weariness, labors, sighs, painful childbirths, and servitude—that is, to serve her husband.

Thus, they were not cursed by God, that they might not perish altogether; but neither were they left unreprimanded, lest they come to despise God. The whole curse, however, fell upon the serpent who seduced them: *And God said to the serpent,* [the Scripture] says, *because you have done this, cursed are you above all cattle and above all wild animals of the earth.*[13] This same thing the Lord said in the Gospel to those who will be found on His left, *Depart from me, ye cursed, into the eternal fire prepared for the devil and his angels,*[14] thereby indicating that eternal fire was not prepared originally for humankind, but for him who seduced humankind and caused humans to sin; for him I say, who is the prince of the rebellion, and for the angels who together with him became rebels.[15] This fire they too will justly experience who, like him, continue in their wicked deeds devoid of penitence and without retracing their steps.[16]

4. For example, Cain, when God advised him to calm himself because he had not made an equitable division of the share of his goods with his brother, but imagined that with jealousy and wickedness he could overcome him, he not only did not calm himself, but added one sin to another, betraying his mind by his deeds. For what he pondered he also did: he overcame him and killed him.[17] God subjected the just one to the unjust one, that the former might be shown as just by the things he suffered, and that the latter might be exposed as unjust by the things he did. But not even by this did [Cain] become gentle, nor did he calm himself in regard to the evil deed; but when asked where his brother was, he said, *I do not know. Am I my brother's keeper?*[18] increasing and multiplying his evil by his answer. Surely, if it is an evil to murder one's brother, it is much worse so audaciously and irreverently to answer the omniscient God, as if one could trick Him. For this reason he too bore a curse, because he excused the sin in himself and did not revere God, nor was ashamed of the fratricide.[19]

5. In the case of Adam, however, nothing of this sort took place. Indeed, all things happened in the opposite manner. To explain, when Adam had been seduced by another on the pretext of immortality, immediately he was seized with fear and hid himself—not as if he could escape from God, but, in a state of confusion at having transgressed God's command, he felt unworthy of coming into the presence of and conversing with God.[20] However, since *the fear of the Lord is the beginning of understanding,*[21] knowledge of the transgression led to repentance—and God bestows His kindness on those who repent. As

it is, Adam showed his repentance by his action in regard to the girdle, namely, when he covered himself with fig leaves, though there were many other leaves that would have been less irritating to his body.[22] But, being awed by the fear of God, he made a garment conformable to his disobedience. He resisted the petulant impulse of the flesh, since he had lost his guileless and childlike mind and had come to the knowledge of evil things.[23] And so he surrounded himself and his wife with a girdle of continence, for he feared God and expected His coming. It was as if he wished to say: Since through disobedience I have lost the robe of holiness that I had from the Spirit, I now acknowledge that I deserve such a garment as offers me no pleasure, but gnaws at the body and pricks it. And he would always have retained this garment, by way of humbling himself, unless the Lord who is merciful had put on him shirts of skin in place of the fig leaves.[24]

So, too, God questions them, that the blame might come upon the woman. In turn He questions her, that she might defer the guilt to the serpent. Indeed, she related what had actually taken place: *The serpent deceived me, and I ate.*[25] The serpent, however, He did not question; for He knew that he was the chief actor in the transgression. But at the first he placed the curse on him, that it might fall on humanity as a secondhand rebuke. For God hated him who seduced humankind; but He gradually, little by little, had pity on the one who had been seduced.[26]

6. For this reason He also cast them [humankind] out of paradise and removed them far from the tree of life.[27] Not that He envied them the tree of life, as some dare to assert,[28] but by way of pitying them, that they might not continue forever as a transgressor, and that the sin that had them surrounded might not be immortal, nor their evil interminable and incurable. So He checked their transgression by interposing death, and He made sin cease by putting an end to it through the disintegration of the flesh, which should take place in the earth, so that humanity, ceasing at length to live in sin, and dying to it, would begin to live to God.[29]

7. With that in mind, He *put enmity between* the serpent and *the woman* with her *offspring,* who *observed* each other.[30] On the one side there is the one whose sole was bitten but who has *the power to tread on the head of his enemy;* on the other side there is the one who bit and killed and hindered the steps of humanity *until the offspring came* who was Mary's child, who was destined beforehand *to trample on his head.*[31]

Of Him the prophet said, *You will tread upon the asp and the basilisk; the young lion and the serpent You will trample under foot.*[32] By this he pointed out that sin (which had made humanity cold), which rose and spread itself out against the human race, would, together with death that held sway, be deprived of its power;[33] and it would be trampled on by Him in the last times,[34] namely, when the lion, that is, the Antichrist, would rush upon the human race; and He would put in chains the dragon, that ancient serpent,[35] and make it subject to the power of the human race, which had been conquered, so that humanity could trample down all his [the dragon's] power.[36]

Now Adam had been conquered, and all life had been taken from him. Consequently, when the enemy was again conquered, Adam received life. *And the last enemy to be destroyed is death,*[37] which had first taken possession of humankind. Wherefore, when humanity has been freed, *shall come to pass the saying that is written, "Death is swallowed up in victory. O death, where is your victory? O death, where is your sting?"*[38] This could not have been said justly if he had not been freed over whom death first had dominion. For his salvation is death's destruction. So when the Lord gave life to humanity, that is, to Adam, death was destroyed.

8. All are liars, therefore, who deny salvation to Adam. These exclude themselves from life forever, because they do not believe that the sheep that had been lost was found.[39] But if it has not been found, then the entire human race is still under the dominion of perdition. So Tatian, the first to introduce this opinion—rather, this ignorance and blindness—is a liar. He was the combination of all heretics, as we have shown.[40] But he invented this error by himself, in order that by introducing something new, different from the rest, and by speaking of empty things, he might prepare for himself hearers devoid of faith, feigning to be esteemed as a teacher, and attempting to make use of sayings of the sort that Paul employed assiduously: *In Adam we all die.*[41] But he was ignorant that *where sin increased, grace abounded all the more.*[42] Since this has been clearly proved, let them all be put to shame who are his followers and who wrangle about Adam, as if some great gain would come to them if he were not saved. Rather, they gain nothing, just as the serpent gained nothing by persuading humanity, except that this showed him to be a transgressor, since he had humanity as the beginning and object of his rebellion.[43] But he did not overcome God.[44] In the same way, those who deny salvation to Adam gain nothing except

this, that they make themselves heretics and apostates from the truth, and show themselves to be advocates of the serpent and of death.[45]

CHAPTER 24
A SUMMARY

1. All of these men,[1] then, have been exposed who introduce pernicious opinions about our Creator and Fashioner, who also made this world and above whom there is no other god. Likewise overthrown are the very proofs of those who teach false doctrines about the nature of our Lord and about the economy that He made for the sake of His own human race.[2] The Church's preaching is everywhere established and continues the same, and has testimony from the prophets and the apostles, and all the disciples (as we have shown) throughout the beginnings and the middle times and the end,[3] yes, throughout God's whole economy and the secure working that tends toward salvation and is operative in our faith.[4] This faith we safeguard, having received it from the Church. It is like some excellent deposit in a suitable vessel,[5] that always, under God's Spirit, rejuvenates itself and rejuvenates the vessel in which it is.[6]

For this, God's gift, has been entrusted to the Church, as the life-breath to the first-fashioned, so that all the members receiving it might be vivified.[7] And in this gift has been deposited the Communion of Christ,[8] that is, the Holy Spirit, the pledge of imperishability,[9] the strength of our faith[10] and the ladder of ascent to God.[11] For *in the Church,* [Paul] says, God *has placed apostles, prophets*...and all the rest of the Spirit's ministries.[12] Of Him [the Spirit] all those do not partake who do not agree with the Church, but defraud themselves of life by their evil doctrines and wicked practices.[13] For where the Church is, there is the Spirit of God; and where God's Spirit is, there is the Church, and all grace; and *the Spirit is truth.*[14]

Those, then, who are not in communion with Him, neither are nourished by the mother's breasts unto life, nor receive from the most limpid spring that proceeds from the body of Christ.[15] No, they dig for themselves broken cisterns out of earthen ditches and drink from the mire the putrid water, fleeing as they do from the faith, lest they be exposed; and rejecting the Spirit, lest they become educated.[16]

2. Moreover, having alienated themselves from the truth, they deservedly wallow in every error, tossed to and fro by it, because they believe differently about the same things as time passes and never have a stable doctrine, because they wish rather to be sophists of words than disciples of the truth.[17] In fact, they have not been founded on the one rock, but on sand, with many stones piled on it.[18]

For this reason they also fabricate many gods, and so have the excuse of always searching, but they can never find them.[19] Really, they are blind! Indeed, they blaspheme the Maker—Him who is truly God, who furnishes also the power to find [Him]—thinking that they have found another god above God, or another fullness, or another economy. For this reason the light that is from God does not shine for them, because they have dishonored and despised God, considering Him of little account, seeing that He comes within reach of human knowledge by reason of His love and immense kindness.[20] But this is not a knowledge relating to His greatness or essence—for no one can measure or touch it—but [a knowledge] that will enable us to know that He is the only true God who made and fashioned us, and breathed the breath of life into us, and nourishes us by means of the creation; who by His Word establishes all things and by His Wisdom harmoniously unites them.[21] But they dream up a god who in actuality does not exist, as being above this God; thus they think they have found a great god whom no one can know, because he does not have fellowship with the human race and does not administer earthly affairs.[22] The Epicureans, for example, invented a god who bestows nothing on them or any others, that is, who takes care of no one.[23]

Chapter 25
Proof That This World Is Ruled
by the Providence of God

1. God, however, does exercise providence over all things. Consequently, He also gives counsel, and by giving counsel He assists those who have a care for morals.[1] It is necessary, therefore, that those who are provided for and governed should recognize their director, since they are not irrational or purposeless, but have received an understanding from God's providence. Consequently, certain ones of

the Gentiles, who were less addicted to allurements and pleasures and were not led away to so great a superstition in idols, though they were moved by His providence only slightly, nevertheless were converted to say that the Maker of this world is the Father who provides for all and arranges this our world.

2. Again, in order that they might take away from the Father the power of reproving and of judging, thinking that it is unworthy of God, and believing they have found a god who is good and free from anger, they asserted that one god judges and the other saves.[2] But they are unaware that thus they deprive [God] both of intelligence and justice. To be sure, if the god with judicial power is not also good, so that he might bestow gifts on those to whom he must and reprove those whom he should, he will appear to be neither a just nor a wise judge. On the other hand, the good god, if he is only that and not also one who puts to the test those on whom he lavishes his goodness, will be without justice and goodness; and his goodness will appear powerless when he does not save all, if this is not done with judgment.[3]

3. Consequently, Marcion, by dividing God in two, asserting the one to be good and the other to have judicial power, destroys God on both counts.[4] For the one who has judicial power, if he is not also good, is not God, because he who lacks goodness is not God. On the other hand, the one who is good, if he is not also just, suffers the same fate as the former, namely, he is deprived of something without which he is not God. Moreover, how do they claim that the Father of all things is wise, if they do not ascribe to Him also judicial power? For if He is wise, He also judges, and one who judges obviously has judicial power. But judicial power is followed by justice, that He might judge them justly, and justice calls for judgment; further, judgment when accompanied by justice will defer to wisdom. Therefore, the Father must excel in wisdom over all human and angelic wisdom, since He is the Lord, the just Judge and Ruler of all. For He is both good and merciful and patient and saves those whom He ought. Neither is goodness lacking to Him on account of His justice, nor is his wisdom deficient. For He saves those whom He ought, and judges those deserving of judgment. Nor is His justice shown to be without meekness, since goodness goes ahead and takes precedence.

4. The God, then, who kindly *makes His sun rise on* all…, *and sends rain on the just and the unjust,*[5] will judge those who have received an equitable share of His kindness yet have not led lives in keeping with

the dignity of His gift, but have spent their time in pleasures and luxury in spite of His benevolence. More yet, they have blasphemed Him who bestowed such great benefits on them.

5. Plato is shown to be more religious than these men, since he acknowledged that the one and same God is both just and good and has power over all things, and even exercises judicial power. Thus he said, "And God indeed, as also the ancient word has it, possesses the beginning and end and middle of all beings; he accomplishes [all things] justly, dealing with them according to their nature. But retributive justice against those who defect from the divine law always follows him."[6] Again, he shows the Creator and Maker of this world to be good. "To the good," he says, "no jealousy ever arises with regard to anything."[7] By this he sets down God's goodness as the beginning and cause of the creation of the world, but not ignorance, nor the Aeon who went astray, nor the fruit of the defect, nor the mother who wept and lamented, nor any other God or Father.[8]

6. Rightly does their Mother weep over the excogitators and originators of such errors. For they have deservedly called this falsehood upon their heads,[9] saying that their Mother is outside the Fullness, that is, outside the knowledge of God, and so their conglomeration has become a shapeless and ugly abortion.[10] In point of fact, she apprehended nothing of the truth, and fell into a void and shadow; for their Wisdom was empty and enveloped in darkness, and Limit did not permit her to enter the Fullness, and Spirit did not receive them into the place of rest.[11] To explain, their Father begat ignorance, and so brought on them the sufferings of death. We are not misrepresenting these things: they themselves confirm, teach, and glory in them. They hold a deep mystery about their Mother whom they assert was begotten without a father, that is, without God, female from a female, that is, corruption from error.[12]

7. We, however, pray that these men do not remain in the ditch they have dug, but will separate themselves from such a Mother, forsake the Profundity, depart from the void, and abandon the shadow. [We pray] that, having converted to God's Church, they may be born legitimately and Christ may be formed in them;[13] and that they may know the Maker and Creator of this universe, the only true God and the Lord of all things. We petition these things for them, loving them more than they think they love themselves. For our love, since it is true, is salvific for them—if only they will accept it. It is like a bitter

medicine that removes the foreign and useless flesh around a wound, for it deflates their pride and haughtiness. Consequently, we shall not grow weary in trying with all our might to extend a hand to them.[14]

In addition to what has already been said, I have put off treating the discourses of the Lord until the following book. Perhaps, by convincing some of these by means of the very doctrine of Christ, I can persuade them to give up this sort of error and desist from the blasphemy against their Maker, who alone is God and the Father of our Lord Jesus Christ. Amen.[15]

NOTES

INTRODUCTION

1. D. J. Unger and J. J. Dillon, *St. Irenaeus of Lyons–Against the Heresies: Book 1*, ACW 55 (New York/Mahwah, NJ: Paulist Press, 1992).

2. J. Smith, *St. Irenaeus–Proof of the Apostolic Preaching*, ACW 16 (Westminster, MD: Newman Press, 1952; repr., Mahwah, NJ: Paulist Press, 1978).

3. The Greek retroversion is an extraordinary work of scholarly reconstruction and an invaluable resource in seeking for Irenaean linguistic continuity and the like; however, it is to be lamented that this Greek translation is too often called upon by readers as authoritative and in some sense original—thus used in citations, quotations, and so on. It is, after all, a modern retranslation.

4. See further comments on the chapter headings in these volumes by Unger at ACW 55, p. 18. The history of the modern printed editions of Irenaeus's works, including a discussion of the advent and inclusion of chapter headings, has recently been offered by Paul Parvis in a paper at the 2009 Edinburgh conference on Irenaeus, entitled "Irenaeus after Rousseau: The Text Past and Future." Students of Irenaeus may eagerly look forward to the publication of this helpful study in the conference proceedings, to be published in 2011.

5. See A. Roberts and J. Donaldson, eds., *The Ante-Nicene Fathers*, vol. 1 (1887; repr., Grand Rapids: Eerdmans, 1987).

6. See P. Bacq, *De l'ancienne à la nouvelle alliance selon s. Irénée: unité du livre IV de l'Adversus Haereses* (Paris: Editions Lethielleux, 1978); M. A. Donovan, *One Right Reading? A Guide to Irenaeus* (Collegeville, MN: Liturgical Press, 1997).

7. See A. Orbe, *La Unción del Verbo*, vol. 3, Estudios Valentinianos 3 (Rome: Gregorianum, 1961), 1–717.

8. See D. J. Unger, "St. Irenaeus and the Roman Primacy," *Theological Studies* 13 (1952): 359–418.

9. But cf. our note on Irenaeus's usage: chap. 1, n. 1.

10. On the implications this holds for the dating of book 3, see ACW 55, pp. 3, 4.

11. On the Word and Wisdom as the Father's "hands," see, e.g., *AH* 4.Praef.4, 4.20.1, 5.1.3, and in various other places in Irenaeus's works.

PREFACE

1. For Simon as the father of all heresies, see ACW 55, p. 81 n. 1, 227–29. Because of the context here and in the rest of the paragraph, we have followed the suggestion of SC 210 (n. 1 to p. 17) that in the first sentence Irenaeus is speaking not of the doctrines of Valentinus alone, but of all his disciples. Lat.Iren. has made a simple mistake in reading the Greek.

2. Lat.Iren. has *propter quod, cum sit unius operis traductio eorum et destructio in multis, misimus.*...Sagnard (SC 34, p. 93) translated, "Mais s'il suffit d'un ouvrage pour les produire à la lumière, il en fair plusiers pour les réduire à néant." SC 211:17 has the same idea in slightly different words. But such a construction by contrast seems scarcely intended here in Lat.Iren., who, by his consistent custom, would have used *quidem...autem*, which SC without warrant added in its Greek retranslation. In our translation we believe we preserve the idea Irenaeus wished to convey.

Traductio et destructio is an allusion to the full title of the *AH*, as also *arguendum et evertendum* in the next paragraph. In the couplet *traductio et destructio*, it is the first term, not the second (*pace* Harvey), that represents the Greek ἔλεγχος ("exposé"); *destructio* is not a false reading for *detectio*, just as *destructa* below is not a false reading for *detecta*, but represents "refuted."

3. Cf. Eph 2:4: *dives est in misericordia*; 1 Cor 13:4: *caritas...non aemulatur.*

4. Cf. Eph 3:20. So Irenaeus presents the economy as flowing forth from God's love; cf. E. Osborn, *Irenaeus of Lyons* (Cambridge: Cambridge University Press, 2001) 85, 105.

5. Lat.Iren. has *distribuit*, which SC 210 (n. 1 to p. 19) claims does not fit, as Irenaeus nowhere else speaks of the Church's distributing faith to her children. *Distribuit* seems to represent διαδίδωσι, which might also mean transmit, and that would be regular in Irenaeus, as also παραδίδωσι (*tradit*) in 5.Pref. But if *distribuit* does represent διαδίδωσι and not παραδίδωσι, it may indeed mean that the Church distributes faith, "hands it out" as a nourishing food. Since the suggested Greek is not certain, we have stayed with the Latin.

Though Irenaeus does not use the title "Mother Church," the idea behind such a term is indicated in the present passage, as again in *AH* 5.Pref. Toward the end of book 3, in 3.24.1, Irenaeus tells us that those who do not partake of the Spirit "neither are nourished by the mother's breasts unto life." From the context it is clear that this "mother" is the Church. In 4.26.5 he singles out the presbyters as "nourished" by the Church. In 4.2.12 he speaks of the nuptials of the Word with the Church of the Gentiles, supposing that the Church is His bride and their mother. In 5.25.2 he uses Gal 4:26, which seems to have been an important source for Irenaeus for the concept of Church-Mother. For the early history of this title, see J. C. Plumpe, *Mater Ecclesia: An · Inquiry into the Concept of the Church as Mother in Early Christianity*, Studies in Christian Antiquity 5, 5 (Washington, DC: Catholic University of America Press, 1943), esp. pp. 35–44 on the title μήτηρ ἐκκλησία in the Church of the Lyonese martyrs and in the works of Irenaeus (on whose feast day the book was dedicated). J. Behr has recently made a new study of the language of "Virgin Mother, Virgin Church" in the patristic age, located in *The Mystery of Christ—Life in Death* (New York: St. Vladimir's Seminary Press, 2006), 115–40.

It should be noted that Irenaeus here also marks the apostolicity of faith, which will be a capital issue against the heretics. See ACW 55, p. 11.

6. Cf. Matt 28:18–20. Irenaeus implies the one Church of the apostles, which guards and hands down to all Christians the doctrine of Christ she received from them. Sagnard (SC 34, p. 95) inserted *precher* and (SC 210, n. 1 to p. 21) *d'annoncer* after "power of"; but even though the power over the Gospel is here limited to preaching it, the expression should be left open, as in Irenaeus. Preaching the Gospel, as he will make clear later, is only the initial step in such power. See H. B. Timothy, *The Early Christian Apologists and Greek Philosophy—Exemplified by Irenaeus, Tertullian and Clement of Alexandria* (Assen: Van Gorcum, 1973), 26.

7. Luke 10:16. Irenaeus here suggests the Church's possession of power to teach all persons authoritatively, as granted by Christ's own authority. To define truth as "the doctrine of God's Son" is as much a beautiful as it is an exact encapsulation of Irenaeus's position. Cf. Osborn, *Irenaeus*, 147.

CHAPTER 1

1. In 1 Tim 3:15 Paul says that the Church is "the pillar and bulwark of the truth"; in 2 Tim 2:15, 19 the "word of truth" is presented as "God's firm foundation." Irenaeus ascribes this function to the Gospel, as itself the foundation of the Church. In *AH* 3.11.8 Irenaeus again alludes to 1 Tim 3:15: *columna autem et firmamentum Ecclesiae est Evangelium.* Because of the similarity to our present passage, SC 210 (n. 2 to p. 21) thinks it possible that Lat.Iren. had originally written here (as there) *firmamentum*, not *fundamentum*. This is possible, but, as indicated above, Irenaeus may also have used 2 Tim 2:15, 19, from which he took *fundamentum*.

The priority of the oral Gospel, "traditioned" and handed on, over the written Gospel as a conduit of revelation is here clearly enunciated. For

Irenaeus, Scripture, as recorded text, is not independent of the living tradition of the Church. On this matter, Behr has recently made insightful comments; see J. Behr, *The Formation of Christian Theology*, vol. 1, *The Way to Nicaea* (New York: St. Vladimir's Seminary Press, 2001), 121–25, and more broadly pp. 17–48. The same author also notes (*Asceticism and Anthropology in Irenaeus and Clement* [Oxford: Oxford University Press, 2000], 30–33) that it is in particular the "scriptural texture" of the apostolic preaching (the tradition) that confirms it as authoritative; and so the new teaching of the apostolic witness is the tradition *of* Scripture, not a tradition opposed to it. So, for Behr, there is an "identity between Scripture and tradition" in Irenaeus (p. 31). See also T. L. Tiessen, *Irenaeus on the Salvation of the Unevangelized* (London: Scarecrow Press, 1993), 193–95; P. Hefner, "Theological Methodology and St. Irenaeus," *Journal of Religion* 44 (1964): 294–309; and J. Ochagavía, *Visibile Patris Filius: A Study of Irenaeus's Teaching on Revelation and Tradition* (Orientala Christiana Analecta 171; Rome: Pontifical Institute of Oriental Studies, 1964), 193–205.

2. Cf. Luke 24:49 ("clothed with power from on high"); Acts 1:8, 2:4. At times it is difficult to indicate by italics precisely which words in quotations and allusions are directly from the Scriptures, as Irenaeus regularly combines texts.

"They had full assurance concerning all things": Lat.Iren. has *de omnibus adimpleti sunt.* Sagnard (SC 34, p. 96) had inserted "with gifts"; but SC 210 (n. 1 to p. 23) points out that Lat.Iren. never uses *de* for such a meaning, but always either the genitive or the ablative. According to the context, they are filled with certitude about all things and, for that reason, have perfect knowledge. SC found a striking parallel to this, both in wording and in idea, in Clement, *1 Cor.* 42.3 (ACW 1:34), where the Greek is πληροφορηθέντες, not πληρωθέντες, as *adimpleti* might suggest. Irenaeus nowhere else employs this word, and so its presence here would seem to confirm that he is indeed using a source, namely, Clement. J. N. D. Kelly (*Early Christian Doctrines*, rev. ed. [New York: Harper, 1978], 36–37) notes parallels to this paragraph in Tertullian, *De praesc.* 21. It is clear that, for Irenaeus, the apostles thus received the fullness of the faith at Pentecost; see Osborn, *Irenaeus*, 86, 109, who also notes that, in light of *AH* 3.3.1, the preaching of these apostles may thus be equated with the truth in its fullness (p. 86), which they have deposited in the Church (p. 122; cf. *AH* 3.4.1).

3. Cf. Acts 1:8; Rom 10:15, 18; Ps 18:5; Luke 2:14. "Gospel of God" occurs a number of times in the NT, e.g., Rom 1:1; 1 Pet 4:17.

4. Chapter 1, a classical passage on the origin of the four Gospels, gives rise to a number of questions. Its context is important: Irenaeus connects this paragraph with the preceding (on the apostles going forth after receiving perfect knowledge, each thus possessing "the Gospel of God") with the connective particle *ita*, supposing οὕτως. The Greek fragment of Eusebius does not have this, though it is considered almost certainly original; Eusebius has changed

the connective to suit his own context, as pointed out by J. T. Curran, "St. Irenaeus and the Dates of the Synoptics," *Catholic Biblical Quarterly* 5 (1943): 39–40. οὕτως, it should be remembered, normally introduces an illustration. From the end of the preface, and from chap. 1 and the end of chap. 2, it is the aim of Irenaeus to prove that the Gospel is apostolic, that it comes from the apostles and is one and the same wherever preached or handed down in the Scriptures, and that through the apostles it comes from Christ Himself, the truth. In other words, he shows, first, that all the apostles possessed the same Gospel of Christ; second, that this one Gospel was first preached orally and only later written down; third, that this same Gospel was preached everywhere, "to the ends of the earth." The present paragraph contains, as the connective particle suggests, an illustrative confirmation of these points.

In order to grasp the construction more easily, we print the paragraph in phrase lines:

(1) Matthew, accordingly,

    (a) produced a writing of the Gospel *among the Hebrews* in their own language,

    (b) whereas Peter and Paul evangelized *at Rome* and founded the Church [there].

(2) But after their departure, Mark, Peter's disciple and translator, handed down to us in writing what was preached by Peter.

(3) Luke too, Paul's follower, set down in a book the Gospel that was being preached by Paul.

(4) Later John likewise, the Lord's disciple who had also rested on His breast, issued the Gospel while living *at Ephesus* of Asia.

The italics are ours, so marked to stress the various geographic centers, and so collectively the universality of the Gospel preaching. As per Irenaeus's comments, Matthew brought out a written Gospel among the Hebrews, supposedly in Palestine; Peter and Paul, who preached the Gospel at Rome orally, had it written down later by their companions Mark and Luke respectively; lastly, John wrote down this same Gospel at Ephesus. There are, then, three geographic centers for the same Gospel. Irenaeus further indicates three periods in the apostolic age for this expansion: first Matthew's, then Peter-Mark's and Paul-Luke's, and lastly John's. This relation or contrast of place in time is carefully noted in the grammatical constructions, with explicit mention of the four authors of the written Gospels. Yet the primary aim is to show not the historical data of composition, but that the Gospels, all four, are the same single Gospel which derives from the apostles, and that it was preached everywhere. The Gospel is thus both apostolic and catholic; or, the catholic Gospel, that which was preached everywhere, is apostolic. Cf. *AH* 3.15.3; 3.31.3.

The individual phrases are worthy of closer examination for what they have to say of Irenaeus's picture of the Gospels and their composition, which differs considerably from the common view of modern scholarship:

(1a) *"Matthew, accordingly, produced a writing of the Gospel among the Hebrews in their own language."* We have already pointed out the force of "accordingly," indicating the connection of this paragraph with the ideas preceding it. The "also" comes from the Greek fragment, which seems to have been omitted by the Latin scribe. Yet it is important, for it implies that Matthew had preached the oral Gospel before he put it into writing, which is precisely what Irenaeus claimed in the preceding paragraph was done by all the evangelists.

Papias is the first written record we have of a Hebrew, or more precisely Aramaic, Matthew. According to a Greek fragment preserved by Eusebius, Papias testified that Matthew used "the Hebrew language" in his exposition of the Gospel; see J. A. Kleist, *The Didache, The Epistle of Barnabas, The Epistles and the Martyrdom of St. Polycarp, The Fragments of Papias, The Epistle to Diognetus*, ACW 6 (London: Longmans, Green, 1948), 118; and see also A. Robert and A. Tricot, *Guide to the Bible* (New York: Desclée, 1960), 386, 390. This ancient testimony has been the subject of decades of heated dispute among scholars, who are of various minds as to the existence of such an original; but it should be noted at the very least that ancient tradition was fairly unanimous in holding it. If such a version did exist, it was certainly not the same as the canonical Greek Matthew, but this of itself does not negate the existence of the Aramaic; see A. Metzinger, H. Höpfl, and B. Gut, *Introductio Specialis in Novum Testamentum* (Rome, 1948), 39–41. Some have argued that Greek Matthew might be a translation of an Aramaic original, but this is unlikely; see A. C. Perumalil, "St. Matthew and His Critics," *Homiletic and Pastoral Review* 74 (1973–74): 31–32, 47–53. It is worth noting, however, that there are some twenty-one citations from the OT in canonical Matthew taken not from the LXX but from the Hebrew, and that some plays on words are not original to the Greek but are of Hebrew origin. Jerome, a multi-linguist himself, refers twice to Aramaic Matthew, and there were thought to have been copies of it in Caesarea, Beroea, Alexandria, and Jerusalem in the fourth century; and the fifth-century Curetonian MS represents the Aramaic Matthew. J. Kürzinger ("Irenäus und sein Zeugnis zur Sprache des Matthäusevangelium," *New Testament Studies* 10 [1963–64]: 108–15) advanced the odd view that Irenaeus knew only Greek Matthew, and that when he says Matthew wrote in the Hebrew language, he is referring not to an Aramaic version but to the Greek written in Hebraic style. This seems wholly untenable.

(1b) *"...whereas Peter and Paul evangelized at Rome, and founded the Church [there]."* Eusebius notes that Peter came to Rome under Claudius (AD 41–54; see Eusebius, *HE* 2.14.6 [GCS 2:138]). Orosius (*Historia Ecclesiastica* 7.6 [ML 31:1072 ff.]) and Jerome (*De viris illustribus* 1 [ML 23:607]) depend on Eusebius for the same information. This harmonizes well with Acts 12:17, where after the martyrdom of James (c. AD 42) St. Peter is said to have gone "to another place," namely, Rome. He returned to Palestine for the so-called

Council of Jerusalem c. AD 50 (cf. Acts 15). The decree of Claudius (issued in 49/50) expelling all Jews from Rome need not have affected Peter, who had already left, though it must have kept him away from Rome until at least AD 54, when Nero recalled the decree. Sometime thereafter he returned, exercising his ministry until being martyred in the city in AD 64, or more probably 67. As for Paul, his letter to the Romans (15:19, 23, 24, 28), as well as the Acts (19:21, 27, 28), makes it clear that he came to Rome for the first time on the occasion of his appeal to Caesar, and that he was imprisoned there for two years (see Acts 28:30). This would be c. AD 61. After his release c. 63, details of his time and activities in Rome are unknown, though it is certain that he did not remain there without interruption, since he visited the East. He was back in Rome certainly for his second imprisonment (see 2 Timothy), leading up to his martyrdom c. AD 67.

Irenaeus is thus justified in his claim that Peter and Paul preached in Rome and there founded the Church. His statement does not require their simultaneous presence in the city, nor that they worked hand in hand to establish the Church, nor even that there was no Church in Rome prior to their arrival. There were Christians there before Peter's arrival, and Paul gives the impression of a well-established Christian community in the city before his own visit. Nevertheless, both Peter and Paul can be considered "founders" of the Roman Church inasmuch as it was their authority by which it was built up, and to whom its establishment was credited among the ancient sources; see Clement of Rome, *1 Cor.* 5.4–5 (ACW 1:12) and Ignatius of Antioch, *Ad Romanos* 4.3 (ACW 1:82).

There was considerable debate in the first part of the twentieth century as to the relationship of (1a) and (1b), namely, over the relative dating of the work of Matthew, on the one hand, and Peter and Paul, on the other. The participial construction of the sentence could be temporal, implying a simultaneity of activity between Peter and Paul's preaching and Matthew's writing of his Gospel, thus c. AD 60–63. So see, for example, the old text of J. Chapman, "St Irenaeus on the Dates of the Gospels," *Journal of Theological Studies* 6 (1905): 566. But this author also put forward that the participial construction could be adversative (see ibid., 563–69). Thus, "Matthew brought out..., whereas Peter and Paul proclaimed...." Irenaeus is concerned not with the dates of the Gospels but with their apostolic origin.

5. Irenaeus here notes that Mark handed down the Gospel of Peter in writing; cf. also *AH* 3.10.5. Again, Papias is the first to record witness to such a tradition (cf. Eusebius, *HE* 3.39.15); see also Kleist, *Didache*, 118, and his note there, as well as his competent study *Reread the Papias Fragment on St. Mark*, St. Louis University Studies, Series A (St. Louis, MO: St. Louis University Press, 1948), 1–17. After Papias it became a common tradition of the ancient Church. It is not to be taken in a restrictive sense, for Mark certainly had other sources than Peter; yet a large share of his Gospel is thought to have

come from Peter's preaching. Some ancient sources, for example, Clement of Alexandria, held even that Peter approved the Gospel after Mark had written it; see Metzinger, Höpfl, and Gut, *Introductio specialis in N.T.*, 74ff.

Mark handed down this Gospel "after their departure." "Their" obviously refers to Peter and Paul in the preceding clause, confirmed by the fact that in this and the next sentence it is Peter and Paul's Gospel that is said to be handed down. And which departure was it? Various answers have been proposed. The Greek term will have been ἔξοδος, used primarily of quitting one place and going to another; but it is also used of death. Lat.Iren. has *excessum*, which Cicero as well as ecclesiastical Latin writers used of death. Rufinus translated Eusebius's fragment with *exitum* (*HE* 5.8). J. E. Grabe (199, n. 3), W. W. Harvey (2:5, n. 2), L. Murillo, and others held that the departure was from Rome on some mission elsewhere, but this does not work with Irenaeus's own time line. Paul's departure from Rome on further missionary travels could not have been prior to the end of his first imprisonment, c. AD 63. But according to Irenaeus, by that time Luke's Gospel was already written, and prior to that Mark's. Scholars such as F. Patrizzi, R. Cornely, A. Camerlynck, and J. Knabenbauer tried to avoid this difficulty by holding that the departure was from Palestine, but this cannot hold in light of the participial construction of the preceding sentence, in virtue of which Peter and Paul would have preached in Rome prior to their departure from Palestine, which is obviously impossible. N. Walker ("Patristic Evidence and the Priority of Matthew," *Studia Patristica* 7 [1966]: 571–75) advanced the view that the departure was from Syria (i.e., Antioch), to which Peter had fled (see Acts 12:17), but this does not work with Irenaeus's statement that before the departure both Peter and Paul had preached in Rome. Walker attempted to get around this difficulty by assuming (indefensibly, in light of both the Latin and Greek manuscripts) that a scribe wrote Rome instead of Syria, and thus he thinks Matthew's Gospel in Aramaic was written c. AD 33, and the Greek version, with additions, c. 35; and Mark's Gospel, according to this tradition, was then written c. AD 45. There can be no probability to this opinion.

The common view has always been that this "departure" of Peter and Paul was from this earth, that is, through death. ἔξοδος has this meaning in Luke 9:31 and 2 Pet 1:15, where it is used for Peter's death. In the letter of the churches of Vienne and Lyons, likely written by Irenaeus, ἔξοδος is used twice for death (cf. Eusebius, *HE* 5.1, 2). The fact that it is nowhere else in the *AH* used in such a way is no absolute argument against such a meaning here. We, like SC 210 (n. 3 to p. 23), read it in this way. But it must be noted that such a reading raises a difficult chronological problem. Paul was martyred c. AD 67, which is also a probable date of Peter's death (though some scholars, as noted above, opt for the earlier date of 64 on both counts). According to Irenaeus's testimony, Mark's Gospel would therefore have to have been written after AD 67 (or 64); but this late date for Mark goes against the whole of ancient tradition (which puts Mark before Luke), as well as the common (though not exclusive) view of modern scholars. Moreover, Irenaeus himself holds that Luke wrote his Gospel while Paul was alive (see above), and no ancient writer is known to have criticized Irenaeus for having made a mistake on this point, though many used his testimony.

It is uncertain, then, how to read the chronological data of the present sentence. It should be remembered, however, that Irenaeus is not attempting a historical study of Gospel origins; his point is that the Gospels were faithfully transmitted by the apostles. Here he is not attempting to offer a date for the composition of Mark's Gospel, only to note that it "was handed down" after Peter's death—which of itself implies that it had its origin earlier.

6. Paul affirms that he preached the Gospel (see Gal 2:2; 2 Tim 2:8; 1 Thess 2:9). That Luke, the longtime companion of Paul, wrote down the latter's preaching is a well-attested tradition of the ancient Church, supported by strong internal evidence that betrays a number of similarities to Paul's theology. Though scholars have often discussed the problem of Luke's composition "after their departure," namely, Paul's departure from this life, that chronological relation was not intended by Irenaeus for Luke, only for Mark (see our previous note). The sentence on Luke's composition is not dependent on "after their departure," as is clear in the Greek καὶ δέ, indicating a procession of thought that makes the sentence coordinate to that on Mark. Irenaeus clearly indicates in the present book (3.14.1) that Luke's Gospel was written during the lifetime of Paul, with his approval, obviously before Acts. As long as the grammatical construction of the present passage does not force us to hold (as it does not) that Luke wrote after Paul's death, we must interpret it in the light of the clearer later passage.

7. Cf. John 13:23; 21:20. Among the ancient writers this is a classical testimony for the Johannine authorship of the fourth Gospel. Irenaeus employs John's Gospel extensively throughout his five books, and appeals to him often by name, for example, 2.2.5; 2.22.3; 3.11.1; 3.22.2; 5.18.2. This "disciple of the Lord" is, according to Irenaeus, this apostle John (see 1.8.5; 1.9.3). The attempts of Harnack and others to prove that Irenaeus is here an unreliable witness rather fail in their attempt. See the old but still useful studies of F. S. Gutjahr, *Die Glaubwürdigkeit des Irenäischen Zeugnisses über die Abfassung des vierten kanonischen Evangeliums* (Graz: Leuschner and Lubensky's, 1904).

8. This sentence is one of what Osborn (*Irenaeus*, 149) calls the "binary or ternary" forms of the rule of faith (as also in *AH* 1.3.6 and 1.10.1). That the apostles all teach the same thing handed down by tradition finds echo in Clement of Alexandria, *Stromata* 7.108.1; see D. K. Buell, *Making Christians: Clement of Alexandria and the Rhetoric of Legitimacy* (Princeton, NJ: Princeton University Press, 1999), 83–86.

9. At the beginning of the paragraph there is an indication of a bipartite confession: "One God...One Christ...." "Despise" harks back to the end of

the preface, where Irenaeus had quoted Luke 10:16 on the fact of those despising Christ who despise the apostles. The Pauline allusions here are to Titus 3:11 (*proprio iudicio condemnatus*—Vulg.) and 2 Tim 2:25 (*qui resistant veritati*).

CHAPTER 2

1. Sagnard (SC 34, p. 99) read this as three objections by the "Gnostics" to the Scriptures: they were corrupt, apocryphal, and did not agree among themselves. SC 210 (n. 1 to p. 27), rejecting this, holds there are only two objections: the Scriptures are not correct and so they are not trustworthy; and they are open to being variously, ambiguously interpreted. We note that *ex auctoritate* means that they do not have the proper authority because they are not authentic—thus they are not trustworthy. SC notes that, in *AH* 3.3.4, *maioris auctoritatis* represents the extant Greek ἀξιοπιστότερον. So *ex auctoritate* in our passage may indeed mean "trustworthy." SC stresses that elsewhere Irenaeus rejects a double-erroneous notion of the Scriptures. In *AH* 3.11.9 the heretics are criticized for discarding many of the Scriptures, or for mutilating them; in 1.8.1–5 they are denounced for ambiguous interpretations. SC appeals also to 4.33.8, but here we believe that the remark about a "harmonious explanation" of Scriptures confirms our view, and Sagnard's, that the third objection in our present passage is to ambiguous interpretations not in themselves but in relation to other texts that they contradict, with the result that they do not give a harmonious explanation of all the Scriptures. According to such groups, the Scriptures state things "variously"; that is, they give a variety of opinions. Irenaeus regularly denounces his opponents for giving an interpretation to one passage which contradicts others, and he consistently argues for the harmony of revelation in all the Scriptures.

2. 1 Cor 2:6. Irenaeus notes here that the heretics also appealed to a tradition. On the matter of the "living voice," see Tiessen, *Salvation of Unevangelized*, 188–93. He follows H. Chadwick, *The Early Church* (Baltimore: Penguin, 1967), 81, in noting that "Marcion was right in at least one thing, the necessity of a canon of authoritative writings of the New Testament." Cf. Y. M. Blanchard, *Aux sources du canon, le témoignage d'Irénée*, Cogitatio fidei (Paris: Cerf, 1993).

The "living voice," which has no grounding in the scriptural proclamation of the Church, is seen by Irenaeus as confounding and distorting rather than elucidating the faith. He is not arguing against inspired teaching or charismatic dynamism (we see elsewhere in book 3 that he views authentic teaching as a charism of the living Spirit), but rather against those who claim that their "voice" adds to or changes the apostolic faith. Cf. his remark at *AH*

1.10.2: "For, since the faith is one and the same, neither he who can discourse at length about it adds to it, nor he who can say only a little subtracts from it."

3. Cf. 2 Cor 4:5. Sagnard (SC 34, p. 99) inserted "Église" as the object of *contra*, but the Church is nowhere in the immediate context. Irenaeus is saying that the heretics claim that the truth—which is a figment of each one's imagination—could be in all those mentioned, and even in those who would contradict them. Their truth is self-contradictory. SC 210 (n. 2 to p. 27) rightly dropped Sagnard's "Église," but it sees in *in illo* a possible corruption of *alio*, noting that elsewhere a list of heretics is followed by "other"; cf. 2.31.1; 4.6.4; and 5.4.1, where *illud* was wrongly introduced for *aliud*. However, in those supposed parallels the "other" is similar to the preceding masters, and so "other" would be logical. But in our passage this *ille* is presented as disputing against the masters, so "other" would be illogical, and *in illo* would be correct in the sense of "in anyone who contradicts them."

4. Irenaeus's language of the Church "guarding" the apostolic tradition reveals an important characteristic of his theological "method," namely, that it is nondevelopmental. It is a characteristic of the heretics that they develop and alter the faith; the Church safeguards and defends it. M. A. Donovan (*One Right Reading?* 12) makes this point emphatically. She provides two helpful references: B. F. Meyer, *The Early Christians: Their World Mission and Self Discovery* (Wilmington, DE: Michael Glazier, 1986); and W. Rordorf and A. Schneider, *L'évolution du concept de tradition dans l'église ancienne* (Traditio Christiana 5; Frankfurt: Peter Lang, 1982). Both of these are worthy of review. It is worth noting that Irenaeus's ecclesiology is thus different in character from his anthropology, the latter of which is intently developmental throughout.

5. Cf. Eph 3:9; Col 1:26. See *AH* 1.12.4. "Highest Authority" is *Summitas*. There is a parallel to our sentence in 4.35.1, where *summitas* is a synonym for *principalitas*, and both most likely translate αὐθεντία, itself translated by *principalitas* in 1.26.1; 1.30.8; 1.31.1; and explicitly interpreted as *summa potestas* in 1.24.1. Because of the contrast to Demiurge and to the Intermediate, the *Summitas* may be the Fullness (*Pleroma*), as SC 210 (n. 1 to p. 29) remarks; but it is also possible that it is specifically the highest authority in the Fullness, namely, Father, or at least Only-begotten, the Father's revelation of all things.

6. The last clause of our translation follows the suggestion of P. Nautin ("L'*Adversus haereses* d'Irénée, livre III: Notes d'exégèse," *Recherches de théologie ancienne et médiévale* 20 [1953]: 185–86) that *errorem* (not *animam*, as in Sagnard, SC 34, p. 100) is the subject of *effugere*. It is not the soul escaping from error, but error fleeing from the soul. Justin has a similar idea: "It is not impossible to put ignorance to flight when truth is brought before it" (*1 Apol.* 12 [MG 6:345A]). This idea is in keeping with Irenaeus's belief that the exposure of error is itself the overthrow of error; see ACW 55, p. 6. See also Osborn, *Irenaeus*, 130, 239; cf. *AH* 3.5.2.

In the first clause of this sentence there is a slight difference between the Greek fragment and the Latin. Following SC 210 (n. 3 to p. 29), we have taken the Greek, which makes it difficult for someone to persuade the soul caught in error to change. Lat.Iren. (*resipiscere*) makes it difficult for the soul itself to change. The Greek seems to fit better with the second clause.

CHAPTER 3

1. Cf. Clement, *1 Cor.* 44 (ACW 1:36).

2. Cf. 2 Tim 2:2 (*qui idonei erunt et alios docere*); 1 Tim 3:2 (*oportet ergo episcopum inreprihensibilem*); Titus 1:6, 7 (*sine crimine est*). Irenaeus draws attention to the care exercised by the apostles in selecting only worthy men as bishops for the office of handing down ("traditioning") the faith. The speculations of D. L. Hoffman (*The Status of Women and Gnosticism in Irenaeus and Tertullian* [Lampeter: Edwin Mellen Press, 1995], 99) that Irenaeus may not have considered that only men could be bishops, seem to us wholly groundless.

3. Irenaeus calls the Roman Church "most ancient" (*antiquissima*), not in an absolute sense, for he knew well that the Church of Jerusalem was the Mother Church of all others (cf. *AH* 3.12.5); and in any case he calls all the Churches founded by the apostles *antiquissimae* in 3.4.1. Still, the Roman Church was "most ancient" because it was among the first of the apostolic Churches founded. A. v. Harnack ("Das Zeugniss des Irenäus über das Ansehen der Römischen Kirche," *Sitzungsberichte der könig. preuss. Academ. der Wissenschaften* [Berlin: J. G. Weiss, 1893], 939–55, esp. p. 942 n. 2) rightly gives *Uralt* as the meaning. But we must disagree with the assertion that Irenaeus is not making a comparison with the older Churches, especially with Jerusalem, on the grounds that it did not then any longer exist. There was, at any rate, still the Church at Antioch, which, as Irenaeus knew, was older than that at Rome. J. N. D. Kelly (*Early Christian Doctrines*, 192–93) refers to this "famous and much debated passage" on the Roman Church, not as revealing an absolute primacy but as an "ideal illustration" of ecclesial organization and function" in view of its preeminent authority." See also J. Comby, *Irénée—Aux origines de l'église de Lyon* (Lyon: Profac, 1977), 13–15. Osborn (*Irenaeus*, 129) paraphrases Irenaeus's intention, stating that it would be "tedious" to list the succession of all the Churches, when that of Rome alone will suffice. Donovan (*One Right Reading?* 63 n. 1) characterizes the SC editions as favoring a "Roman interpretation" of the passage, "i.e., that every church must necessarily agree with the church at Rome for reasons connected with its origin." This tendency is indeed visible in some of the SC notes on the text, though Donovan argues that it is also evident in the French translation and Greek retroversion.

L. Abramowski ("Irenaeus, Adv. Haer. III, 3, 2: *Ecclesia Romana* and *Omnis Ecclesia*; and ibid. 3, 3: Anacletus of Rome," *Journal of Theological Studies* 28 [1977], 101–4) objects to Rousseau's translation for just such reasons. See Tiessen, *Salvation of Unevangelized*, 199 n. 19 for multiple further resources on the debate.

"Built up" (*constitutae*) is missing in the Greek; but in section 3, the Greek for *fundantes et instruentes* is θεμελιώσαντες καὶ οἰκοδομήσαντες ("having founded and built up"). So here *fundatae et constitutae* seems to suppose the same Greek verbs, with their suggestion of laying the foundation and building upon it.

4. Cf. Rom 1:8.

5. *Sententia mala* occurs a number of times in *AH*; cf. 3.3.4 (*perversae sententiae* is κακογνωμόνων), 3.4.3; 3.12.12; 4.Pref.1. It does not mean "false judgment" as Sagnard translated (SC 34, p. 103), or "doctrinal error" as in SC 210 (p. 33).

6. On the questions raised by this portion of *AH* 3, see our treatment above in the introduction, pp. 9–11. One scholar has called attention to a text in Caesar, writing about the chief Druid (*De bello gallico* 6.13):

His autem omnibus druidibus *praeest* unus, qui *summam* inter eos habet *auctoritatem*. Hoc mortuo aut si qui ex reliquis excellit dignitate succedit, aut, si sunt plures pares, suffragio druidum, nonnumquam etiam armis de *principatu* contendunt. Hi certo anni tempore, in finibus Carnutum, quae regio totius Galliae media habetur, *considunt* in loco consecrato. *Huc* omnes undique, qui controversias habent, *conveniunt* eorumque decretis iudiciisque parent.

We have emphasized in the above those words which, it has been argued, bear a similarity to Irenaeus's passage. V. White ("Chief Druid and Chief Bishop: A Parallel in Caesar's *Gallic War* with Irenaeus *Against the Heresies*, III, 3," *Dominican Studies* 4 [1951]: 201–3) pointed out the similarities in words and ideas and thought it natural for a second-century Gaul to think of the pope in terms of the Chief Druid, and that in this light it would be easier to understand Irenaeus's passage as a clumsy adaptation of Caesar, modified to fit his needs. Scholars rightly concede no probability to such a use of Caesar by Irenaeus or the translator of Lat.Iren.

7. Lat.Iren., which we follow here hesitatingly, has *Lino episcopatum administrandae Ecclesiae tradiderunt*. The Greek is more concise: ἐπισκοπῆς λειτουργίαν, namely, the bishopric is a public ministry (genitive of apposition). The Greek appeals, but it is difficult to see how Lat.Iren. would have intro-

duced *Ecclesiae* if it was not in the original, and why he would have changed the concise Greek at all. Both have substantially the same idea. Cf. 2 Tim 4:21. Linus was pope c. AD 67–79 (on some lists c. 67–76).

8. Anacletus was pope c. 79 until c. 90 (on some lists c. 76–88). This Anacletus is likely identical to the "Cletus" that appears on other lists.

Clement of Rome was pope c. 90 until c. 99 (on some lists c. 88–97, or as late as 101). There seem to have been two traditions about the place of Clement in the sequence after the apostles. Irenaeus has him as the third pope *after* Peter, which seems to have been the usual ordering. It was accepted by Jerome, who notes that among the Latins several held that Clement was second after Peter (see *De viris illustribus* 15 [ML 23:631]). One of these Latins was Tertullian, *De praesc.* 32 (CCSL 2:213): *sicut (ecclesia) Romanorum, Clementem a Petro ordinatum edit. Edit* is according to some MSS; the *est* of CCSL is out of place. The question is complicated by the fact that Tertullian certainly knew of Irenaeus's opinion in this book. M. Bévenot ("Clement of Rome in Irenaeus's Succession-List," *Journal of Theological Studies* n.s. 17 [1966], 98–107) attempted a solution in favor of Tertullian by arguing that Irenaeus did not intend a strict chronological succession for the first three popes. In fact, so this argument goes, Linus and Anacletus were only auxiliaries of Peter, and so Clement is really the first to follow Peter as pope. Counting in Peter and Paul, he would therefore be "third." But that would mean that Paul succeeded Peter as pope, which is entirely untenable. D. F. Wright ("Clement and the Roman Succession in Irenaeus," *Journal of Theological Studies* n.s. 18 [1967]: 144–54), in a closely reasoned article, fairly demolished Bévenot's position. Linus and Anacletus were popes and Clement followed them. He is the third after Peter and Paul, who were never considered bishops by Irenaeus, but always apostles.

9. Namely, from Clement of Rome, *1 Cor.* (ACW 1). As we indicate in the note to follow, the points Irenaeus mentions are indeed found in Clement's letter, save for the reference to hell.

10. The scriptural references are Gen 1:1 (Creator), Gen 2:7 (Fashioner of man), Gen 7:6ff. (deluge), Gen 12:1 (Abraham), Exod 3:4ff. (Moses), Exod 20:1ff. (giving of law), Deut 18:15–18 et passim throughout OT (sending of prophets), Matt 25:41 (devil). Irenaeus refers frequently to this last point: see 2.7.3; 3.23.3; 4.22.2; 4.33.11; 4.40.1; 4.41.3; 5.27.1; 5.28.1. The references to Clement's letter are to *1 Cor.* 2–7 (ACW 1:10–13), 13 (p. 48), 19 (p. 21), 54 (p. 42), 42 (p. 34), 47 (p. 38), 19–20 (pp. 21–22), 33 (p. 29), 9 (p. 14), 10 (pp. 14ff.), 51 (pp. 40ff.), 43 (p. 35), 53 (pp. 41ff.), 17 (p. 20), 43 (p. 35), 42 (p. 34).

11. Here Irenaeus uses *apostolicam traditionem*, rather than his more usual *ab apostolis traditio*. He clearly wishes to tie the tradition to the apostles in the most direct and binding way.

12. "Glorious witness" is in Greek "glorious martyr," the word that had already become a title for those who witnessed to Christ by their blood. The

dates of Popes Evaristus, Alexander, Sixtus, and Telesphorus are uncertain (some lists tentatively offer the dates of c. 97–105/7, 105/7–115, 115–125/7, and 125/7–136/8 respectively; of these, the dates of Telesphorus are the most agreed upon among scholars).

13. Hyginus was evidently the eighth pope, since he is preceded by seven predecessors, as is clear from the rest of the data given here and as Irenaeus says explicitly in 3.4.3. J. Chapman ("La chronologie des premières listes épiscopales de Rome, I, II, III" *Revue Bénédictine* 18 [1901]: 399–417; 19 [1902]: 13–37; 19 [1902]: 145–70), discussed the dependence of the accounts of Julius Africanus, Hegissipus, and Hippolytus on Irenaeus. Since all have "ninth" (as do Irenaeus in 1.27.1 and Eusebius, *HE* 4.11; 6.11), Chapman concludes that "ninth" is correct and that "eighth" in 3.4.3 was the error of a scribe who recalled that Irenaeus said shortly after that Anacletus was "tenth" but that Pius came between him and Hyginus. This conclusion is not acceptable. Irenaeus's calculation seems to amount to this: that Hyginus is the eighth pope after Peter. Eusebius himself (*HE* 5.Pref. [GCS 2.1.400]) has Eleutherus as the twelfth pope after the apostles, so he must have counted Hyginus as the eighth at this point. Therefore, "ninth" in 1.27.1 was a scribe's error already in the Greek text. See ACW 55, pp. 91 n. 2, 249. Anicetus was pope c. 155 to 166/7.

14. Eleutherus was pope from AD 174/5 until 189. See ACW 55, p. 4 on the date of the composition of the *AH* that can be gathered from this information.

15. In 3.25.1, near this book's end, Irenaeus will return to this notion of the universal, unchanging faith as "life-giving," and there will, rather poetically, also stress that it is ever young, even in its antiquity, and by its stability in the Spirit rejuvenates those who participate in it.

16. According to Tertullian (*De praesc.* 32.2 [CCSL 1:213]), John appointed him bishop of the Church of Smyrna.

17. Irenaeus's explanation of the old age of Polycarp is added so that the reader would understand how Irenaeus, writing in the latter part of the second century, could have seen Polycarp, though the latter had been appointed by the apostles. Polycarp was an old man when he was martyred c. AD 155/156. He therefore would have been born about AD 65 and could have been appointed bishop as early as 95, at which time John was still living. Early suggestions of AD 98 (Dodwell) or 120 (Lightfoot) for Irenaeus's birth have largely given way to the "between 130 and 140" of Osborn (*Irenaeus*, 2) based on Irenaeus's recollections of Polycarp, as in our present location, whom he saw "as a young man." For a fuller survey of studies on the dates of Irenaeus, see M. C. Steenberg, *Irenaeus on Creation: The Cosmic Christ and the Saga of Redemption* (Leiden/Boston: Brill, 2008), 14 n. 39.

18. Cf. Polycarp's letter to the Philippians, 7, 9 (ACW 6:79ff.). "To the Church" is here, and in the following paragraph, according to the Latin. This

makes sense in the context of handing down tradition in succession, and thus we have stayed with the Latin, against the Greek, which has "Church" in the nominative—namely, it is the Church that hands down. This too makes sense in Irenaean thought, but since the dative in Latin is more unusual a case to fall into than the nominative, there is an added reason for accepting the Latin text. Sagnard (SC 34, pp. 110, 111) followed the Greek, and SC 210 (n. 1 to p. 41) strongly defends it as original.

19. Lat.Iren. has only "in the city," which the Greek makes more specific by adding "at Rome."

20. See n. 18 above.

21. Eusebius repeats this story in *HE* 3.28.4, 5 (GCS 2:258). Epiphanius has it in *Panarion* 30.24 (GCS 1:365), but he speaks of Ebion, not Cerinthus. Theodoret has it too (*Haereticarum fabularum compendium* 2.3 [MG 83:389C]). Lat.Iren. presents the statement in indirect discourse; the Greek has it as direct discourse, which we have followed here.

22. Both the Greek excerpt and the better Latin reading have the imperative, not an interrogation: "Do you recognize us?" Jerome has this incident take place in Rome (*De viris illustribus* 17 [ML 23:683C]).

23. Titus 3:10ff. "or twice" is omitted in Latin. It could have been inserted into the Greek by a scribe copying the whole text as it was in the Bible. It could also have been dropped by the Latin scribe, since it is present in 1.16.3.

Here Irenaeus touches, as Sagnard notes (SC 34, pp. 113–15), on the mystery of the hardening of one's heart against the faith. That which is to unite one authentically with the Word of God is rejected, and one imposes one's own ideas over and against those of the Lord. See below, 3.7.1, 2.

24. Cf. Eusebius, *HE* 3.23.4 (GCS 2:238).

Chapter 4

1. Cf. Rev 22:17; John 7:37; and *AH* 3.24.1. Here an interesting metaphor for the Church's possessing, within itself, the fullness of the truth.

2. Cf. John 10:1.

3. Irenaeus again stresses the priority of tradition over written Scripture; cf. above, 3.1.1, and our n. 1 to chap. 1. If the apostles had left no Scripture at all, the Church would nevertheless have their tradition, which it would gratefully accept. "Certain and clear" in the preceding sentence is a doublet, according to SC 210 (n. 1 to p. 47), since in 4.26.1 the Greek fragment has the one word ἀκριβεστάτης, for which Lat.Iren. has the same two words as in our present passage: *liquidam et certam*.

4. Cf. 2 Cor 3:2; Rom 2:15; Heb 8:10; also 2 John 12 (*per cartam et atramentum*).

5. Cf. Exod 20:11; Ps 145:6 (LXX); Neh 9:6; Acts 4:24; 14:15; Rev 10:6.

6. Cf. Eph 3:19. For Lat.Iren. all MSS have *per Christum Iesum*, that is, Jesus Christ is mediator of faith in the one God. SC 210 (n. 4 to p. 47) thinks it probable that *per* was originally *et* (which seems reasonable, and thus we have followed it in our translation), and that we have here in nascent form the second great theme of the later Creed, stressed in book 3 and introduced in 3.1.2. Yet Irenaeus himself (*AH* 1.23.1) has the idea of Christ's mediating this faith; as do also Acts 3:16 and 1 Pet 1:21.

Irenaeus here has a bipartite "creed" of sorts, with a longer development of its soteriological dimension. In it there are a number of scriptural allusions, for example, 1 Tim 3:16; Matt 16:27; 25:31; 25:41. Irenaeus gives God's immense love as a reason for the incarnation, and union with God as its end.

The fact that Irenaeus expressed the idea of birth from the Virgin with the finite, independent verb, but what follows with participles, emphasizes grammatically his theological perception of the priority of the virginal birth: the other acts (union with God, suffering, and so on) were dependent on the birth from the Virgin. From this starting point, Irenaeus develops a strong view on Mary's active role in human salvation. It is in her giving birth that humankind's salvation is begun; see Osborn, *Irenaeus*, 113. We shall have more to say on Irenaeus's Mariology in our notes to chaps. 21–23.

7. Cf. Justin, *1Apol.* 60.11 (MG 6:420). According to Comby (*Irénée*, 15), this passage further demonstrated that, for Irenaeus, tradition and Scripture were not to be conflated.

8. Sagnard (cf. SC 34, p. 119) read this last sentence as a title for the following paragraph, and SC 210 (n. 1 to p. 51) strongly defends this, against the view of Nautin (*L'Adversus haereses*, 186–88; see above, our n. 6 to chap. 2). Their reasons are not convincing, and we have kept the text as the older editors had it: a conclusion to this paragraph that sets the scene for the following. Irenaeus has been saying that the "barbarian" Christians would not listen to the heretics, and in fact there never were any assemblies or schools of heretics among the [presumably Lyonese] people. *Doctrina* here, as elsewhere at times, stands for διδασκαλεῖον, with which Nautin (p. 186) agrees; but SC 210 (p. 51) takes the normal meaning of doctrine, thus διδασκαλία in its Greek retranslation.

9. See above, n. 13 to chap. 3; and ACW 55, pp. 91 n. 2, 249.

10. This following the Greek, which does not have *saepe* as does Lat.Iren. On this and the whole problem of "confession," see ACW 55, pp. 37 n. 17, 166–67.

11. See above, n. 13 to chap. 3.

12. One of the instances when Irenaeus uses the proper title "Gnostics" (*Gnostici* / Γνωστικοί) in identification of a particular group of heretics. See also 1.11.1; 2.13.10; 3.10.4.

13. See *AH* 1.23.5.

14. This paragraph confirms our statement above (n. 4 to chap. 2) that Irenaeus regards doctrinal or theological "development" as an act of the heretics, not the Church. See also Tiessen, *Salvation of Unevangelized*, 201.

CHAPTER 5

1. Cf. John 14:6; 1 John 5:6; also John 8:45ff.; 1 Pet 2:22; Isa 53:9; 1 John 2:21. SC 210 (n. 2 to p. 53) thinks *ex quibus* makes no sense, and so changed it to *in quibus (Scripturis)*. This emendation we accept.

2. Ps 84(85):12.

3. 1 John 2:21; 2 Cor 6:14.

4. Sagnard (SC 34, p. 122) rightly filled in the missing word "utterable" in Lat.Iren.: *per parabolas et aenigmata, inenarrabile <narrabile> fecisse mysterium*. In the context Irenaeus suggests that the heretics held that the apostles adapted their message to the capacity of their hearers. Since he is clearly speaking ironically, he might have said that the apostles declared an unutterable mystery to those who comprehended the unnamable Father. *Fecisse mysterium* can mean "reveal a mystery," as *doctrinam facere* means to teach. W. W. Harvey (2:19, n. 2) thinks it possible that Lat.Iren. read πλάσασθαι, which could have been a corruption of φράσασθαι ("to declare"). But S. Lundström (pp. 123–24) seems to have found the best solution by the aid of a parallel in 1.14.1; namely, *narrabile* had fallen out, as noted above. SC 210 (n. 1 to p. 57) would rather change *fecisse* to *dixisse*: "They uttered the unutterable mystery," but again this change is not necessary.

5. Cf. Deut 27:18.

6. Luke 5:31, 32. The designation of Jesus as the divine physician is found already in Ignatius, *Ad Ephesios* 7.2 (ACW 1:63).

7. "Without partiality" was for Irenaeus an important characteristic of the apostles. Such sincerity is frequently inculcated in Scripture: cf. Matt 22:16 (the Pharisees recognized it in Jesus); for God, see Rom 2:11; Eph 6:9; Col 3:25; Gal 2:6. Irenaeus's mentioning that Christ brought "knowledge" must have been an intentional jab at the "gnosis falsely so-called" of his foes. The full title of the present volume, *The Refutation and Overthrow of Knowledge Falsely So-Called*, makes this clearer than our commonplace abbreviation: *Against Heresies*. Throughout the volume, as particularly here, Irenaeus wishes to refute the "so-called gnosis" of those who purport wisdom. See further details on the naming of this text in M. C. Steenberg, *Of God and Man: Theology as Anthropology from Irenaeus to Athanasius* (London: T&T Clark/Continuum, 2009), 21 n. 17.

Such taunting and teasing were regular tools in Irenaeus's rhetorical arsenal; see *AH* 1.4.4 for a classic example of early patristic mockery, and a still more famous example in 1.11.4 (this latter may be a deliberate parody of the Naasene *Hymn to Attis*, found in Hippolytus, *Refutatio omnium haeresium* 5.9.8; in this assertion we follow R. M. Grant, *Gnosticism: A Source Book of Heretical Writings from the Early Christian Period* [New York: Harper & Brothers, 1961], 105). Osborn has more recently made a careful study of Irenaeus's use of parody: see "Irenaeus on God—Argument and Parody," *Studia Patristica* 36 (2001): 270–81. See also M. C. Steenberg, "An Exegesis of Conformity: Textual Subversion of Subversive Texts," in *Discipline and Diversity*, edited by K. Cooper and J. Gregory, Studies in Church History 43 (Woodbridge: Boydell & Brewer, 2007), 25–35.

8. Lat.Iren. has *incorrupte haereditatem*, which cannot be correct. Sagnard (SC 34, p. 126) corrects it to *incorruptelae haereditatem*, which Irenaeus uses elsewhere. See also 1 Pet 1:4: *in haereditatem incorruptibilem*.

9. Cf. Acts 14:14ff.; Wis 14:21; 1 Pet 1:18; and Isa 27:19. This paragraph is a mosaic of a number of scriptural words and allusions.

10. See 1 Thess 1:10; Eph 1:7; 5:26; Titus 2:14; 1 Pet 2:9; Heb 13:12. We have capitalized "Rebellion" because with SC 210 (n. 1 to p. 63) we believe that Irenaeus here implies Satan himself; cf. *AH* 5.1.1.

11. Cf. Matt 24:30; 25:31–46; John 15:10.

12. Cf. Eph 2:20, 14, 17.

13. Gen 9:27. "Enlarged Japhet" follows Lat.Iren. It is possible, however, as SC 210 (n. 2 to p. 63) holds, that "Japhet" was originally not in the accusative but in the dative ("make room for"), as in *AH* 5.34.2; *Proof* 21. The enlargement of Japhet (cf. Gen. 9:27) is a theme of importance for Irenaeus: the divergent lineages of Sem and his brother set the groundwork for the lineage of Abraham, "God's friend" (see *AH* 4.13.4; cf. Jas 2:23), and through him the incarnate Christ. Justin's reading of Japhet's enlargement follows the same lines; see *Dial.* 140. Irenaeus will take this further, ascribing to the Church's mission to all humankind, and especially its calling to salvation of the Gentiles, the realized fulfillment of this scriptural foretelling: Japhet is enlarged when the human race is encouraged to obedience and raised to life in Christ; cf. *Proof* 21, 42. See Steenberg, *Irenaeus on Creation*, 205–9.

CHAPTER 6

1. Lat.Iren. uses *ex* (or *a*) *persona sua* six times in book 3 (6.1; 6.3; 6.5; 9.1; 10.1; 10.5) and twice in book 5 (both in 25.2). The phrase has been given a variety of translations. E. Klebba in *Bibliothek der Kirchenväter* (1912) has "ohne Vorbehalt"; ANF has "in their (his) person," which is ambiguous. Sagnard (SC 34, p. 129) correctly called attention to the underlying Greek αὐτοπροσώπως ("franchement, sans ambages")—a term used of actors who

did not wear a mask, did not impersonate anyone else, but spoke *in their own name*. See Irenaeus's paraphrase in 3.6.3. It can be translated "candidly, straightforwardly, absolutely." SC 210 (n. 1.3 to p. 65) has the correct explanation and translates "de façon absolue"; but that can have the meaning of unconditionally, which would be ambiguous here.

SC 210 (n. 1.1 to p. 65) objects to the subjunctive mood in Lat.Iren. *nominassent...appellassent*, which should state a simple fact, as in 6.3; 8.1; 9.1. But the subjunctive mood expressing the hypothetical makes good sense here, emphasizing Irenaeus's point.

2. Cf. Matt 28:18.

3. Ps 109(110):1. Justin, *Dial.* 56 (MG 6:601) uses these same texts. Perhaps Irenaeus copied from him; perhaps both used a florilegium.

4. Cf. Ps 2:8; 1 Cor 15:21–28.

5. Gen 19:24; cf. also Gen 18:17–22.

6. We have translated "He" (the Spirit) rather than "it" (the scriptural passage), as Irenaeus is continuing his exposition of the Spirit revealing both the Father and Son as "Lord," begun at the opening of the paragraph. That this project continues becomes clear through Irenaeus's language following the next scriptural quotation.

7. Ps 44(45):7, 8.

8. Ps 81(82):1; cf. a similar argument by Tertullian, *Adversus Praxeam* 13.4 (CCSL 47:1174). SC 210 (n. 2 to p. 67) argues strongly that Irenaeus had written "assembly of God" not of "the gods," as in Lat.Iren., as otherwise there would be no reference to the Son in this scriptural passage, though He is expressly mentioned in the commentary that follows. It is worth reading the longer defense in the SC. Behr (*Asceticism and Anthropology*, 69–71) treats well of Irenaeus's claim here that the "assembly of the gods" in Ps 81(82):1 refers to filially adopted human persons, whom Irenaeus thus does not hesitate to call "gods." Behr notes that this adoption ought therefore not to be considered simply a matter of regard, but as the genuine establishment of men as sons of God.

9. Cf. Rom 8:15.

10. Ps 49(50):1.

11. Ps 49(50):3.

12. Isa 65:1, according to Rom 10:20.

13. Ps 81(82):6.

14. Rom 8:15; also Gal 4:5, 6. In the present paragraph Irenaeus has unequivocally called the Son "God" (ὁ Θεός) in the same manner as he calls the Father "God." While he does not always apply this direct nomenclature to the Son, our current passage is clear evidence that Irenaeus is moving beyond the hesitation of previous generations, as well as some of his contemporaries, to call the Son θεός directly. Cf. Justin's circumscript language of the Son as δεύτερος θεός, in *Dial.* 56, *1 Apol.* 13.3; found also in Philo and Origen.

15. Exod 3:14. This is used also in *Proof* 2, where Irenaeus adds: "those who do not worship the God who really is, are the 'ungodly.'"

16. Cf. John 1:12.

17. Exod 3:8. Irenaeus ascribes this to the Son, since He is God and He "descended" through the incarnation for the deliverance of the people. See the same use in *Proof* 46; cf. Osborn, *Irenaeus*, 260.

18. Cf. Eph 4:10; also John 3:13.

19. Cf. Exod 3:15; John 17:21; John 14:10ff. SC 210/211 (cf. n. 2 to p. 71) reads the phrase thus: "He who is God was manifested."

20. See John 5:37; 17:26. This whole section is deeply Johannine in tone and content. For the indwelling of the Father and the Son, see also John 1:1, 5; 17:6, 14; 1 John 5:9. For the Father's revealing the Son, see also Matt 16:17; John 6:44; 8:54; 12:28. For the Son's revealing the Father, see also Matt 11:27; John 11:41ff.

21. Isa 43:10.

22. Ps 95(96):5. Neither the Hebrew nor the LXX has "idols," but Sagnard (SC 34, p. 135 n. 2) notes that it is found also in Justin, *Dial.* 55.2; 73.2 (see E. J. Goodspeed, *Die ältesten Apologeten* [Göttingen: Vandenhoeck & Ruprecht, 1915], 154, 83); and in *1 Apol.* 41.1 (*Die ältesten Apologeten*, 54–55); though it is omitted in *Dial.* 73.3; 79.4; 83.4 (*Die ältesten Apologeten*, 183, 191, 195).

23. Ps 80(81):10. The LXX has the singular "strange god." But cf. Jer 35[42 LXX]:15.

24. Isa 44:9, 10; 43:10.

25. Jer 10:11, for which the LXX reads "and from under the heavens."

26. 3 Kgdms 18:21.

27. 3 Kgdms 18:24.

28. A combination of 3 Kgdms 18:36 and 37. Donovan (*One Right Reading?* 69) draws attention to the fact that all the citations in this passage are from the OT. Only the reference to Rom 8:15 (at the end of 3.6.1) is from a NT text, placing the Christians fully into the tradition of the OT revelation. The revelation of the "prophets" is one and the same with the revelation of the Church.

29. We have followed SC 210 (n. 1 to p. 77) and read *donationem* (δωρεά), which is in keeping with Irenaeus's use elsewhere (cf. *AH* 4.18.6, where the reading is corroborated by the Armenian MS).

30. On Irenaeus's use of the term *scriptura* (γραφή) here in reference to his own writing, and its implications for his understanding of "scripture," see M. C. Steenberg, "Scripture, *graphe*, and the Status of Hermas in Irenaeus," *St. Vladimir's Theological Quarterly* 53, no. 1 (2009): 29–66. Cf. ACW 55, pp. 9 n. 39, 118.

31. This whole paragraph is a fine example of spontaneous prayer among the early Christians. Noteworthy is the place the Holy Spirit occupies. See also *AH* 3.11.8, 9; 4.21.3; 5.20.1. The passage is a mosaic of scriptural

ideas: cf. 3 Kgdms 18:36; 2 Cor 1:3; 11:31; Eph 1:3; 1 Pet 1:3; Col 1:3; Ps 105(106):7, 45; John 17:3; Isa 37:10; 1 Chr 29:12; Isa 37:16; Acts 2:38; 10:45; Ps 85(86):10; Ps 90(91):6; John 17:3; 4 Kgdms 19:15.

32. Gal 4:8, 9.
33. 2 Thess 2:4.
34. 1 Cor 8:4–6.
35. Deut 5:8; Exod 20:4.
36. Deut 4:19.
37. Cf. Exod 7:1.
38. Heb 3:5; Num 12:7.

CHAPTER 7

1. 2 Cor 4:4. Tertullian (*Adversus Marcionem* 5.11 [CCSL 1:697]) claims that Marcion originated this reading of 2 Cor 4:4, which Irenaeus refutes, and which Tertullian too rejects. The "god of this world" is Satan. Such an interpretation is further contained in a fragment ascribed to Irenaeus (Harvey, 2:510), but which cannot be authentic. See N. Brox, "Ein vermeintliches Irenäus-fragment," *Vigiliae Christianae* 24 (1970): 40–44.

2. Cf. Eph 1:21; Col 1:16. Lat.Iren. reads *principatum et initium et potestatem*. SC 210 (n. 1 to p. 81) claims that the first two nouns are a doublet translation of ἀρχή. This is a possibility. But as such, Lat.Iren. would have varied his translation of the same Greek word. *Initium* here most certainly stands for ἀρχή; but *principatum* could translate κυριότης (*dominatio*) and *potestas* ἐξουσία—the three terms that occur in Col 1:16. Or, *principatum* could translate ἐξουσία and *potestas* δύναμις—terms found in Eph 1:21.

3. Here Irenaeus's reading challenges the text, in which the genitive needs to be read with God: "God of this world," who would be Satan; see John 12:3; 14:30; 16:11, though not in the sense that he made the world and is a rival of the true God. The genitive could be one of apposition: the world is the god, which the unbelievers would worship by their actions. In the next sentence Irenaeus promises a proof from Paul on this matter. He does not get to this until *AH* 4.29.

4. This sentence is a combination of 1 Cor 15:50 ("will not inherit the imperishable") and Eph 1:21 ("the coming world").

5. Gal 3:19.
6. 2 Thess 2:8, 9.

CHAPTER 8

1. Cf. Matt 22:21.

2. Matt 6:24.

3. John 8:34.

4. It is difficult to determine whence Irenaeus got this "Mamuel" for mammon, "with a suffix." In Luke "mammon of inquity" could come from the Hebrew *māmôn 'iwel*, which might have been contracted into *mamuel*. This would have a resemblance to "memule," a transcription of the Hebrew passive participle "filled" or "gluttonous." Thus Harvey (2:28, n. 1). SC 210 (n. 2 to p. 91) thinks the Lat.Iren. *adiunctive* (in the Salamanca MS *adiective*) means the adjectival form of mammon is mamuel. But SC admits that this is only a conjecture, and no satisfactory answer has been found.

5. Matt 12:29.

6. Jer 31:11.

7. Cf. John 1:3.

8. Cf. Col 1:16.

9. Cf. above, *AH* 3.6.2.

10. John 1:3; for the introductory clause, see John 1:1–2. God created even the angels; this is Irenaeus's steady contention against any variant reading. See 1.23.2–5; 2.2.3; 3.8.3; 4.7.4; *Proof* 10. As created beings, the angels are thus not able to be "creators" in the same sense that God is Creator—a particularly anti-Valentinian, anti-Saturninan, and anti-Basilidean point; see 1.23.5; 1.24.1, 3, 4; 4.20.1.

11. Pss 148:5; 32(33):9. The introductory clause alludes to Ps 148:1–4.

12. Ps 32(33):6. Cf. ACW 55, pp. 80 n. 3, 226.

13. Cf. Ps 113:11 (115.3). One notes Irenaeus's emphasis on God's freedom in creating, stressed against the necessitarianism he attributes to the heretics. See Osborn, *Irenaeus*, 64, 65.

14. A concept that will be of great importance later, in Irenaeus's argument throughout *AH* 4.38–39. Irenaeus here establishes his fundamental anthropological doctrine of man's dependence on God, arising from his distinction from Him. Only God is uncreated and unchanging. That which He creates is, by virtue of its being created, "liable to dissolution," subject to change, and ever in requirement of God for sustained existence. Irenaeus's claims, in 4.38, that humanity must have been created as "imperfect" (ἀτελειότης) stem from this notion: if "perfection" is the state of being at one's *telos* or fulfilled end (as the Greek term suggests, without the negative moral implications of the English), then that which shall change and grow over time is yet to be at this *telos* and must therefore be described as *a-teleiotēs*, "imperfect." In this lies the heart of Irenaeus's dynamic vision of human creation into growth and development, by which vision he is so often characterized. See R. F. Brown, "On the Necessary Imperfection of Creation: Irenaeus' Adversus

haereses IV, 38," *Scottish Journal of Theology* 28, no. 1 (1975): 17–25; G. Wingren, *Man and the Incarnation: A Study in the Biblical Theology of Irenaeus,* trans. R. Mackenzie (Edinburgh: Oliver & Boyd, 1959), throughout; and M. C. Steenberg, "Children in Paradise: Adam and Eve as 'Infants' in Irenaeus of Lyons," *Journal of Early Christian Studies* 12, no. 1 (2004): 20–22.

CHAPTER 9

1. Donovan (*One Right Reading?* 70–75) draws attention to the "somewhat loose example of chiastic organization" evidenced in this chapter and the next. Her treatment there is deserving of consideration. We quote for reference only her outline from p. 70, demonstrating the chiasmus:

A. The Baptist, Matthew (*AH* III. 9, 1)
    B. The Infancy Narrative, Matthew (*AH* III. 9, 2)
        C. Jesus' Baptism, Matthew (*AH* III. 9, 3)
    B'. The Infancy Narrative, Luke (*AH* III. 10, 1–5)
A'. The Baptist, Mark (*AH* III. 10, 6)

2. Cf. Gen 15:5. SC 210 (n. 1 to p. 101) makes an interesting observation on Irenaeus's use of "as the stars of heaven," namely, that it does not refer to the multiplicity of the stars (as Sagnard, SC 34, p. 153, implies by "multiplier"), but to the illuminating property of the stars. As these give light to the world, so Abraham and his posterity, especially through Jesus, would bring the light of God's Word and faith in it to the world. SC uses *AH* 4.5.3–5; 4.7.1–3 as parallels, where Irenaeus makes his mind clear by introducing Phil 2:15 and Matt 5:14 into the explanation. We can accept this, with the reservation, however, that Irenaeus likely did not mean to exclude the obvious meaning of multiplicity; as is his wont, he merely wished to draw out a special symbolic significance from something natural to stars.

3. Rom 9:25; Hos 1:10; 2:23 (25 in LXX). See also *Proof* 93 for the same idea. This connection of Matthew's words to the prophecy of Hosea draws together the temporal expanse of God's economy and refutes the general pretension that the Creator of the Old Testament is not the Father of Jesus Christ.

4. Lat.Iren. has *varium autem et omni malitia completum sensum habebant.* SC 210 (n. 2 to p. 101) rejects as unnecessary and unproved the suggestion of F. J. A. Hort and J. A. Robinson that *varium* (which we have translated as "capricious") is a corrupt reading for *uane.* SC sees *varium* as a translation of ποικίλος, which can have meanings other than varied, namely, tortuous, filled with tricks. Its translation is "tortueux," and it appeals to *AH* 4.41.3: *secundum similitudinem animalium in varietate ambulantes.* But in this latter text the meaning is that the animals suddenly change, in an unpredictable fashion; they are capricious. "Erratic" might also do, or "writhing."

5. Matt 3:7.

6. Luke 3:4–6; Matt 3:3; and Isa 40:3–5.

7. Cf. John 1:14.

8. Here Irenaeus stresses as the reason for the incarnation the fact that man desires to see his God, and so God made Himself visible to man. This reason holds independently of man's sin, and speaks for the incarnation of God's Son prior, in God's intention, to Adam's sin. See D. J. Unger, "Christ's Rôle in the Universe according to St. Irenaeus," *Franciscan Studies* 5 (1945): 14–18. This builds on the motivation for the incarnation expressed earlier in chap. 4, namely, God's love (see our n. 6 to chap. 4, above).

9. Matt 1:20; 2:13.

10. Matt 2:15; 1:23; Isa 7:14.

11. Ps 131(132):11. The RSV for this passage is less literal: "One of the sons of your body." Stressing the word *womb*, which is true only of woman, Irenaeus sees a reference in this Psalm to the virginal conception (cf. *AH* 3.21.5). The womb is Mary's, who is herself of David's lineage. But how does this correlate to the words of the Psalm, *De fructu ventris tui* [Davidis]? One readily thinks of Jesus, the fruit of Mary's womb (cf. Luke 1:42). In other words, to explain this Psalm as a reference to the virginal conception one needs but add the genitive construction *ventris*, namely, *Virginis*. But Irenaeus himself does not go about things in this manner. He places what is in Lat.Iren. the ablative construction *ex Virgine* parallel to *de* (or *ex*) *fructu ventris; De hoc qui est ex Virgine Emmanuel dixit se ex Virgine...et...Filius qui ex fructu ventris David, hoc est, ex David Virgine, est Emmanuel.* Clearly *ex David* (gen.) *Virgine* is parallel to the whole phrase *ex fructu ventris David.* Yet this is where SC 210 (n. 3 to p. 105) claims to have a "contresens," namely, by putting *ex Virgine* parallel to *ex fructu ventris.* Lat.Iren., SC suggests, was putting Jesus parallel to Mary, showing that the translator did not understand the construction; but with this we cannot agree. *De fructu ventris* means "someone, some child from the womb," which is essentially the same as "a child," who is Jesus (cf. 3.21.5). But *ex Virgine* also means "someone, some child" of the Virgin, which is then the same as *ex fructu ventris.* In Latin, therefore, both nouns would be in the ablative; but in Greek they would be in the genitive after ἐξ. The genitive παρθένου would explain the genitive καρποῦ; it is not a genitive of possession following *ventris* (κοιλίας). This explanation agrees entirely with the very similar sentence in *AH* 3.21.5: *De fructu ventris eius (Davidis) aeternum suscitaturum se Regum, hic est qui ex Virgine quae fuit de genere David generatus est.* There, *ex Virgine* is not in place of a genitive of possession modifying *ventris* but a parallel to *de fructu.*

Though LXX and Vulgate have "your throne," Lat.Iren. has *sedem meam,* as is clear from the MSS evidence (only A and Erasmus have *tuam*). "My" seems likely to have been original with Irenaeus, since it is not probable that a scribe would have changed *tuam* to *meam* against the clear reading of Scripture. And as SC 210 (n. 2 to p. 105) observes, by this change Irenaeus shows that he considers Christ to be God's Son, possessing the very throne of God, though He is also David's son through Mary.

12. Ps. 75(76):2, 3.

13. Num 24:17. "Leader" is also in *Proof* 58, and in Justin, *Dial.* 106 (Goodspeed, *Die ältesten Apologeten,* 222, 223). The Hebrew Bible has *'sēbet* ("scepter") and LXX "man." Lat.Iren. has *in Israel,* which is questionable, as LXX, *Proof* 58, and Justin have *ex Israel.*

14. Matt 2:2; and for what follows see Matt 2:11. This passage is preserved in a Syriac fragment.

15. Luke 1:33.

16. Ps 75(76):2.

17. Cf. Rom 10:20; Isa 65:1. Such an explanation of the threefold gift of the magi was held by other patristic writers and became traditional in the Church. See Origen, *Contra Celsum* 1.9 (GCS 1:111); Leo I, *Sermo* 31 (ML 54:236); *Sermo* 33 (ML 54:241, 42); *Sermo* 36 (ML 54:254). Prudentius put it into verse in his *Cathemerinon,* hymn 12 (M. P. Cunningham, *Aurelii Prudentii Clementis Carmina* [CCSL 126; Turnholt: Brepols, 1966], 65–72).

18. Matt 3:16, 17. Here we have followed SC in utilizing the Greek fragments (including the Oxyrhynchus Papyrus [P.Oxy. 405], dated to c. 200 and thus nearly contemporary with Irenaeus himself); cf. SC 211:106–9; SC 210 (n. 1 to p. 109).

19. The false tenet expressed is described in *AH* 1.2.6 as pertaining to the Ptolomaean Valentinians. The previous refutation, to which Irenaeus refers in the next line, could be 3.8.2; but SC 210 (n. 2 to p. 109) think it might also be 2.24.1, 2. Irenaeus clearly states what he considers the right doctrine as far back as *AH* 1.10.1. For a thorough (and astoundingly long) treatment of Jesus' baptism and anointing by the Holy Spirit for the new economy of salvation, see Orbe, *La Unción del Verbo,* 1–717. Osborn (*Irenaeus,* 133, 34) treats in summary fashion of the baptism of Jesus, as does Donovan, *One Right Reading?* 72, 73. Behr offers a succinct summation of Irenaeus's view: "Jesus, at his baptism, was anointed by the Father with the Spirit so that man might share in the abundance of his Unction which made him Christ" (*Asceticism and Anthropology,* 67). Thus, it is first in the person of Jesus Christ that the accustomization of the Spirit to dwell in man, described in *AH* 3.17.1, takes place.

Many articles have been written over the past twenty-five years exploring the baptism of Jesus in Irenaeus from different angles. Among the most pertinent of these are A. Houssiau, "Le baptême selon Irénée de Lyon," *Ephemerides Theologicae Lovanienses* 60, no. 1 (1984): 45–59; A. Orbe, "El Espiritu en el bautismo de Jésus (en torno a san Ireneo)," *Gregorianum* 76, no. 4 (1995): 663–99; idem, "¿San Ireneo adopcionista? En torno a *adv. haer.* III,19,1," *Gregorianum* 65, no. 1 (1984): 5–52. Orbe was the first to dedicate a study to the question of Irenaeus's "adoptionistic" language in *AH* 3.19.1 in relation to Jesus' baptism. The subject was taken up again more recently by D. A. Smith,

"Irenaeus and the Baptism of Jesus," *Theological Studies* 58 (1997): 618–42; with a response issued by K. McDonnell, "Quaestio disputata: Irenaeus on the Baptism of Jesus," *Theological Studies* 59 (1998): 317–19. The main point of contention in all these studies is whether Irenaeus's language of the Son "receiving adoption" (3.19.1), taken together with the language in our present paragraph of Jesus "becoming Jesus Christ" at the baptism, represents an adoptionist christological statement. It is agreed by all that it does not (Irenaeus is stringently anti-adoptionistic elsewhere, and such locations provide a context of interpretation that prohibits such a reading here); but the language still remains something of a puzzle to commentators.

20. Isa 11:1—4. Lat.Iren. has *gloriam* for "appearance," but this is simply an alternative meaning of the Greek δόξα of the LXX.

21. Isa 61:1, 2. The change of sequence from "anointed me; he has sent me to bring..." is according to Lat.Iren. here and in Irenaeus's commentary, as also in *Proof* 53; namely, "anointed" governs "to bring." This is the fine observation of SC 210 (n. 2 to p. 111). Cf. Donovan, *One Right Reading?* 73.

22. Cf. Matt 1:1.

23. John 2:25 and 24. In the following sentence "console" stands for *advocabat*, which translates παρεκάλει. Lat.Iren. gave a slavish translation of the Greek and thus took out one of its basic meanings, "to defend and aid." We do not agree with SC 210 (n. 4 to p. 111) that Lat.Iren. here gave a false translation—rather only an overly rigid one.

24. Prov 5:22.

Chapter 10

1. Luke 1:6.

2. Luke 1:8, 9. For Gabriel's belonging to God in the text that follows, see Luke 1:11, 19.

3. Luke 1:15–17.

4. Matt 11:9, 11; cf. Luke 7:26, 28.

5. Ps 57:4 (58:3).

6. Cf. Luke 1:17.

7. Luke 1:26, 32, 33.

8. Cf. Luke 3:6; Isa 40:5. Lit., "to all flesh" (*omni carni*/πάσῃ σαρκί).

9. Again the ideas of seeing God and of union with Him are advanced as reasons for the incarnation. See Unger, "Christ's Rôle," 14–20. The title "Son of Man" is encountered here, as is frequent in the Gospels. For man's becoming a son of God, see John 1:12; 1 John 3:1.

10. Luke 1:46, 54–59. It is worth noting how Irenaeus has the Church identified with Christ's mother in this joy and prophecy. Mary prophesies on

behalf of the Church, inasmuch as the Church will rejoice with her in the Savior and His redemption of God's people. See D. J. Unger, "Sancti Irenaei Lugdunensis Episcopi, Doctrina de Maria Virgine *Matre*, Socia Iesu Christi Filii Sui ad Opus Recapitulationis," in *Maria et Ecclesia: Acta Congressus Mariologici Mariani in Civitate Lourdes Anno 1958 Celebrati* (Rome: Academia Mariana Internationalis, 1959), 4:99ff. SC 210 (n. 1 to p. 119) retains *Maria* here as after all the Latin MSS, but hesitates because in *AH* 4.7.1, Arm.Iren. and two Latin MSS ascribe the Magnificat to Elizabeth, as they do here (3.10.2). "Mary" could be an intentional adjustment of a Latin copyist. However, this seems impossible in the present location, as but a little earlier the advent of the Savior is presented as coming through the Virgin. To Irenaeus's mind Mary alone, and not Elizabeth, prophesied here for the Church.

11. Luke 1:78, 79.

12. Cf. Luke 1:64, 67.

13. Rom 3:30. Irenaeus thus emphasizes that, though connected with all that has gone before, what is offered in Christ is a new life. Osborn notes, "Newness is shown in a new spirit, a new order, a new worship of one God" (*Irenaeus*, 117; see also 118).

14. Luke 1:68–75.

15. Luke 1:76, 77.

16. John 1:29, 30; and 1:15, 16.

17. Lat.Iren. has *Mater Ogdoados*, but, as Sagnard remarks (SC 34, p. 169 n. 2), this genitive does not mean that she is the mother of the Ogdoad by giving birth to it. This is a genitive of apposition; the mother is the Ogdoad; see *AH* 1.5.2–3.

18. Gen 49:18.

19. Isa 12:2.

20. Ps 97(98):2. LXX has σωτήριον; RSV has "victory." σωτήριον may rightly mean "saving power," as SC 210 (n. 2 to p. 125) observes. Cf. Titus 2:11.

21. Lam 4:20. Irenaeus introduces the quotation from Lamentations with these words, in the Latin: *etenim Salvator quidem, quoniam Filius et Verbum Dei; Salutare autem, quoniam Spiritus.* A. Houssiau (*La christologie de saint Irénée* [Louvain: Publications universitaires de Louvain, 1955], 67 n. 6), holds that *salutare* in Irenaeus is the manifestation of the Word through the incarnation, and so he believes that someone incorrectly exchanged *Salutare* and *Salvator* in this sentence. SC 210 (n. 3 to p. 125) rightly defends the word order as it is in Lat.Iren., for Jesus Christ is "salutary," that is, the saving power, precisely because He is Spirit—that is, He is divine. For Irenaeus it is the Spirit, the spiritual, that actively (transitively) saves; and it is the flesh that is saved (see *AH* 5.6.1; 5.9.1). The spiritual may save either because it is strictly divine or because it shares in the divine. The Holy Spirit is salvific in the first sense: He is divine, as being one of the "hands" of the Father. But the Father too is Spirit (see 2.13.2; 2.28.4); and the Son is Spirit, as is presented in our present pas-

sage via the quotation from Lam 4:20. In this text it is clear that Christ is *Salutare* not because of some manifestation of the Word in Christ, but because He as Son is Spirit-Divine. He became man and so was visible and manifested, but that alone does not render Him salutary; He is such because He is divine Spirit. See 5.14.2: *quod fuit qui perierat homo, hoc salutare factum est Verbum*, the saving Word, that is, the Spirit-Word, the divine Word, became what man is. See *Proof* 71: again quoting Lam 4:20, Irenaeus comments, "Scripture tells us that Christ, being Spirit of God, was to become man...." See also *AH* 3.20.4; 3.9.1. This passage is a good demonstration of the kind of fluid language that was applied to descriptions of the divine persons prior to the linguistic clarifications of a later age.

22. John 1:14. There is in this collation of scriptural texts an expression of the divine and the human in Jesus, by which it is possible for Him to redeem man, united as He was with God and with man in the one person of God's Son and Word. So Donovan (*One Right Reading?* 71) remarks, "What Irenaeus is concerned to do is unite in the one figure, Christ, attributes the Gnostic myth splits among several figures."

23. John 1:29. This true "knowledge of salvation" is in opposition to the false gnosis of the heretics. Salvation is presented as consisting, like eternal life, in knowing the one true God and His Son; see John 17:3.

24. Luke 2:8, 11–14. Irenaeus has added "his."

25. Luke 2:11. It is interesting that Irenaeus, here quoting from the scriptural usage of his opponents, has the normal and complete text of Luke, namely, with "city of David," not "house"; and "to you today," all of which he skipped above.

26. See Luke 3:23.

27. Cf. Ps 131(132):11. See n. 11 to chap. 9, above.

28. Ps 120(121):2. In the introductory clause to this quotation, the Greek fragment has "this universe," which is in concert with the general policy of Irenaeus to use the demonstrative pronoun with "universe": cf. 1.10.3; 1.19.1; 1.Pref.1; 2.11.1. Lat.Iren. has "entire universe," which we have followed. See SC 210 (n. 2 to p. 129).

29. Ps 94(95):4–7.

30. Luke 2:14. Irenaeus reads the angel's song as implying that there is but one God, not two; and that this one God is the Creator of the world and the supreme Father. The Creator of this world is herein the same as the Creator of the highest heavens—a deliberately anti-Valentinian point.

31. Luke 2:20.

32. Luke 2:22–24; cf. Exod 13:2; Lev 12:8.

33. Luke 2:29–32. Irenaeus uses the song of Simeon in the sense preserved in the Lucan Gospel, namely, of Simeon's (and pedagogically any other's) being released from this world through death; cf. *AH* 3.16.4; 4.7.1. This is admitted in SC 210 (n. 1 to p. 135), but there it is also posited that in

our present passage Irenaeus applies it to the liberation from servitude to the law, which is paralleled to the redemption of Jerusalem about which the prophetess Anna speaks. SC has a point, inasmuch as throughout the present section Irenaeus is aiming to prove that there is only one God who through His Son brings liberty from servitude. We would wish, however, to speak somewhat more reservedly on the matter. If Irenaeus has such a meaning here as SC 210 suggests, he would likely not be using it to the exclusion of the more standard meaning, maintained elsewhere in his corpus. The meaning of liberation from the law would be but an additional overtone.

34. Luke 2:36, 38. According to the Latin MSS the reading of the sentence following this quotation is as follows: *Per haec autem omnia unus Deus demonstratur, [nullam] <novam> libertatis dispositionem per novum adventum Filii sui testamentum hominibus aperiens.* This reading raises a number of problems. We have bracketed *nullam* because it makes little sense, though witnessed by CVA. Scholars unanimously insert *novam* in its place.

With *per adventum* in the accusative, *testamentum* must be governed by *aperiens*; but then there is no verb for *dispositionem*. Various solutions to this challenge have been offered. One suggestion is that *adventus* should be genitive. This releases *aperiens* as the verb for *dispositionem*, which is grammatically correct but is an unusual expression and is not found elsewhere in Irenaeus. One might suggest that since *testamentum aperiens* is found elsewhere, Irenaeus may have written *dispositionem aperiens*, especially since *testamentum* and *dispositio* are connected. Another solution was begun by Grabe (217, n. h)—and then followed by R. Massuet (MG 7:877–78, n. 61), A. Stieren, and W. W. Harvey (2:38–39, n. 5): Grabe dropped *testamentum* and kept *adventum* in the accusative. But this would present the same problem as the above, with *aperiens* governing *dispositionem*. Moreover, *testamentum* is witnessed by CVAS. SC 210 (n. 3 to p. 135), satisfied with neither of these solutions, took an entirely new approach: by a scribal accident *dispositionem* and *testamentum* must have exchanged places, which gave rise to other changes. The text so changed would originally have read: *...novum libertatis testamentum per novam adventus Filii sui dispositionem hominis aperiens.* All the phrases now fit the style of Irenaeus admirably. (a) *libertatis testamentum* is found in 3.12.14; 4.16.15; 4.33.14; 4.34.3, always with *novum* modifying *testamentum*. (b) For *per novam adventus Filii dispositionem*, see 3.16.3; 5.14.2; and 3.10.2, wherein the economy was actualized by the Son's coming. (c) That coming was the inaugurating of the new covenant; see 4.34.3; 4.4.1; 4.9.1, 3. (d) Lastly, *aperiens* governs *testamentum* in 3.17.2; 4.34.3; 5.9.4. SC's observation is ingenious, and we have accepted it in our translation. We have done so reluctantly, however, due to the solid MSS witness to the arrangement usually followed. There seems but one way out of this. If a verb such as *faciens* (governing *dispositionem*) fell out, *aperiens* could continue to govern *testamentum*. *Adventum* would remain accusative; but that in a weak aspect, as *testamentum* would then not be modified by *novum*—an unusual, though not impossible, situation. This would have the advantage of not requiring so many changes to the text. *Videant periti.*

35. Mark 1:1–3; cf. Mal 3:1; Isa 40:3. "Before our God" may come from a text similar to our codex Bezae, which has "the paths of *your* God." Isa 40:3 in the Hebrew has "paths for our God," and LXX has "paths of our God."

36. Cf. Luke 1:17.

37. Mark 1:3.

38. Cf. *AH* 2.25.3. "Abundant and rich" may have been inspired by such texts as Isa 55:7 and Rom 10:12. The phrase occurs (with the words inverted) also in *AH* 3.16.7 and 4.20.11.

39. Mark 16:19.

40. Ps 109(110):1.

41. For the first clause, see Matt 22:37; Deut 6:5; for the last, see Exod 20:11; Ps 145(146); Acts 4:24, 14:15.

CHAPTER 11

1. See *AH* 1.24.3 and ACW 55, pp. 85 n. 10, 233. Cf. Rev 2:6, 15.

2. The Latin alternates in the present sentence between *Monogenen* (*monogeni* in Q and Erasmus) and *Unigeniti*, with no extant Greek for comparison. It seems likely that this is a case of Lat.Iren.'s propensity to vary vocabulary, since both terms are clearly in reference to the same being. SC's Greek retroversion translates each with Μονογενῆ, and follows suit in its French translation (SC 211:141).

3. "Located" translates *subiecta*, which might seem to imply "was cast down"; but here it likely represents ὑποκειμένης, which Lat.Iren. often translates by *subiaciens*. For all the erroneous views mentioned, see *AH* 1.1.1.

4. A concise statement on the unity and continuity of the Word's economic activity.

5. John 1:1–5. For the punctuation of v. 3, see ACW 55, pp. 44 n. 45, 177.

6. Cf. *AH* 2.2–8.

7. John 1:10, 11. Lat.Iren. has *in hoc mundo*, but as *hoc* is not in the Greek NT, it is likely a translation of the definite article, as elsewhere in *AH*.

8. Cf. *AH* 1.27.2–4.

9. Cf. *AH* 2.2.1–5.

10. Cf. *AH* 1.5.

11. John 1:14.

12. Cf. *AH* 1.7.2; 1.12.4; 1.26.1; 1.30.13. That the Word did not become flesh is, according to Osborn (*Irenaeus*, 152), one of the "four common denials that run through the variety of heretical opinion." He lists the others

as a denial of the OT Scriptures; a profession that the saving God is not the same as the Creator; and a belief that the flesh cannot be saved. Cf. A. Benoît, "Irénée et l'hérésie, les conceptions hérésiologiques de l'évêque de Lyon," *Augustinianum* 20 (1980): 63–67.

13. *AH* 1.7.2, and ACW 55, pp. 39 n. 8, 170.

14. Cf. *AH* 1.7.2.

15. Cf. *AH* 1.25.1; 1.26.1.

16. John 1:14. Docetists thus deny, ultimately, that God is involved in, active in, the creation He has fashioned. This denial of God's immediacy to creation is far more offensive to Irenaeus than the actual metaphysical details of docetic Christology. He comments further on the matter in 3.18.3–5, summing up his emphasis in 3.18.6: "[Christ] was a man, fighting for the fathers," that is, directly involved with and active in the world of man. See M. Slusser, "Docetism: A Historical Definition," *Second Century* 1 (1981): 172; cf. idem, "Theopaschite Expressions in Second-Century Christianity as Reflected in the Writings of Justin, Melito, Celsus and Irenaeus" (D.Phil., University of Oxford, 1975), 222ff.; and P. L. Gavrilyuk, *The Suffering of the Impassible God: The Dialectics of Patristic Thought*, Oxford Early Christian Studies (Oxford: University Press, 2004), 80 n. 58, who comments on the above sources.

17. John 1:5–8.

18. Cf. Luke 1:17. For the allusions prior to this short quotation, see Luke 1:19; Mark 1:2; Mal 3:1. SC 210 (n. 2 to p. 151) correctly observes that *praeparaturum*, as well as the preceding *missurum*, are future infinitives and both depend on *promisit*. Thus, Irenaeus presents God Himself as preparing the way, and not John, as is the case in Scripture. This is not necessarily contrary to what Scripture relates, as God is clearly working through John; otherwise the quotation from Luke, which Irenaeus understands in reference to John, would make little sense.

19. To what scriptural passage is Irenaeus referring? Nowhere in the Scriptures is Elias presented as making such proclamation expressly. Elias professes belief in the Lord as "the God of Abraham" (cf. 3 Kgdms 18:36; Irenaeus has quoted this in *AH* 3.6.3, above); and as "God of hosts," namely, of the heavens (cf. 3 Kgdms 18:15). SC 210 (n. 3 to p. 151) enforces this by noting that one who believes in the God of Abraham also believes what Abraham believed about Him, namely, that He is Creator of heaven and earth (see Gen 14:22, which Irenaeus quotes in 4.5.5).

20. Matt 11:9 and Luke 7:26. For the coming allusion to the Father's light foretold by the prophets, see, for example, Isa 60:1; for the desire to see Him, see Matt 13:17; for John the forerunner and Baptist, see John 1.29.

21. 1 Cor 12:28. So it is clear that, for Irenaeus, though the prophets are the valid and important conduits of God's activity, whose value remains even in the new covenant, nonetheless the apostles preach a greater message; see Osborn, *Irenaeus*, 178–79.

22. Cf. John 2:1, 3, 10.

23. Cf. John 2:2, 10. "In a summary way" is *compendialiter* in Lat.Iren. It is a summary in time, inasmuch as it was made miraculously, over against the elaborate and drawn-out process of nature. Compare *compendiosam* in 3.11.8; and *compendii poculo* in 3.16.7. See Osborn, *Irenaeus*, 116, 187.

24. John 6:11 (took bread and gave thanks); Matt 22:2–10; Rev 19:9 (invitation to a wedding; cf. John 6:11).

25. Cf. Gen 1:11; 1:9; 2:5; Ps 103(104):10. For the following Irenaean idea, see also *AH* 4.20.5; 3.16.6.

26. John 1:18. For "Only-begotten Son of God," see ACW 55, pp. 44 n. 43, 176.

27. Cf. Matt 11:27 and 25.

28. John 1:47, 49.

29. Matt 16:17 and 16.

30. Matt 12:18–21, from Isa 42:1–4; cf. also Matt 3:17. "Victory" is according to the NT, in Greek νῖκος. Lat.Iren. has *contentionem*, which most probably comes from a false reading as νεῖκος.

31. "Cardinal points" for *principia*. Sagnard's "commencements" (SC 34, p. 191; retained by SC 211) is not true to the context. Irenaeus does not treat of merely the beginning statements of the Gospels.

32. *Ex ipsis (Evangeliis) egrediens* was translated by Sagnard (SC 34, p. 193) incorrectly, since he inserted "de l'Église" (p. 193) as if it were a question of the heretics leaving the Church. The Church is nowhere in sight in this context. That *egrediens* means "using as a starting point," namely, as a source for doctrines, is confirmed by a passage in 4.Pref.4; *ex differentibus locis egrediantur*. P. Nautin ("Notes critiques sur Irénée, Adv. haer III," *Vigiliae Christianae* 9 [1955]: 34–36) observed that *egrediens*, which supposes ἐξελθόντα, might be a misreading for ἐξελόντα; namely, each one snatches from the Gospels something to confirm his doctrine. SC 210 (n. 1 to p. 159) accepts this. Since, however, the Latin makes good sense as it stands, there is little need for this correction.

The "authority" (*firmitas*) is that of the Gospels as sources of teaching. It is not of tradition, as Sagnard (SC 34, p. 193) interpolates. If it were the authority of tradition, it would not help the heretics to use the Gospels. Irenaeus is showing that these groups used the Gospels as a starting point for their teachings precisely because of the authority of the Gospels, not of tradition in general, concerning which Irenaeus has not been speaking. This passage is a valuable witness to the authority of the Gospels among the early Christians; even those termed heretics did not dare sidestep them completely. See Behr, *Way to Nicaea*, 113–14.

33. Cf. *AH* 1.24.23 and ACW 55, pp. 85 n. 7, 231–32.

34. Cf. *AH* 1.27.2–4. SC 211:159 translates *circumcidens* with the French "amputée," which we also find a fitting rendering.

35. Cf. 1.8.5; 9.1–3.

36. The witness is not given "to us," as Sagnard (SC 34, p. 193) has it, but to the Gospels.

37. "Cardinal" is for *principales* in Lat.Iren. and καθολικά in the extant Greek (via a fragment from Anastasius the Sinaite, *Quaestio* 144)—thus the four cardinal (i.e., general) winds.

38. Cf. 1 Tim 3:15, adapted, for in Timothy the Church is the bulwark of the truth; here the Gospel is the bulwark of the Church.

39. Ps 79(80):2; Cf. Wis 1:7.

40. Ps 79(80):2.

41. Rev 4:7; for the "four faces," see Ezek 1:6, 10.

42. The nature of Christ is said to be "powerful and sovereign and kingly." A little later Irenaeus speaks of the generation of Christ from the Father as sovereign. "Sovereign" in both cases translates the extant Greek ἡγεμονικόν, for which the Latin translator gave *principale.* See discussion of this term in ACW 55, pp. 11 n. 59, 120.

43. Rev 4:7. "Ministerial and priestly rank" is in the Greek τὴν ἱερουργικὴν καὶ ἱερατικὴν τάξιν. Lat.Iren. gave this as *sacrificalem et sacerdotalem ordinationem.* The word order is the same in both. Later in the same paragraph, Irenaeus says that Luke's Gospel is sacrificial in nature (thus the calf is the symbol), and so the priest Zacharias begins by offering sacrifice. The Greek here is ἅτε ἱερατικοῦ χαρακτῆρος...ἱερέως θυμιῶντος, in Lat.Iren. *sacerdotalis characteris est, a Zacharia sacerdote sacrificante.* Still later Irenaeus again has two terms in Latin: *sacerdotalem et ministerialem actum,* but the extant Greek has only ἱερατικήν for *sacerdotalem,* and nothing for *ministerialem.* In these three places *sacerdotalis* consistently translates ἱερατικήν. In the first instance the first term is ἱερουργικήν, with the Latin *sacrificalem,* which would more correctly have been translated by *ministerialem* in place of the more specific *sacrificalem.* In the final passage the second term is *ministerialem,* for which the Greek is missing. But here Lat.Iren. used the more generic term, and it seems almost certain that the Greek was ἱερουργικήν, and not λειτουργικήν as Harvey (2:48) suggests.

In the last set the noun is *actum* in Lat.Iren., which supposes πρᾶξις in Greek; but the Greek has τάξις, as in the first place, and should be translated *ordinem.* Here we have favored the Latin *actum*-πρᾶξις because in the context there is a contrast in regard to how the Lord operated in patriarchal times (according to divinity and glory) and in Mosaic times (in a priestly and ministerial function). The Greek scribe seems to have misread τάξις for πρᾶξις, though this is not absolutely certain. Perhaps the contrast is between "characters": in the Old Testament it was the divine glory, and in the New, the priestly and ministerial rank. In such a case the Latin translator would have misread πρᾶξις for the original τάξις.

44. Rev 4:7.

45. Irenaeus's account of the symbolism of the four Gospels is the oldest on record. How did he understand these symbols? What does he assert about them? How does he prove them? It must be remembered that Irenaeus earlier suggested that the criterion for the genuineness of the Gospels is apostolicity. He went to some lengths to show that even Mark and Luke, though written by non-apostles, are apostolic inasmuch as Mark wrote down Peter's preaching, and Luke wrote down Paul's (cf. 3.1.1). By this means he defended that there are four and only four Gospels. Irenaeus is also aware that John said the whole world could not contain all the words and deeds of Jesus, and that each evangelist wrote from his peculiar viewpoint. If now he adduces arguments from Scripture about the symbolism of the Gospels, these "arguments" can scarcely be for him more than illustrations of a fact already proved by apostolicity. Furthermore, if the symbolism is true, and especially if it was intended by God, then one has a further justification for the fourfold Gospel, which is, however, established rather *a posteriori*, after having proved the existence of the four by a strict argument of apostolicity and acceptance by the Church.

Irenaeus finds a scheme of fourfold things in creation and the economy of salvation, listing two schemes from creation and three from the economy. In creation he notes four zones and four cardinal winds. One notes immediately that he sees in these zones and cardinal winds a resonance of "catholicity," in that they cover the whole world, and thus he immediately adds that the Church "is spread out over the whole earth." There may seem to be an inextricable mixture of figures here, but the zones are not mentioned without cause. The pillars are introduced as an explanation of them, inasmuch as the winds blow from the four corners, supported by the pillars. It may be that some words fell out of the Latin text, or perhaps already in the Greek used by Lat.Iren.: *quattuor habere eam columnas <in regionibus, ubi sunt> spiritus undique flantes.* As the Latin stands in the present MSS, as well as the Greek, the pillars would do the blowing, but this is clearly illogical. In any case, in the application to the Church the pillars are the four Gospels and the "breath of the life" is the Spirit. Behr (*Way to Nicaea*, 113) notes that Irenaeus's reasoning here is "hardly likely to persuade anyone who does not already accept the fact" of these Gospels' canonicity.

Irenaeus's first illustration from the economy of salvation is the four-faced image of the Cherubim, which he takes from Ezek 1:1 and Rev 4:7. J. Hoh ("Zur Herkunft der vier Evangelisten-symbole," *Biblische Zeitschrift* 15 [1918]: 229–34) surmises that Irenaeus received this symbolism from the Christian Jews, since he betrays contact with them more than once (cf. *AH* 1.18.4; 2.25.3; 3.21.1; 4.31.3; 4.33.4), and since these Jews highly revered the vision of Ezekiel. After noting that Mark's Gospel has a "prophetic" character, namely, that it proclaims God's Word, Irenaeus remarks that the Word of God spoke to the patriarchal age, then to those under the law of Moses, and then, as the enfleshed Word, to present humanity. If he had noted the "prophets" in the third group, to whom he refers so often in his work, he would have had a fourfold symbol even here. His second illustration from the economy is of the four main covenants that God made with humanity.

It should be observed that this symbolism of the Gospels expressly involves a symbolism of Christ's person and functions. Only one of the symbols, that of the face like a man, refers to his human nature. The other three refer to His salvific functions: they are kingly, priestly, and prophetic, symbolized by the lion, the calf, and the eagle, respectively. For the "prophetic character," see the expanded explanation in the following paragraphs.

46. John 1:1–3. Before the quotation the words "the Gospel according to John" are from the Greek fragment, and are called for as a parallel to the remark about the Lucan Gospel below.

47. Cf. Luke 1:5–9.

48. Cf. Luke 15:23.

49. Matt 1:1 and 18.

50. Cf. Matt 11:29.

51. Mark 1:1, 2. "Winged": we have taken *volatilem et pennatam* as a doublet translation.

52. See n. 43 to the present chapter above.

53. Cf. Ps 16(17):8; 60(61):5; 90(91):4.

54. "Principal" is supplied from the Greek, καθολικαί. Elsewise, the Latin appears more authentic than the Greek fragment, which differs considerably. See the discussion in SC 210 (n. 2 to p. 171).

55. On such claims, see Timothy, *Early Christian Apologists*, 7–9. In the present paragraph, Irenaeus presents his readers with the first closed Gospel canon in the Christian tradition.

56. "Part of": Massuet followed earlier editors, reading *pariter* in place of *partem*. But the latter, which is in all the MSS except Q and Erasmus, is surely correct, for by clipping from the Gospel, Marcion had only part of it left; see 3.14.4 and especially 1.27.2. SC 210 (n. 3 to p. 171), after some hesitation, defends *partem*.

57. Cf. Acts 2:16, 17; Joel 3:1; John 15:26.

58. Sagnard (SC 34, p. 202) did not understand what Irenaeus wished to say, and so erroneously changed *volunt* to *nolunt*.

The group targeted in Irenaeus's comments here is unclear. For a long time it was thought to be the so-called Montanists, with claims to exclusive possession of the Spirit denied to the rest of the Church (and so it is noted in the ANF edition). Naturally such a group would reject the Gospel that contains a frequent promise of the Paraclete "to everyone"; cf. L. Nasrallah, *"An Ecstasy of Folly": Prophecy and Authority in Early Christianity*, Harvard Theological Studies 52 (Cambridge, MA: Harvard University Press, 2003), esp. chaps. 1 and 5. Such Montanist attribution is, however, now widely rejected; see R. E. Heine, "The Role of the Gospel of John in the Montanist Controversy," *Second Century*

6 (1987): 14 n. 74. Irenaeus certainly rejected the Montanist proposition (he is widely believed to have been a partner in, if not in fact the author of, the letter of the churches of Vienne and Lyons against the Montanists of Asia); but it seems unlikely that he has them in mind here.

Perhaps the group described are the Encratists or the Severians. E. Schüssler Fiorenza ("Word, Spirit and Power: Women in Early Christian Communities," in *Women of Spirit: Female Leadership in the Jewish and Christian Traditions*, edited by R. R. Ruether [New York: Simon & Schuster, 1979], 39–40) argues that the group may in fact be the *Alogoi* known from chap. 27 of the *Acts of Thomas*. Yet scholarly opinion here is far from unanimous.

59. Cf. 1 Cor 12:31, 10–29; 14:1–40; cf. also 1 Cor 11:4–5. Recently, much has been made of Irenaeus's specific mention here of women prophesying in the Church. See Hoffman, *Women and Gnosticism*, 94–95, and esp. his n. 89 (p. 126).

60. Cf. Matt 12:31, 32.

61. That Irenaeus may here refer to the *Gospel of Truth* as preserved in the Nag Hammadi Codices (NHC I,3 and XII,2; see J. M. Robinson, *The Nag Hammadi Library in English* [San Francisco: Harper, 1991]) has been suggested since at least W. C. Van Unnik, *Newly Discovered Gnostic Writings: A Preliminary Survey of the Nag Hammadi Find*, Studies in Biblical Theology 30 (London: SCM Press, 1960), 60. An extensive catalogue of modern scholars who agree with this assessment is cited in Tiessen, *Salvation of Unevangelized*, 44 n. 30; see also Steenberg, *Irenaeus on Creation*, 13 n. 33.

The *Gospel of Truth* may be rather firmly dated to c. 140–145, or at least before Valentinus's departure from Rome (c. 160): in this we follow Tiessen, *Salvation of Unevangelized*, 58; van Unnik, *Newly Discovered*, 63; and R. M. Grant, *Gnosticism and Early Christianity* (rev. ed.; New York: Harper & Row, 1966), 128–29. Van Unnik takes the suggestion from H. C. Puech and G. Quispel, *Evangelium Veritatis* (Zurich: Rascher Verlag, 1956) xiv, stating it with more certainty than do those earlier authors. That Valentinus was the author has been challenged in a serious way only by A. Orbe, based primarily on a comparison of style between the tractate and the Valentinian homily quoted by Clement, but this view has not found widespread support. See A. Orbe, "Los hombres y el creador según una homilia de Valentin (Clem. Strom IV 13,89,1–91,3)," *Gregorianum* 55, no. 2 (1974): 339–68. Orbe's main statement against Valentinus's authorship of the *Gospel of Truth* comes only in a brief paragraph at the end of his English summary; cf. Tiessen, *Salvation of Unevangelized*, 58 n. 67. For an early witness to the more widespread view of Valentinus's authorship, see Quispel's comments in F. L. Cross, ed., *The Jung Codex: A Newly Rediscovered Gnostic Papyrus* (London: A. R. Mowbray, 1955), 53. But cf. H. Ringgren, "The Gospel of Truth and Valentinian Gnosticism," *Studia Theologica* 17, no. 2 (1963): 65, for a more cautious analysis.

62. *Ex principiis* is not "guiding principles" but "capital points." See n.

31 to the present chapter above. The words of the Lord that Irenaeus promises are given in book 4; see 3.25.7; 4.Pref.1.

CHAPTER 12

1. Acts 2:16–17, 20; Pss 168(169):26; 108(109):8.
2. Acts 2:15–17; Joel 2:28. The allusions before the quotation are to Acts 2:4, 13, 15.
3. Acts 2:22–27; Ps 15:8–10.
4. Cf. Acts 2:29.
5. Acts 2:30–36, with internal references to Ps 131(132):11; and Ps 109(110):1.
6. Acts 2:37, 38.
7. The Greek fragment has ἀναστήσαντα ("rose"), but Lat.Iren. has *sursum volaverit*, which supposes ἀναπτάντα. The idea of flying upward is present also in 3.11.1.
8. Cf. Acts 2:36.
9. Acts 3:6–8; cf. 3:2.
10. Acts 3:12–26. Irenaeus here follows the Western text (D) for a number of words: for example, "wished" for decided; "oppressed" for disowned; "putting in order" for restitution. For the subquotation "from Moses," see Deut 18:15, 19.
11. Gen 22:18; also 12:3.
12. Acts 4:8–12. For reference to the cornerstone, see Ps 117(118):22.
13. Acts 4:22.
14. Acts 4:24–28, with the implicit quotation from Ps 145(146):6 at the beginning. For the words of David, see Ps 2:1, 2.
15. "Mother City" is according to the Greek fragment (μητροπόλεως); that is, the Jerusalem Church, from which Irenaeus says every church has its beginning. Lat.Iren. has *civitatis magnae*, which could stand for a misreading of the Greek. But we ought not to rule out the possibility of the inverse: that the Greek excerpter misread the original μεγαλόπολις as μητρόπολις.
16. Acts 4:24; Ps 145(146):6. The Greek fragment has the addition "who are truly perfect," which SC 210 (n. 2 to p. 197) defends. It is possible that the simpler Latin is correct.
   This paragraph is a notable statement on the apostolicity of the Church, and on the perfection of the apostles through the gifts of the Holy Spirit, as opposed to the false perfect, the "Gnostics falsely so-called." On the perfecting role of the Spirit vis-à-vis the apostles, see Ochagavía, *Visibile Patris Filius*, 129–30; and vis-à-vis the Church at large, pp. 131–34.
17. Acts 4:31.

18. Acts 4:33.

19. Acts 5:30–32. "Killed," earlier in the paragraph, is only one word also in the Greek NT, which etymologically means laying hands on someone to kill him. Lat.Iren. tried to express both ideas by using two verbs: *apprehendistis et interfecistis.* "Glory" (δόξα) is in place of "right" (δεξιά), as in the Western text (D) of the Bible.

20. Acts 5:42.

21 Cf. Ps 95(96):5; Gal 4:8; and elsewhere in Irenaeus at 3.6.3; 4.24.2.

22. Acts 10:2–5, 15.

23. Acts 10:34, 35.

24. Acts 10:37–43.

25. Cf. Acts 8:27.

26. Acts 8:32, 33; Isa 53:7, 8.

27. Acts 8:35, 37.

28. Cf. Acts 9:19, 20; for the introductory clauses, see Acts 9:4, 5; 9:10, 18; and 9:24 ("with all boldness").

29. Phil 2:8. For the preceding allusions, see Eph 3:3; Gal 1:12 (about the mystery revealed); and Matt 28:18 (on full power from the Father).

30. Acts 17:24–31. "Jesus" is added here by Irenaeus from the Western text (D). For v. 29 of Acts, Lat.Iren. has *concupiscentia* (supposing ἐπιθύμησις); Acts has ἐνθύμησις (thought or imagination). Lat.Iren. must have misread the Greek. "As some of your own have said, 'For we are indeed His offspring'": this reference in Acts is to Aratus, a third-century BC Cilician poet, from his *Phaenomena,* 5.

31. Deut 32:8, 9. "Angels of God" is from the LXX; the Hebrew Bible has "sons of God." That angels had a role among various peoples was an ancient tradition; see Dan 10:13–21 (angels of Greece and Persia). Jewish apocalypses were replete with this idea, as was also Philo. See J. Daniélou, *The Angels and Their Mission According to the Fathers of the Church,* translated by D. Haimann (Westminster, MD: Newman Press, 1957), 15. The angels were ministers of salvation already in creation; see G. Bentivegna, "L'angelologia de S. Ireneo nella prima fase dell'opera di salvezza; l'economia 'secundum providentiam,'" *Orientalia christiana periodica* 28 (1962): 5–48.

32. Cf. Acts 14:8, 10–13.

33. Acts 14:15–17, with a quotation from Ps 145(146):6.

34. This single sentence is a concise summary of Irenaeus's exegetical "method," insofar as he can be described as having one discretely. It is only from within the scriptural heritage of the Church that an exposition of her beliefs is possible; to turn away from this heritage and attempt an explanation by other means is to rebel, not to explain.

35. The Latin *martyrii* is evidently a transliteration of the Greek, which literally means "witness." But in the context it is a witnessing by blood, and so it is, technically, the Christian "martyrdom." For Christ's "martyrdom," see

Rev 17:3; and 1:5 (the faithful witness); 1 Pet 2:21 (footsteps). In section 3 above, Irenaeus calls Jesus "the Teacher of martyrdom."

36. Acts 7:2–8. For the internal references, see Gen 12:1 and 15:13, 14.

37. Cf. Gen 17:10.

38. Cf. Acts 7:9, 16 (on the patriarchs); Acts 7:17–44 (on Moses).

39. See *AH* 2.30.2, 5.

40. 1 Tim 6:4.

41. Cf. John 1:17.

42. That the heretics believe themselves to have discovered something more than the apostles did is the same idea given in *Proof* 99. See also *AH* 3.2.2.

43. Cf. *AH* 1.27.2–4; and Tertullian, *Adversus Marcionem* 4.5.3–6 (CCSL 1:551); Epiphanius, *Panarion* 42.11.7 (GCS 2:117ff.), especially 42.12 (p. 183).

44. Cf. *AH* 1.27.4, where Irenaeus makes the same promise. Some scholars think Irenaeus never got to writing this promised book; but perhaps the promise was kept in the rest of book 3, and in books 4 and 5.

45. Cf. *AH* 1.27.2; and book 2 passim. With SC 210 (n. 2 to p. 233), we have accepted *intolerabiliorem* (witnessed only by Q and Erasmus; accepted also by SC 211:232) over against *tolerabiliorem* of the other MSS. "More tolerable" does not fit the error of a second god who created evil.

46. Cf. *AH* 1.5. "Thesis" is *propositum* in Lat.Iren., as also a few sentences earlier, for which SC has "thèses," while Sagnard (SC 34, p. 243) has "thème." See Lundström's discussion of this term (pp. 32–34). He translates it by "Absicht." Behr's comments on the "hypothesis" of Scripture are pertinent here; see *Way to Nicaea*, 32–33, 38, 74.

47. Cf. Heb 2:10; 7:28; 8:1.

48. Cf. Acts 7:55, 56.

49. Acts 7:60. For "martyrdom," see n. 35 to the present chapter above.

50. Hos 12:10.

51. Cf., for example, Acts 4:29, 31.

52. Cf. Acts 15:1; 11:26.

53. Cf. Acts 15:2.

54. Acts 15:7–11.

55. Acts 15:13–20. For the internal quotation, see Amos 9:11, 12. In this and the next long quotation, the *suffocates* of the scriptural text was skipped, but the "golden rule" was added, as in the Western text of D. Throughout, the text differs from the Vulgate inasmuch as synonyms are given. This is again a clear indication that Lat.Iren. made his own translation of Scripture from the Greek of Irenaeus.

56. Acts 15:23–29. The last sentence of this quotation about the "golden rule" is not in the critical text of the NT. It is in the Western text of D and in a few of the ancient translations, such as the Syrian and Sahidic. The last phrase, "walking in the Holy Spirit," is also not in the NT, but in codex D, though there the participle is φερόμενοι, not πορευόμενοι.

57. Acts 10:28, 29.

58. Acts 10:47.

59. Cf. Gal 2:12, 13.

60. Cf. Acts 1:8; John 15:27.

61. Cf. Mark 5:37; Matt 17:1; 26:37. At the beginning of this paragraph the James spoken of is the bishop of Jerusalem, who is not the brother of Peter in the trio of most beloved apostles, as Irenaeus errantly indicates.

CHAPTER 13

1. Cf. Eph 3:3; Gal 1:15ff.; and Acts 9. The "those" mentioned were the Marcionites, who admitted the corpus Paulinum and Luke's Gospel.

2. Cf. Gal 2:8.

3. Rom 10:15, from Isa 52:7, with phrases inverted.

4. Though the Latin codices have *Deum* here and after the quotation, Irenaeus most likely wrote *Dominum* (as presumed also in SC 211:252). The abbreviated forms of these two names are easily misread.

5. 1 Cor 15:11.

6. John 14:9, 11, 7. Cf. v. 8 for the introductory phrase.

7. Cf. Matt 10:5, 6.

8. Cf. Luke 10:1.

9. Matt 16:17.

10. Gal 1:1. Between this quotation and the clause to follow there is a problem, of which Grabe (234, n. 1) and Massuet (MG 7:911–12, n. 88) were already aware. Lat.Iren. reads:

Sicut ergo Paulus apostolus non ab hominibus neque per hominem, sed per Iesum Christum et Deum Patrem <factus est, sic et Petrus et reliqui apostoli cognoverunt Filium et Patrem,> Filio quidem adducente eos ad Patrem, Patre vero revelante eis Filium.

The clause in angular brackets is the suggested correction of SC 210 (n. 1 to p. 255). *Ergo* obviously introduces a sentence that sums up what preceded. In the beginning of chap. 13 it is clear that Irenaeus is refuting the Marcionite tenet that Paul alone possessed the truth. In section 1 he refutes them by Paul's own statements. In section 2 he adduces three examples of apostles who had the same knowledge as did Paul: Philip, for instance, according to John 14; then the twelve apostles and all the seventy-two disciples; lastly, Peter according to Jesus' own testimony in Matt 16:17. Then follows the concluding sentence. *Sicut ergo* supposes a comparison was made, yet the participial clause at the end cannot be the second part of such a comparison. Something has

fallen out. How much? In angular brackets above we have indicated what SC
would insert, stressing thus the knowledge of the Father and the Son. This is
well and good, but if this is inserted into the second half of the comparison,
it would seem to be necessary also in the first half, and one would have to suppose that words such as *cui per revelationem mysterium manifestatum est* (cf. section 1) also fell out. This is possible, but then the text supposed to have fallen
out would be rather long. It is preferable to keep it is as short as possible. This
in mind, since the idea of knowledge through revelation for Paul and for all
the apostles has been stressed sufficiently in Irenaeus's explanation already,
his conclusion may have spoken merely about the others being apostles just
as Paul was, then noting again the knowledge through revelation in the final
clause. So we have translated.

11. Gal. 2:1, 2. For the reference in the introductory clause, see Acts 15:2.

12. Gal. 2:5. Irenaeus omits the negative here, thus changing Paul's
meaning. This omission is in the Western text (D) also, as in Tertullian,
Victorinus, and Ambrosiaster.

CHAPTER 14

1. Acts 15:39.

2. Acts 16:8, 9. Lat.Iren. has *venimus* where the Vulgate has *descen-
derunt*, in agreement with the Greek NT. But below, with reference to Acts
20:6, Irenaeus also has *venimus*, as in the Greek NT and Vulgate.

3. Acts 16:10, 11.

4. Acts 16:12, 13. "Journey" is for Lat.Iren. *adventum*, which here cannot mean arrival, as it is modified by *reliquum omnem* (SC 210, n. 4 to p. 259).

In *primum sermonem locuti sunt*, the *primum* should not be translated as
an adjective modifying *sermonem*. It is an adverb, which in Greek would have
had the same form as the adjective. And *sermo* here seems to have the same
meaning as it does in Acts in many places, even in 16.6, with which we are now
dealing: it is God's word that is proclaimed. Cf. SC 210 (n. 5 to p. 259).

5. Acts 20:5, 6.

6. Cf. Acts 20:7–21; 21:17–23, 35.

7. Cf. Acts 25–26.

8. Cf. Acts 27–28 for the rest of Irenaeus's paragraph.

9. "Puffed up" is *elatus*, supposing ἐνεχθείς, which seems to be the correct reading, against Harvey's (2:75, n. 2) ἐλεγχθείς ("convicted"). The word
must be a coordinate of "liar" in view of the *nec...nec* construction. The term
occurs again in 3.15.2.

SC 210 (n. 1 to p. 263) thinks that the Latin of this sentence is grammatically faulty. By retranslating into Greek, it puts *constarent* in the infinitive,

and like *esse* and *ignorare* makes it subject to the preposition διά, which is thought to stand for *eo quod.* Perhaps. But if one takes *constarent* to mean "they are clear," as it can mean, and then makes the two infinitives (*esse* and *ignorare*) subject to it as an exemplification, the Latin makes sense as it stands. Thus have we translated.

10. 2 Tim 4:10, 11.

11. Col 4:14.

12. Acts 20:25–28. For the references to the events prior to this quotation, see Acts 20:17, 16, 18–24. Irenaeus follows the Western text (D) in writing "church of the Lord," instead of "church of God," and "for Himself." In the quotation Paul is speaking only of bishops, but in his introduction to this quotation Irenaeus speaks of both bishops and presbyters, while Luke (Acts 20:17) mentions only the presbyters who were assembled. This would fit with an observation that, at this period in history, the bishops were presbyters, but not all presbyters bishops.

13. Acts 20:29–30, and 27.

14. Luke 1:2.

15. Cf. ACW 55, pp. 21 n. 2, 125, for "discard."

16. Cf. Luke 1:5—2:52 for all the points mentioned.

17. Cf. Luke 3:1–23.

18. Luke 6:24–26.

19. Cf. Luke 5:1–11.

20. Cf. Luke 13:10–17.

21. Cf. Luke 14:1–6.

22. Cf. Luke 14:7–11.

23. Cf. Luke 14:12–14.

24. Cf. Luke 11:5–8.

25. Cf. Luke 7:36–50.

26. Luke 12:16–20, esp. v. 20. "His crops" is *nata* in Lat.Iren., which is found also in the old Latin of the Bible and in the Syriac. The Greek NT has καρπούς, "fruits/crops."

27. Cf. Luke 16:19–31.

28. Luke 17:5, 6.

29. Cf. Luke 19:1–10.

30. Cf. Luke 18:9–14.

31. Cf. Luke 17:11–19.

32. Cf. Luke 14:16–24.

33. Cf. Luke 18:1–8.

34. Cf. Luke 13:6–9.

35. Cf. Luke 24:13–32. It is of interest that already in Irenaeus's time readers were aware of the extra material in Luke's Gospel and had made lists of such items.

36. Cf. n. 45 to chap. 11 above.

37. "Danger of ruin" is *periculum*, which in ecclesiastical Latin has such a meaning. We note again the corrective intention behind Irenaeus's polemic, stated clearly here.

CHAPTER 15

1. Acts 9:5; 22:7, 8; 26:14, 15; 9:15, 16.

2. See our comments below, n. 20 to chap. 22, on the type of exegesis evidenced in this comment on God revealing certain facts only to Luke in order to force the heretics to admit his authority.

3. Cf. Acts 20:20, 27.

4. The heretics called the Christians names, namely, *communes* and *ecclesiasticos*. Below Irenaeus notes that the Catholics called their opponents "heretics." Cf. Acts 11.26, where the Gentiles first called the followers of Christ "Christians." Harvey (2:79, n. 6) thinks that the Greek for *communes* might have been καθολικούς, with the meaning of "general" (see *AH* 3.11.8, where it means principal or general). There would thus have been a beginning for the name "Catholics" similar to that of "Christians." But in *AH* 4.7.1, *communiter* means "in general"; so also in 5.12.2 (twice), where the Greek is κοινῶς. In 3.12.5, from Acts 10:28, 29, Peter is told to call no one *communem*, which is κοινόν in the NT. The nickname κοινοί would be quite intelligible in various "Gnostic" contexts as a reference to all others, since members of such groups often thought of themselves as the *perfect*. Lundström (p. 91) and Sagnard (*La gnose valentinienne et le témoignage de saint Irénée, Études de Philosophie Médiévale* [Paris: J. Vrin, 1947], 85 n. 1) reject Harvey's postulations.

The *ecclesiastici* are evidently the orthodox believers. Origen, *In Leviticum*, hom. 14.14 (GCS 6:480) takes the terms as synonymous; see also his *In Isaiam*, hom. 7.3 (GCS 8:283); *In Lucam*, hom. 16 (GCS 9:109); *In Ezechielem*, hom. 2.2 (GCS 8:342). For this see P. Galtier, "«...Ab his qui sunt undique...»" (Irénée, «Adv. Haer.,» III, 3, 2.)," *Revue d'Histoire Ecclésiastique* 44 (1949): 419ff.

5. "Discern" is certainly the sense of the verb in this context, but whether it was *discernere*, as J. Billius, F. Feuardentius, R. Massuet (MG 7:918, n. 26), A. Stieren (1:502 n. 4), and SC 210 (n. 1 to p. 281) hold, or *discere*, as in Harvey (2:80, n. 3) and all the MSS save V (which has *dicere*), may be doubted. Sagnard (SC 34, p. 272) wrote *discernere*, but in his earlier study (*La gnose valentinienne*) he had *discere*. At the end of this paragraph there is an allusion to Matt 11:25.

6. Irenaeus makes a keen point in calling error "plausible" as a general principle. Heresies are often simplifications: attempts at rendering the mystery of the faith fully comprehensible and rationally explicable. A few centuries after Irenaeus, this would be pointed out by many with reference to the procla-

mations of Arius, Eunomius, Aetius, and their ilk. It might seem a stretch to regard the cosmologies of the Valentinians as "plausible," as any reader of, for example, the *Apocryphon of John*, would protest; but the principle still applies. Intricate aeonic mythologies serve the purpose there of rendering explicable the presence of evil in the cosmos—a reality more challenging to grasp in an authentic Christian theology.

7. "Imitating" as translated from Lat.Iren. *imitationi* (the dative, one of means as in Greek syntax, is in all the MSS) makes good sense; such a one achieves redemption by imitating the teachers, in whatever they do to obtain redemption; cf. *AH* 1.21.1–5. But we have hesitated to retain that reading, as *imitationi* could be a corruption of *initiationi*, as SC 210 has (n. 1 to p. 283), following the suggestion of early editors such as Grabe (237, n. 1). The idea of redemption by initiation is certainly found in such groups (besides the reference above, see also 2.Pref.1). In that case the line would read, "and has by their initiation attained even to redemption." Though the Valentinians spoke of imitation in the emission of the Aeons, there is nothing in Irenaeus about redemption by imitation. Of course, if "imitating" is correct, that would include their rite of initiation.

8. "Place of refreshment" (*locus refrigerii*) was used for heavenly beatitude. See Leclercq, *DACL* 14 (1948): 2179–90.

9. Cf. Col 1:18; also Matt 28:18.

Chapter 16

1. Cf. *AH* 1.12.4.

2. Cf. *AH* 1.7.2; 1.26.1; 3.12.2.

3. "All": though Lat.Iren. has *Christum*, which Sagnard and SC 211 retained. Harvey (2:82, n. 1) had also kept it, but in a footnote asked whether *totum* might not have been written instead. The explanation offered by Irenaeus in what immediately follows seems to demand such an "all." See 1.2.6; 2.12.7.

From this description of one heretical Christology, it is evident that Irenaeus attacks what was but an accidental union between Word-Christ and Jesus; namely, he is attacking what amounts to a proclamation that Jesus was not God in truth.

4. See *AH* 3.11.1–4, and John 1:1, 14, 18. Behr (*Way to Nicaea*, 124–25) notes that the "one and the same" in this paragraph and the next is frequent in Irenaeus, and "thereafter became one of the basic assertions of the unity of the one Jesus Christ." He draws attention to its presence in the definition of Chalcedon. See Kelly, *Early Christian Doctrines*, 147–48.

5. Cf. Ps 131(132):11.

6. Cf. Gen 15:4.

7. Matt 1:1.

8. Matt 1:18; see also v. 19.

9. Matt 1.20–23 (cf. Isa 7:14). In v. 20 the NT has "what has been conceived in her," but Irenaeus has as translated here; so also in 4.23.1, where the Armenian agrees. On the event of the angelic reassurance, see also 3.21.4; 4.23.1.

10. Cf. John 1:13, 14.

11. Irenaeus is insistent here, as he will be later, that Jesus is at once God the Father's Son and the Christ, born of the Virgin: God and man. Though Irenaeus nowhere uses the title *Theotokos*, "Mother of God," the thought of this paragraph hints at the idea. "The Son of God was born of the Virgin" from whom He took His human nature, and so He was perfect man as God's Son born of woman. This is a consistent refrain: see *AH* 3.9.2; 3.16.5; 3.19.2; 3.21.10; 4.6.7; 4.9.2; esp. 4.33.11 (the Word of God would Himself be flesh, and the Son of God, the Son of man); and 5.19.1 (the same is both God and man, so Mary the Virgin bore God in her womb). It is echoed in Tertullian, *De carne Christi* 20 (ML 2:830–31), despite his broader lack of sympathy for her person. For Mary's divine motherhood according to Irenaeus, one may consult longer studies: for example, J. F. Moholy, "Saint Irenaeus: The Father of Mariology," *Studia Mariana* 7 (1952): 139–45; J. A. de Aldama, *María en la Patrística de los Siglos I y II*, Biblioteca de Autores Cristianos 300 (Madrid: Biblioteca de Autores Cristianos, 1970), 67–78, 251–60. Irenaeus's view of Mary will consume much of the coming chapters.

12. Rom 1:1–4.

13. Rom 9:5. The last clause has been a puzzle to exegetes. The words are clear, but not so the punctuation. Of all the opinions advanced, two have been accepted most widely and alone have probability. The one reads the clause as an exclamation of praise to God after having spoken of the incarnation; thus "and to their race, according to the flesh, is the Christ. God who is over all be [is] blessed forever." The other view reads the last clause as an exclamation of praise for Christ Himself; thus "and to their race, according to the flesh, is the Christ, who is over all things, God, blessed forever." By such a reading the terms form a direct statement that Christ is God—a point Irenaeus has already made above. A majority of Christian interpreters read it this way, as this best fits Paul's usage for christological doxologies. Lat.Iren. reads as such, and the Greek must have had this meaning, as Irenaeus's subsequent reasoning calls for it.

14. Gal 4:4, 5. For the full Marian content of this passage according to Irenaeus, see *AH* 5.21.1, where he treats it more explicitly.

15. This is an allusion to Rom 1:3, which Irenaeus has just quoted. It is interesting to note that as early as Irenaeus this text from Romans was taken as an indication of the Davidic lineage of Mary, through whom Christ, on account

of the virginal conception (thus without heredity from the paternal line), had Davidic lineage.

16. Cf. Rom 1:4 (cf. v. 3).

17. Cf. Col 1:18 and 15.

18. "Human nature," lit., "man" (*homine*, ἀνθρώπου). See Unger, "Christ's Rôle," 18–20, on divine adoption as reason for the incarnation. This reason holds true apart from the station of sin. In becoming man, Christ becomes fully Savior; as per Donovan (*One Right Reading?* 79), "From Irenaeus' perspective, the genuine humanity of Christ is of key soteriological significance."

19. Mark 1:1, 2. Mark refers specifically to "Isaias the prophet," but Irenaeus speaks only of "the prophets."

20. Isa 7:14; Ps 131(132):11; cf. Isa 9:6.

21. Cf. Luke 1:69, 78; cf. Zach 3:8; 6:12; Jer 23:5.

22. Ps 77(78):5.

23. Ps 77(78):5–7.

24. Luke 1:32.

25. Cf. Rom 14:9.

26. Cf. Ps 109(110):1.

27. Cf. Luke 2:26 and 28. "Firstborn": see Luke 2:23; 2:7. SC 210 (n. 2 to p. 301) states that all editors, even up to Sagnard (cf. SC 34, p. 284), put a comma between *Iesum* and *hunc* in the clause: *nisi prius videret Christum Iesum, hunc manibus accipiens*, as we have translated. However, SC thinks this incorrect, because a comparison with Luke's text will show that the comma should be between *Christum* and *Iesum*, and that *hunc* is here but a literal translation of the Greek definite article for *Iesum*, as so often the case in Lat.Iren. So SC argues that it should read: "...until he had seen the Christ, when he received [this] Jesus in his hands...." SC also thinks the comments later, that Simeon professed as Christ, as God's Son, the Jesus whom he held, confirm this punctuation. Though this opinion has some merit, we yet think the old punctuation is correct. Irenaeus wishes to show the identity of Christ and Jesus in the one child Simeon is holding. So in his introductory remarks he unites the two titles and says that Mary's child, whom Simeon holds, is Christ Jesus. In his later comments, Irenaeus separates them to clarify their identity. *Hunc* seems here not a translation of the definite article, for if Lat.Iren. were being so slavish, he would have followed also the word order of the Greek, as he does elsewhere, and *hunc* should precede *Iesum*. Finally, Irenaeus's account, though quite similar, is not entirely like Luke's in construction. In Luke, the titles *Christ* and *Jesus* are separated by a number of words.

"Firstborn" seems to have been taken from the quotation of Exod 13:2 (internal to Luke 2:23); but Luke wrote only some verses earlier that Mary (whom he called "the Virgin" in 1:27) gave birth to "her firstborn" (Luke 2:7). Irenaeus could scarcely have been unaware of the allusion to this when he wrote of "the Firstborn of the Virgin." In what sense, then, does he call Jesus "Firstborn of the Virgin"? H. Koch (*Adhuc Virgo: Mariens Jungfrauschaft und Ehe in der altkirchlichen Überlieferung bis zum Ende des 4 Jahrhunderts*, Beiträge zur historischen Theologie [Tübingen: Mohr Siebeck, 1929]) asserted that this necessarily implied other natural children by Mary after Jesus, but this was immediately challenged by other scholars. Koch attempted to answer his critics in a second text, *Virgo Eva—Virgo Maria: Neue Untersuchungen über die Lehre von der Jungfrauschaft und der Ehe Mariens in der ältesten Kirche*, Arbeiten zur Kirchengeschichte 25 (Berlin/Leipzig: de Gruyter, 1937).

Irenaeus could have used "firstborn" merely as the title given to Christ even by the evangelists, one that implies He is heir of the parental rights and possessions. But Irenaeus did not use the title firstborn by itself, as he might have done in such a case: he added "of the Virgin." In the context, as our earlier notes have shown, he is proving that Christ had a real human nature, and that He received it from the Virgin. When Simeon receives this child in his arms as the Savior of Jews and Gentiles, it is significant that in such a setting Irenaeus should call the child the Firstborn of the Virgin.

28. Luke 2:28–32.

29. Again Irenaeus emphasizes that Christ is both man and God's Son, a kind of simple prolepsis of later discussions on two natures. On Mary's divine motherhood, see n. 11 to the present chapter above.

30. Isa 8:3.

31. Cf. Luke 2:28.

32. Cf. Luke 2:20.

33. Cf. Luke 1:41.

34. See *AH* 3.9.2 above.

35. Cf. Matt 2:11, 12; see also *AH* 3.9.2.

36. Isa 8:4.

37. Cf. Exod 17:16 (LXX). The "hidden hand" was the Word incarnate.

38. Cf. Matt 2:16; 2:4, 5; Luke 2:11. It is a faithful and optimistic spirit that causes Irenaeus to view this martyrdom as a "happy lot." See also Rev 14:4ff. SC 210 (n. 2 to p. 305) has a long and interesting note on the idea of "sending on ahead," which is found also in *AH* 4.31.3; 4.33.9, where the Church is spoken of as sending her martyrs on ahead to heaven. In the letter of the churches of Vienne and Lyons, this idea is used to describe the mother Blandina, who nobly exhorted her children and then was "sent on ahead" through martyrdom (see Eusebius, *HE* 5.1.55 [GCS 3:424]). As SC rightly remarks, this characteristic Irenaean concept is a further indication that he wrote that letter.

39. Luke 24:25, 26.

40. Luke 24:44–47.

41. Luke 9:22; Mark 8:31; Matt 16:21. Irenaeus has "crucified" in place of the NT's "killed." Justin, *Dial.* 76.7 (Goodspeed, *Die ältesten Apologeten*, 187) has the same.

42. John 20:31. "Eternal" in this quotation is not in the NT critical editions, but is found in several Greek as well as Vulgate MSS.

43. Irenaeus's attack on those who claim that the Lord is from two *substantiae* continues his rebuttal of those who separate the "human" from the "divine" in Jesus—namely, in this passage, the adoptionists who claim that the divine Christ descended as a distinct entity upon the human Jesus. Here Irenaeus employs all four evangelists to show that "the Son of God is this Jesus Christ who was born." See Behr, *Way to Nicaea*, 124–26. Lat.Iren.'s use of *substantia* only serves to clarify—if such clarification were needed—the lack of specific focus to christological terminology in the early Church. Irenaeus clearly intends the term to mean that Jesus Christ was not two beings fictionally united (see section 8 below), thus not two hypostases or persons (apart from *substantia*), as later christological convention would have it.

44. 1 John 2:18–22.

45. The line from "and that this is Jesus" until "and that this is Christ" was restored by Sagnard (cf. SC 34, p. 290) from the Syrian fragments.

46. "Either": Lat.Iren. MSS have *autem*, but according to two Syrian fragments this should be corrected to *aut eum*, which Sagnard (SC 34, p. 290) accepted, and SC 210 followed him.

47. "Closely grafted," *consparsus* in Lat.Iren., indicates a very intimate union. Cf. *commixti* in 3.19.1, said of the heretics who are not "united with the Word"; and *commixtus*, said of the Son of Man united to God's Word. But in those cases it is a question of humanity or human nature being united with God's Word, whereas in our present case it is God's Word being united with humanity. The Word permeates the whole man, as the soul itself does; but not vice versa. The parallels are not entirely parallel. Sagnard's interpolation of "impregnée de sa divinité" (SC 34, p. 291) is not correct; it is not merely the divinity, but concretely God's Word united with or implanted in human nature. Irenaeus may well have chosen this word because the heretics had spoken of the spark of the Aeon implanted or deposited in creatures. Grabe (241, n. 6), followed by Massuet (MG 7:925, n. 73) and Harvey (2:82, n. 5), suggested that the Greek was πεφυρμένος ("mixed" or "mingled"), but B. Reynders seems more correct in suggesting συμφυραθείς ("kneaded together" or "mixed up with," that is, in a close union; see Reynders, *Lexique comparé du texte grec et des versions latine, arménienne et syriaque de l'Adversus Haereses de saint Irénée* [Louvain: L. Durbecq, 1954], 66; and SC 211:313). Behr's translation (*Way to Nicaea*, 126–27) retains "mingled."

48. This sentence has an inconsistent grammatical construction in Latin. *Et rursus venturus* is followed by three phrases that obviously express purposes of the Word's coming: *ad resuscitandam…et ad ostensionem salutis, et*

regulam...ostendere [*extendere* as evidenced from the Syriac] *omnibus*....SC
211:312, both in the French translation and in the Greek retroversion, gives
them as three coordinate purposes in identical constructions. But in the
Syriac fragment (cf. Harvey 2:438ff.) the construction is varied, as in Lat.Iren.
There seem to be, in fact, two main (coordinate) purposes: resurrection and
final judgment. Whether these were originally expressed in like grammatical
constructions cannot be determined. In Syriac they are alike, and equivalent
to *ut resusciandam*; namely, the purpose of the resurrection is the manifestation of salvation. In Irenaean thought the resurrection will be the manifestation of complete salvation, as book 5 discusses at length. In keeping with the
Syriac fragment, we have omitted the "and" before *ostensionem*, which makes it
more clearly a subordinate clause. We have, however, retained *ostendere* in
place of *extendere* as suggested by the Syriac, because it seems most consistent
with Irenaeus's thought: at the final judgment the standard of just judgment
"will be manifested to all" is as good as "will be extended to all."

49. Cf. Eph 1:10. This section is almost creedal in tone. "Who comes":
the cryptic Latin is *veniens per universam dispositionem. Universa* often stands for
πᾶν, in the sense of every or all. Irenaeus here enunciates a reality so frequent
in his work, namely, that the Word was present in every one of the "lesser
economies," not simply that He was present in the whole of the final economy; much less that He is in the universal economy, as Sagnard (SC 34, p.
293) has it. See Kelly, *Early Christian Doctrines*, 172–73.

50. Cf. Ignatius of Antioch, *Ad Polycarpum* 3 (ACW 1:97); and below, *AH*
3.20.2.

51. An evident allusion to Col 1:15–18 and Eph 1:22.

52. Cf. John 12:32. In this passage we have again reason for the incarnation that is not dependent on sin and redemption from it. Christ's sover-
eignty over all creation and the union of humanity with God through Christ,
which Irenaeus sums up in the term *recapitulation*, is made primatial in the
human economy through the Word's becoming man.

53. "Unplanned": Lat.Iren. has *incomptum*, which is incorrectly given as
"incomplete" by ANF (1.443). Sagnard (SC 34, p. 293) has "desordinné" correctly.
Cf. 4.4.2: *non mensum...incompositum*, where the Greek is ἄμετρον...ἀναρίθμητον,
"not measured and not counted," with a reference to lack of order and time.
Cf. section 7 below.

54. Cf. John 2:4. "Compendious cup" is *poculum compendii*, namely, a cup
that contains something in a compendious manner. It is a summary. In *AH*
3.18.1, Irenaeus speaks of having "recapitulated in Himself the long unfolding of mankind," and immediately explains that with a participial clause: *in
compendio nobis salutem praestans*. So Harvey is scarcely correct in thinking that
the Greek in our passage was ἀνακεφαλαίωσις, though that word might catch
the meaning, as we note from 3.18.1. The miraculous wine, produced by the
shortcut of a miracle, is a symbol of the recapitulation through Christ's pas-

sion. In 3.18.2, borrowing from 1 Cor 10:16, Irenaeus speaks of the "cup of benediction." Perhaps we have in these an allusion to the cup of the Eucharist, which in turn is the compendious symbol and "sign" of salvation.

"Untimely" (*intempestivam* in Lat.Iren.) is how Irenaeus characterizes Mary's haste in asking for the miracle. This term was used in the beginning of the paragraph to say that in God's planning there is nothing "untimed." All happens in due time: *apto tempore*. Mary's action was, for Irenaeus, not timed properly, not in tune with the plan God had originally intended. Grabe (241, n. 11) and many others were quick to see in this Latin term (the Greek is not extant) an argument from tradition that Christ's mother was not sinless, a reading carried on by Kelly, *Early Christian Doctrines*, 493; cf. Tertullian, *De carne Christi*, 7. This seems, however, to refocus somewhat Irenaeus's point of address. In his presentation, Mary knows not a time that has not yet been revealed. The fitting time for beginning Christ's public miracles was known to the Father alone. For her this occasion seemed propitious, but her haste need not imply imprudence. Jesus repelled her haste not as sinful but simply as untimely. As Irenaeus explains, "He was waiting for the hour that was fore-known by His Father."

More significant is Irenaeus's observation that Mary hastened to the wondrous miracle because of what it would mean for her and for the disciples: the witness of the miraculous wine, produced in a "compendious manner," not by the long process of nature (cf. 3.11.5, where *compendialiter* was used for the same miracle). She was anxious to taste the gift of faith to be wrought in the disciples through the miracle. On this whole question, see Unger, "Doctrina de Maria Virgine Matre," 93; de Aldama, *María*, 321–24. As noted above, Irenaeus uses eucharistic language in this account. If he has in mind that this miracle symbolizes the Eucharist, then he has Mary hastening to taste not merely of the miraculous wine and the faith of the disciples, but also the Eucharist. SC 210 (n. 3 to p. 315) suggests this strongly, and notes that if Abraham could by special illumination share in the sacrifice of Christ by a readiness to sacrifice his own son (see *AH* 4.5.4, 5), why could not Mary, who is also a prophetess (cf. 3.10.2; 4.33.11), have had a prophetic illumination about the relation of the wine at Cana and the Eucharist, of the wedding at Cana and the wedding between Christ and the Church?

55. John 2:4. Irenaeus rightly holds that the "hour" is a time set by the Father, not solely of the passion, but of some significant event in Christ's life, such as His capture, and this miracle.

56. John 7:30.

57. Hab 3:2.

58. Gal 4:4.

59. Again here, as in *AH* 3.6.1 and elsewhere, Irenaeus directly refers to the Son as "God" (ὁ θεός). See our n. 14 to that chapter, and n. 14 to chap. 19 below.

60. Cf. *AH* 1.4.5.

61. Cf. Matt 7:15.

62. Tiessen (*Salvation of Unevangelized*, 208–10) posits implications here for the status of one who thus subscribes to heresy.

63. "The above mentioned letter" is John's second, since that is what he is actually quoting. However, in book 3 thus far he has quoted only from John's first epistle. Grabe (242, n. 6) concluded that Irenaeus had a lapse of memory. But in context it seems that Irenaeus considered the two letters of John as one, given that immediately after our present quotation from 2 John, he speaks again of "in this letter," and then proceeds to quote from 1 John.

64. 2 John 7, 8.

65. 1 John 4:1–3. See n. 63 above on Irenaeus's conflation of 1 and 2 John.

66. John 1:14.

67. 1 John 5:1.

68. There is an allusion here to Ps 23(24):7–9, which was early taken in reference to Christ's ascension: see Justin, *Dial.* 35.4–6 (Goodspeed, *Die ältesten Apologeten*, 131–32). In the final sentence there is possibly an allusion to Matt 16:27.

At the end of this testimony from John's Gospel and letters, SC 210 (n. 2 to p. 321) spends several pages explaining the fine structure and symmetry of the present section, which is but one example of many such carefully designed passages. SC's analysis deserves close attention. There the passage is divided into five parts; but we divide it here into three, though largely to the same effect:

I. (1) Scripture (John 20:31; 1 John 2:18–20), showing that Jesus is the Christ, the Son of God.
    (2) Irenaeus (A) denounces the heretics;
                  (B) states the truth.

II. (1) Scripture (John 2:4; 7:30; Hab 3:2; Gal 4:4), showing that the Father works all things at the "hour" assigned by Him beforehand.
    (2) Irenaeus (A) states the truth again;
                  (B) denounces the heretics once more.

III. Scripture (2 John 7–8; 1 John 4:1–3; John 1:14), showing that the one Jesus Christ is the Word of God become flesh.

69. Rom 5:17. The epistle's "of the gift" is omitted, as also in the NT codex Vaticanus and the Sahidic version, as well as in Origen, Chrysostom, Ephrem, and Augustine.

70. Rom 6:3, 4.

71. Rom 5:6, 8–10.

72. Cf. Luke 22:54; John 18:12; Matt 26:55; Mark 14:48.

73. Rom 8:34. Harvey (2:91, n. 3) says that the words "at the same time" have been wrongly printed hitherto as part of the scriptural quotation; yet they are also in Papyrus 46, and could well have been in Irenaeus's NT.

74. Rom 6:9.

75. Rom 8:11. The bracketed words of introduction seem necessary (see SC 211, n. 1 to p. 327).

76. The Latin *unum quod non* is a slavish rendition of the Greek μονονουχί, "all but." ANF 1.444 has "This he does not utter to those alone who wish to hear," which misses completely the grammatical connections.

77. 1 Pet 2:23.

78. Luke 23:24.

CHAPTER 17

1. Cf. Matt 3:16; Luke 3:22; Mark 1:10; John 1:32.

2. Isa 11:2.

3. Isa 61:1; Luke 4:18.

4. Matt 10:20.

5. Matt 28:19. Irenaeus thus makes clear that "the power of regeneration" is the sacrament of baptism. Cf. *AH* 1.21.1, where baptism is similarly regeneration unto God. See also *Proof* 3, 7.

6. Cf. Joel 2:28, 29; Acts 2:17, 18; Isa 11:2; 1 Pet 4:14. For the allusion in the next sentence, see 1 Pet 4.14 ("rest among").

7. Cf. Rom 7:6; 6:4. In this paragraph we thus see two prominent and interconnected Irenaean themes: that God gradually leads humanity to glory, and that the incarnation is a means to precisely this end. For a good treatment on the eschatological dimension of human perfection implicated in this idea, see Behr, *Asceticism and Anthropology*, 57–85. See also his comments on p. 67 on the connection with the baptism of Christ. Cf. our n. 19 to chap. 9 above.

8. Ps 50(51):14.

9. Acts 2:1–4.

10. Cf. Acts 2:4, 11. Only the Latin is extant, but it seems clear that Irenaeus believes that the people sang God's praises in various languages: *et omnibus linguis conspirantes hymnum dicebant Deo.* They were united in this by the Spirit: *Spiritu ad unitatem redigente distantes tribus.* In *AH* 5.6.1 we have the same: *et omnibus linguis loquuntur per Spiritum [Dei], quemadmodum et ipse loquebatur.* This latter passage is an important clarification: the people spoke with the various tongues just as the Spirit did. In Irenaeus's time this charism was apparently found among many Christians, as he comments on having himself heard them (ibid.).

11. Cf. John 15:26; 16:17. "Prepare us for God" is *aptaret Deo*, which could mean "fashion for"; but the illustrations indicate that the former meaning is intended. Water (see n. 5 above) and the Spirit together procure the life of God.

12. Cf. 1 Cor 10:17; Rom 12:5; Gal 3:28. In the next sentence "dry wood" may allude to Luke 23:31; and "gratuitous rain" to Ps 67(68):10.

13. Baptism is this bath (cf. Titus 3:5; Eph 5:26; and *AH* 5.15.3). Lat.Iren. reads, *Corpora enim nostra per lavacrum illam quae est ad incorruptionem unitatem acceperunt, animae autem per Spiritum.* The contrast between bodies-bath and souls-Spirit is obvious. It is also certain that *unitatem ad incorruptionem acceperunt* must be supplied in the second half. SC 210 (n. 2 to p. 333) argues that the Latin indicates unity leading to imperishability. In another context that might be so, but here it is clear that this is not a union of bodies with one another, and of souls similarly, that leads to imperishability—whatever that might mean. *Unitatem acceperunt ad* simply means they are united with imperishability: the bodies through baptismal water, and the souls through the (baptismal) Spirit. This SC explains correctly, with the aid of the clear statement in *AH* 3.19.1: *we* are united with imperishability and immortality. Here it is our bodies and souls that amount to "we." For water and Spirit, see John 3:5.

14. Cf. John 4:14; for the circumstances noted, see John 4:9, 10, 16–18. "Sinner" is *praevaricatrix* in Lat.Iren. SC 210 (n. 3 to p. 333) observes that this word occurs a number of times in the Vulgate of Jer 3:7, 8, 10, 11, where it translates ἀσύνθετον, "the unfaithful one," namely, Israel. So SC has translated it with "infidèle." Yet the Vulgate *praevaricatrix* of Jeremias can be no sure guide to the underlying Greek of Irenaeus or for its meaning. *Praevaricatrix* does not occur elsewhere in Irenaeus, but *praevaricatio* does, and this always means a transgression, usually found in a context with some form of *transgressio.* This would suggest that in our passage it simply stands for "sinner," which in the context surely implies infidelity but does not affirm it expressly.

On Irenaeus's notion about repeated marriages, see ACW 55, pp. 93 n. 5, 256–57.

15. This entire paragraph is among Irenaeus's more beautiful on grace, baptism, the Holy Spirit, and the body of the Church. The Holy Spirit is the principle of life and unity in the body of Christ. See also *AH* 3.24.1, and our notes there; and A. d'Alès, "Le doctrine de l'Esprit en Saint Irénée," *Recherches de Science Religieuse* 14 (1924): 497–538; A. Orbe, *La teología del Espíritu Santo,* Estudios Valentinianos 4 (Rome: Libreria Editrice dell'Università Gregoriana, 1966), 1–784, mainly on the Valentinian tenets; Houssiau, *Christologie,* 174.

16. Cf. Judg 6:36–40.

17. Isa 5:6.

18. Isa 11:2–3.

19. See Luke 10:18; John 15:26; Rev 12:9, 10.

20. Cf. 1 John 2:1.

21. *Suum hominem*: It is unclear—perhaps meaningfully—whether this is Christ's own individual humanity (as the phrase is used elsewhere in the corpus) or the nature of all humankind, united with Him in the incarnation. For the possibility of the former, cf. 3.17.4: *incarnato in homine,* that is, in

human nature, and thus his own individual human nature. For the latter, cf. 3.24.1 and our note there. We differ here from Behr's translation of this passage (*Asceticism and Anthropology*, 122), where he renders *Suum hominem* as "his own man," thus referring to the human plasma. This is not necessarily a contradictory meaning—indeed, Irenaeus's whole point here is to conflate the nature of Christ as man and all humankind as human, thus showing that what He undergoes Himself is of consequence for the whole human race.

22. Cf. Luke 10:30–37.

23. Cf. Matt 22:20 and parallels. On the increase of denarii, see Matt 25:14–30; Luke 19:12–27. As is readily apparent, Irenaeus here weaves together elements from three parables.

24. Gal 4:4.

25. "Dodecads": Lat.Iren. reads *octonationes et quaternationes et putativas*. Sagnard (SC 34, p. 309) translated "de prétendues Tétrades." However, the *et* must be eliminated for such a translation. In the critical apparatus he indicates that the original was *decades* or *dodecades* for *putativas*, which was misread as δοκήσεις. This seems fairly certain. As Sagnard notes, in *AH* 1.15.1, the Greek excerpt has four terms (tetrad, ogdoad, decad, dodecad), but the Latin three, skipping decad. SC 210 (n. 4 to p. 339) accepted Sagnard's suggestion into the text.

26. Pliny, *Natural History* 36.59 (edition Teubneriana, p. 372/Loeb Classical Library 149, pp. 144–45) tells of a nobleman who killed himself by a potion of liquid gypsum.

27. Cf. ACW 55, pp. 21 n. 12, 128; and 1.Pref.2.

CHAPTER 18

1. John 1:1–3. In the following sentences, for "with the human race," see John 1:10; for "became man," John 1:14.

2. "Unfolding" is in Lat.Iren. *expositionem*, which makes good sense; Harvey's suspicion (2:95, n. 4) that the original might have been ἀπόθεσις (*depositio*) is unnecessary. SC 210 (n. 2 to p. 343) thinks the Syriac fragment, which has *taš'itā* (ἱστορία), is to be accepted in place of *expositio*. Yet, though *expositio* may be an awkward translation, it is not opposed to the same meaning. SC supposes that the Greek was ἱστορία, and that here it means the whole unfolding of human "history." Lat.Iren. used *historia* for Zacharias's events in Luke 1, in *AH* 3.14.2. What the Greek was there we do not know for certain. We have stayed with "unfolding," which conveys the correct idea. Behr (*Way to Nicaea*, 128) translates "long narration."

"Compendium" is *in compendio*, for συντόμῳ. Behr (*Way to Nicaea*, 128) has "résumé." Inasmuch as He recapitulated all humankind in Himself by the incarnation, He initially saved all in Himself by the incarnation; that is, the incarnation was of itself soteriological.

Irenaeus's argument here should be proof enough for his readers not to accuse him of thinking that the second person of the Trinity was not eternal precisely as Son, and that in the strict sense. Still, some scholars continue to suggest that Irenaeus, though he did not deny the eternity of the Son, did not affirm it either. See D. J. Unger, "The Divine and Eternal Sonship of the Word According to St. Irenaeus of Lyons," *Laurentianum* 14 (1973): 357–408; also G. Abey, "Les missions divines de saint Justin à Origène," *Paradosis* 12 (1958): 184–86. For a view more in accordance with Irenaeus's thought here, see Behr, *Way to Nicaea*, 127–28.

3. Cf. Gen 1:26. This is one among the many occasions on which Irenaeus quotes this passage in a specifically christological context. For fuller studies on the image and likeness in Irenaeus, see Wingren, *Man and the Incarnation*, 14–26; A. Orbe, *Antropología de San Ireneo* (Madrid: Biblioteca de Autores Cristianos, 1969), 107–48. Behr (*Asceticism and Anthropology*, 90 n. 18) corrects the assertion of R. M. Grant (*Irenaeus of Lyons*, Early Church Fathers [London: Routledge, 1997], 52) that Irenaeus here claims humanity lost its character as image-bearer, noting that it is in reference to being in the image *and likeness* that Irenaeus makes his claim in the present passage. See also G. T. Armstrong, *Die Genesis in der Alten Kirche: Die drei Kirchenväter* (Tübingen: Mohr Siebeck, 1962), 70–72; J. Fantino, *L'homme, image de Dieu chez saint Irénée de Lyon* (Paris: Editions du Cerf—Thèses, 1986), 106–74; Osborn, *Irenaeus*, 212–16.

4. 1 Cor 9:24; for "even to death" later in this paragraph, see Phil 2:8. In what follows, Irenaeus points out two impossibilities proving that humanity could not save itself. The second seems clear: while he was in sin, he could not receive salvation on his own. The construction of the first, however, creates a doubt. Lat.Iren. has *hominem qui semel victus fuerat...per inobaudientiam replasmare et obtinere bravium victoriae*. In this it is clear that if he was conquered, he could not be victorious on his own. *Replasmare* does not seem to fit, at least not in the active voice. Perhaps *se* fell out, representing the presence of a middle-voice verb in Greek. SC 210 (n. 1 to p. 345) reads the verb in the passive, *replasmari*, and then takes it to refer to creation: humanity could not be re-created, made a new creation (even by God), because it would then be different from the old and the old would not be saved. But since this victory was for the soul more than for the body, or at least as much, this could not mean creation as such. It must mean that humanity could not be made a new spiritual creature; and again one must supply "on its own," if this is not expressed in the middle voice or with a reflexive pronoun, as the context demands. This is a restoration of the primitive integrity, including grace. For other suggestions, see D. Minns, *Irenaeus*, Outstanding Christian Thinkers (London: Geoffrey Chapman, 1994), 101 n. 18; and Behr, *Asceticism and Anthropology*, 52 n. 62, where he draws a parallel to a similar state of confused vocabulary in *AH* 4.24.1.

5. Rom 10:6, 7. "Believe this" is *cui* in Lat.Iren., which could refer to *salus* (Sagnard, SC 34, pp. 312, 313) or even to *Christus* (SC 210, n. 2 to p. 345). We consider that it refers to what was said just previous, which will be explained in the following quotations, not specifically as belief in Christ, but as belief in the saving events of Christ.

In the NT of Rom 10:7 we read ἀναγαγεῖν ("to bring up"). Lat.Iren. has either *eliberare* (AQ and Erasmus) or *liberare* (CVS), both of which mean to free. In *AH* 1.25.4 Lat.Iren. used the passive *eliberari* for ἀπαλλαγῆναι, where the prefix *e* seems to be simply a literal translation of the preposition of a compound verb, as often in Lat.Iren. So it is possible that in our 3.18.2, Irenaeus wrote ἀναγαγεῖν, but Lat.Iren. misread ἀπαλλάττειν, as SC 210 (n. 4 to p. 345) thinks. However, it is also possible that Lat.Iren. read the Greek correctly but gave the derived meaning (to free) instead of the primitive meaning (to bring up). More probable yet, Irenaeus may have written ἐρρίθη (*dictum est*) as in Rom 10:7, and some scribe misread it as ἐρρύθη (*liberata*), or Irenaeus himself made that mistake, or Lat.Iren. did. In any case, that this is possible is backed by *AH* 4.20.12, where Lat.Iren. has either *liberata* or *eliberata* (VAQ Erasmus), but the NT of Rom 9:26, there being quoted, has ἐρρέθη. This correction was suggested already by Massuet.

6. Rom 10:9.

7. Rom 14:9.

8. 1 Cor 1:23.

9. 1 Cor 10:16. Irenaeus will have more to say on the Eucharist in books 4 and 5.

10. Cf. *AH* 1.4.1. Lat.Iren. offers *id est Fini* as an explanation of *Horos*, which would be tautological in Greek.

11. Isa 7:14, 15.

12. Jer 17:9 (LXX).

13. 1 Cor 15:3, 4.

14. 1 Cor 15:12.

15. 1 Cor 15:21.

16. Rom 14:15.

17. Eph 2:13.

18. Gal 3:13; cf. Deut 21:23.

19. 1 Cor 8:11. In the next sentence the wording "lay...rose" may allude to Ps 3:6, and "descended also ascended" to Eph 4:10.

20. Cf. John Damascene, *De fide orthodoxa* 3.3 (ed. B. Kotter, *John of Damascus—De fide orthodoxa*, Patristische Texte und Studien 12 [Berlin: de Gruyter, 1973], 10–11). He speaks of Christ anointing Himself: as God He anoints, as man He is anointed, and His divinity is the unction.

21. Isa 61:1; Luke 4:18. See *Proof* 47: "And the oil of anointing is the Spirit." In quoting the scriptural text, Irenaeus has "Spirit of God," though both Isaias and Luke have "Spirit of the Lord."

22. Matt 16:13.

23. Matt 16:16; cf. 16:17.

24. Matt 16:21, and parallels.

25. Cf. Matt 16:22, 23. Cf. John 12:34; Luke 24:25, 26, 44–46.

26. Matt 16:24, 25; Mark 8:34–35; Luke 9:23–24. "Save" for the NT's "find"; but in the next paragraph Irenaeus does have "find."

27. Cf. Matt 10:32ff.

28. Cf. *AH* 1.7.2; 1.26.1; 3.12.2.

29. "Stake" supposes σταυρός in Greek, which means stake and alludes to the name of one of the Aeons; cf. *AH* 3.1.5.

30. Matt 16:25. A similar idea occurs in Matt 10:39.

31. Matt 23:34; 24:10.

32. Matt 10:18; 23:34; cf. Mark 13:9.

33. Matt 10:28; Luke 12:4, 5.

34. Matt 10:32, 33; Luke 9:26. The "ashamed" clause is from Mark 8:38. Behr (*Asceticism and Anthropology*, 76–80) offers one of the best treatments of Irenaeus's views on martyrdom as evidenced by this passage. In joining the sacrifice of the martyrs to His own passion, Christ bestows on the martyr a full participation not only in His death but also in His resurrection. There is in this, then, a particular route to the attainment of the divine likeness.

35. Cf. Luke 11:50. Earlier in the paragraph there might be an allusion to Matt 24:10 (being killed for confessing the Lord), and 1 Pet 2:21 (following in Christ's footsteps).

36. Luke 23:34.

37. Matt 5:44; Luke 6:27, 28.

38. This paragraph represents Irenaeus's clearest explanation of his conception of God's impassibility. He takes pains to deny, here and elsewhere, that God's being impassible removes Him from the realm of involvement with the world and the created order (see, for example, his refutation of the Epicureans, in 3.24.2, with their god who "takes care of no one"); and at various points in book 1 he denies with great emphasis that the passionate gods of the Gnostics or pagans have anything in common with the one God who is supremely divine, omnipotent, and sovereign and not driven to any necessity by the activities of His creation. So God is not uninvolved with the cosmos, but neither is He inappropriately involved (as, for example, the passionate divinities with the Nephalim; or the fallen Ptolomaean Sophia in her unabated longing and desire; or the Demiurge in his rage). God is not impassible in a sense of removal or separation from the cosmos He has fashioned; but His passibility in the person of Christ (stressed in the present book) is strictly delimited by our current passage: the manner of Christ's suffering in the passion reveals those emotions which can truthfully and faithfully be ascribed to God in theological discourse. His suffering reveals that He is "more patient, and truly good"—attributes that Irenaeus feels cannot be ascribed to a deity removed

from the world (the one who "flew away" at the cross), but that equally cannot be ascribed to one who is bound by his desires and overly human characteristics (such as the Gnostic *Pleroma*, as Irenaeus sees it). For an excellent study on impassibility used in the patristic sources in such a manner as we see here in Irenaeus, see Gavrilyuk, *Suffering of the Impassible God*, esp. chaps. 2–5.

39. Cf. Luke 6:29; Matt 5:39. In the following there is an allusion to Matt 10:24 (being above the teacher). Though both Matthew and Luke give Christ's statement in direct speech, but Irenaeus in indirect speech, Irenaeus is clearly using Luke's wording rather than Matthew's. Luke wrote: "To him who strikes (τύπτοντι), offer the other [cheek] also." Lat.Iren. has both *vapulare* and *praebere* as infinitives. *Praebere*, because of indirect speech; it depends on *adhortans*. But why *vapulare*? It should be a participle for a conditional clause: *nos vapulantes*, "when we are struck." Yet *vapulantes* has passive force, though active in form. SC 210 (n. 1 to p. 363) thinks Lat.Iren. wrote *vapulantes*, which a scribe changed to *vapulare*. This we may accept. It should be noted that the use of this Lucan passage later in *AH* 4.34.4 supports the participial construction: *percussi et alteram praebent maxillam*.

40. "For" is *pro*, which, as Harvey (2:100, n. 1) guesses, might suppose *anti* in Greek, in the sense of "in place of." If so, we might have an expression here of vicarious satisfaction. A similar thought is found in *Proof* 31: "So that He might join battle on behalf of His forefathers." But we must be cautious of suggesting a reading of vicarious activity here; Irenaeus is more wont to emphasize Christ's actions in solidarity with, rather than substitutionally in the place of, humankind. See Behr, *Asceticism and Anthropology*, 61.

SC 210 (n. 1 to p. 365) argues at length against the four *enim* in a row in Lat.Iren., and claims that logic demands changing *adligavit enim* to *adligavit autem*. But we read this clause as an explanation of the preceding, and so have retained *enim*. Irenaeus had said "He destroyed the disobedience," and now he explains that He bound the strong one, and so on, and so *destroyed sin*.

41. In this brief phrase there is the doctrine of the typical relation between Christ and Adam, as developed more fully later. For the allusions, see Rom 5:19; Matt 12:29. In the last sentence the ideas may have been borrowed from Ps 102(103):8 and John 3:16. Cf. Titus 3:4.

42. "Adhere to…": Lat.Iren. has two terms, as we translated. The Greek fragment from Theodoret has only one, ἥνωσεν. Even SC 210 (n. 2 to p. 365) does not treat the Latin as a doublet, but thinks the Greek excerpter dropped the one term. Irenaeus spoke of this function of the God-Man already in *AH* 3.4.2.

This is the first location in which Irenaeus speaks of the devil's having been overcome by Christ "justly." The idea occurs again in *AH* 3.23.1; 5.1.1; 5.2.1; 5.21.1, 3. Because of it there have been those who argued that Irenaeus considered the devil as having a strict right over humankind, and that by a mutual contract God offered the life of His Son in exchange for the souls of humanity. Thus, for example, the early twentieth-century study of A. Sabatier, *The Doctrine of the Atonement and Its Historical Evolution,* translated by V. Leuliette (London: Williams & Norgate, 1904), 42–48, 60–68. J. Rivière (*The Doctrine of the Atonement: A Historical Essay,* 2 vols. [St. Louis: Herder, 1909], 1:113–16) writes of this doctrine in a manner that almost makes Irenaeus out to be an ignoramus. Rivière was rightly refuted by P. Galtier, "La redemption et les droits du Démon dans S. Irénée," *Recherches de Science Religieuse* 2 (1911): 1–24. Rivière tried to vindicate his position in "La doctrine de saint Irénée sur le role du démon dans la redemption," *Bulletin d'ancienne littérature et d'archéologie chrétiennes* 1 (1911): 178–88. He admitted that as far as God is concerned, "justice" here means "wisdom" or "great propriety." But Galtier was not satisfied; he returned in "Les droits du Démon et la mort du Christ," *Recherches de Science Religieuse* 3 (1912): 345–55, insisting that, according to Irenaeus, Christ's death had genuine/effective satisfactory value. Rivière wrote another article ("La mort du Christ et la justice envers le démon," *Recherches de Science Religieuse* 4 [1913]: 57–60), in which he claimed that the voluntary acceptance of the onerous redemption by Christ was in a material and passive sense submission to Satan. In a rejoinder (P. Galtier, "La mort du Christ et la justice envers le démon," *Recherches de Science Religieuse* 4 [1913]: 60–73), Galtier rightly rejected this, because there is not the slightest sense of a submission by Christ to Satan in Irenaeus. Kelly (*Early Christian Doctrines,* 173–74) continued this flawed reading of Irenaeus, suggesting that, though the notion of the devil's rights over humankind is present in Irenaeus's thought, "it is not fully integrated with it." But cf. Behr, *Asceticism and Anthropology,* 61. For more general comments on sacrifice, atonement, and the role of Christ, see F. M. Young, *Sacrifice and the Death of Christ* (London: SPCK, 1975); and F. W. Dillistone, *The Christian Understanding of Atonement* (London: SCM Press, 1984), esp. 93–95, where he treats of Irenaeus.

An investigation of the texts of Irenaeus seems in order. He regularly uses the term *juste.* Sometimes it implies strict justice; e.g., where there is question of external punishment (3.23.3; 3.16.6; 4.4.3; 4.8.3; 4.15.2; 5.28.2). More frequently it implies propriety (1.11.4; 2.7.7; 2.16.4; 2.18.7; etc.). So does it mean strict justice or mere propriety when used of God's liberating humankind from the devil's power? The context must determine. It is certain that Irenaeus considers the devil as having *unjust* power over humanity through sin, and that humankind does not belong to the devil by nature. See *AH* 5.1.1: "And since the Rebellion ruled unjustly over us and alienated us against our nature, since by nature we belonged to the omnipotent God, the Word of God…redeemed from it [the Rebellion] what was His own." In *AH* 5.2.1 Irenaeus declares that God was not unjust, as if He came into another's territory and snatched another's possessions. God came to what really belonged to Himself. In 5.21.3 he says emphatically that the devil's "power [over humanity] is transgression and apostasy"; humans "were held captive by him, whom he exploited unjustly."

There can be no doubt that for Irenaeus the devil possessed the human race and ruled over it unjustly, holding no genuine rights over humanity, and God was not obliged to him in any way. In consequence, Christ, who took back His own through the redemption, paid no price as such to the devil. Christ had no debts because the devil had no rights over humanity, much less over Christ.

What, then, does he mean by the repeated statement that God redeemed humanity "justly" from the devil? He means, as he himself explains, that God outsmarted the devil: He redeemed humanity precisely through a human being, through the very nature the devil had enslaved (cf. *AH* 3.23.1). So "justly" takes on the meaning of "rightly" or "wisely," as we have seen it have in many other contexts. Moreover, in 5.1.1 Irenaeus explains that God "justly" turned against the Rebellion itself and redeemed from it what was His own, not by force—as the Rebellion ruled over humanity in the beginning by snatching away greedily what was not his own—but by persuasion. By this Irenaeus implies God's respect of human free will, and He persuades humans to return, but does not force them. So God's justice here is entirely toward humanity and toward Himself, not toward the devil. The misinterpretation of Irenaeus on this matter is largely a case of taking a word in its modern, technical meaning and reading it into Irenaeus, instead of reading him in his own context.

43. "Mediator"; cf. 1 Tim 2:5; see also Gal 4:5; John 1:14. We have here a beautiful laconic statement by Irenaeus, but the reading is not certain, since the Greek excerpt differs from the Latin text. We have accepted as fairly certain the Latin, which reads, *in amicitiam...utrosque reducere, et facere ut et Deus adsumeret hominem et homo se dederet Deo.* The Latin *reducere*, which supposes ἀναγαγεῖν, we hold correct against the Greek fragment's συναγαγεῖν, "to bring together." *Et facere* is necessary in order to give the two infinitives a controlling verb; the action of the two is not in fact the result or the purpose of "leading back to friendship." SC 210 (n. 1 to p. 367) thinks this is a doublet. SC rightly rejects *AH* 4.40.7 as a parallel to our passage, but thinks 5.17.1 a true parallel. However, it is difficult to find in the second part such a genuine parallelism. In 5.17.1 God gives to humankind association and submissiveness; in our case humankind gives itself to God. 5.17.1 says only indirectly that humankind gives itself to God, through God's gift to the human race. But even this indirect parallel points to the Latin *dederet* as correct, over against the Greek idea of making God known to humans.

Throughout this paragraph, Irenaeus places stress on the incarnation of God's Son as necessary for humanity's adoption as son of God, thus again suggesting the incarnation as part of the original plan of God's economy.

44. See *AH* 2.22.4, 6, about Christ's sharing life with humans in every age of life (i.e., every age level).

45. "Extend patronage to sin" is in Latin *advocationem praebentes peccato.* Since the Greek is lost, we are dependent on parallel expressions for the meaning. In *AH* 4.34.4 (*Iudaeis advocationem praestans*); and in 3.23.8, of the heretics

as *advocates serpentis et mortis,* that is, supporting or promoting the cause of the serpent and death. Irenaeus's meaning seems clearly to be that of giving aid to someone, in context, for an evil purpose.

46. Rom 5:14.

47. For "witness to sin" see Rom. 7.12. Some raise questions as to what the subject is ("it"): the sin of death, or the devil. It seems certain, however, that the subject is sin, here personified. The change of gender to the masculine is due to the masculine of *peccator,* not to the masculine of the underlying Greek for death, θάνατος. Sin, as Irenaeus says, is homicidal in the sense that Paul explains in Rom 5:12–14, which he just employed. It has a kingdom, as below Irenaeus will say that it held sway over humankind.

In the rest of this paragraph and in the next there are other allusions: Rom 7:14 ("guilty of death" and "law as spiritual"); Rom 7:7 ("manifested sin"); Rom 5:12, 6:20ff. ("held by sin"); Gen 2:5 ("untilled earth").

48. Cf. Rom 5:19. The parallelism in construction and ideas is both beautiful and noteworthy. It is clearly built upon the style of Rom 5:19, which was partially quoted, and may be diagrammed as follows:

For, just as	so it was fitting also
through the disobedience	through the obedience
of one man	of the one man,
who was fashioned first	who was born first
from untilled earth	of the Virgin,
many	that many
were made sinners	be made just
and lost life,	and receive salvation.

In the Greek fragment we do not have the usual "firstborn," but an adverbial phrase, τοῦ πρώτως ἐκ...γεγεννημένου, "of the one who was born first of the Virgin." Lat.Iren. has an adjective (*primus*), but with adverbial force.

The main clause is a clear statement of the typology of opposition between Christ and Adam, or in Irenaeus's language, of recapitulation, which he mentioned in the last sentence. In this section, his intention is to show that Christ is true man by the fact that He genuinely redeemed humankind (which could only "justly" be done by a human; see n. 42 above), having obtained real human nature from the Virgin. The link in this parallelism by opposition is the likeness of nature between Adam and Christ, and their likeness, further, in being "firsts" from a virgin, which Irenaeus expresses in a subordinate phrase. Adam was "fashioned first out of untilled [that is, virgin] soil"; Christ was "born first of the Virgin."

But why did Irenaeus employ this peculiar phrase here? His overarching desire is, as noted above, to show that Christ had real human nature because He was born of the Virgin, and thus as truly human He could redeem the entire human race, including Adam. In Greek, "born first of the Virgin" is expressed by the perfect participle and an adverb, making the phrase a kind of title:

"born-first-of-the-Virgin." It indicates that Christ was not only conceived of a virgin, but actually born of one who so remained—otherwise the phrase makes no sense. Mary's virginity in childbirth will be treated more in book 4.

But why is it said that He was born "first"? Surely, to strengthen further the likeness between Adam and Christ: just as Adam was first, so Christ was first; as Adam was the father of the human race, so Christ was the author of salvation for all. Just as Adam had "second-born," so Christ had "second-born"; and so this "first" is also in contrast to "many" who in Adam's case are sinners, but in Christ's, the just. "First" brings out the fact that others depend on Adam as sinners, and on Christ as just. But does only the first Adam depend on "virgin soil," or do all the many who come from him depend on the virgin soil as well? Does only the first Christ depend on the Virgin, or do all the just also so depend? All humans depend on, come from, the virgin soil indirectly, since they have the same nature as Adam. All the "second-born," the many just, also depend on the Virgin; otherwise it would have been purposeless to speak of Christ as "born first of the Virgin." He would simply have said, as so often, "born of the Virgin." The second-born get their life also through the Virgin, as does the firstborn. Irenaeus holds elsewhere that the Virgin did cooperate in the regeneration of all whom Christ saved. See 3.22.4; 4.22.1; 5.1.3; 5.19.1; *Proof* 33. I. M. MacKenzie (*Irenaeus's Demonstration of the Apostolic Preaching: A Theological Commentary and Translation* [Aldershot, England: Ashgate, 2002], 101–3) notes that the language in this passage demonstrates the manner in which creation and redemption are "bracketed together" in the typological relationship of humanity as originally created and humanity as redeemed of the Virgin-born Savior. Cf. M. C. Steenberg, "The Role of Mary as Co-recapitulator in St Irenaeus of Lyons," *Vigiliae Christianae* 58 (2004): 126–27.

That the expression "born first" implies that Mary had other children by natural generation was the assertion of H. Koch (Adhuc Virgo, and our n. 27 to chap. 16, above). Yet if it were to mean that she had other natural children, then these too would have had to be conceived and born of her as a Virgin, by virtue of the phrasing "born first of the virgin," which would be true not only of the firstborn but also of the second-born. Irenaeus tells us, however, that they are the many just. This passage seems in fact to be among the more compelling in Irenaeus for Mary's perpetual virginity. It would be fruitless to object that, as the untilled soil from which Adam was made did not remain untilled, virginal, neither did Mary remain as virgin. The parallel between the virgin soil and the Virgin may not be extended beyond the author's intention. Besides, for the untilled soil there is no perfect participle as for the Virgin, indicating a permanent state, even in and after begetting the many second-born. See Unger, "Doctrina de Maria Virgine Matre," 102ff., and our n. 27 to chap. 16, above.

49. Deut 32:4 (LXX). In the next sentence Irenaeus uses 2 Tim 1:10 for "destroy death and give life."

CHAPTER 19

1. Cf. *AH* 1.25–26.1.

2. These heretics are said not "as yet" to be united with God. "United" is *commixti*, for which the Greek is not extant. Certainly, *commixti* does not in this case mean "commingled." Later in this paragraph the Son of Man is said to be united with God's Son, and Lat.Iren. again has *commixtus* there for the extant Greek χωρήσας, which really ought to be rendered *capiens*. In 1.Pref.2, Irenaeus spoke of brass being mixed with silver, which used ἐπιμιγῇ and was translated *commixtum*. In 4.20.4 we read of a *commixtio et communio* of God with humanity through the incarnation. The idea of *coniungere* preceded. So the meaning of *commixtus* in the present passage is properly "united" and not "commingled," as Lat.Iren. might seem to indicate. Certainly, there is no justification for Harvey (2:103, n. 4) to claim that *commixtus* bears the taint of Eutychianism. F. R. M. Hitchcock (*The Treatise of Irenaeus of Lugdunum against the Heresies* [London, 1916], 133 n. 1) already criticized him for this. Yet the Greek excerpt from Theodoret, who is known to have changed the text when it seemed to him to smack of monophysitism, might have been tampered with. See section 3 below.

3. John 8:36.

4. Cf. Isa 7:14. The expression *qui ex Virgine est Emmanuel* holds more meaning than one might suspect, and Irenaeus continues to focus on its implications throughout the remainder of book 3. The Virgin's Emmanuel is the God-Man, and since He is the Virgin's, she is implicated in the liberty He offers. See our n. 48 to chap. 18 above.

5. Cf. John 4:10, 14.

6. "The antidote to life" is Christ, whom humanity must accept. Ignatius of Antioch used the same expression of the eucharistic Christ; see *Ad Ephesios* 20 (ACW 1:68).

7. Ps 81(82):6, 7.

8. What does Irenaeus mean by "incarnation of the pure generation of the Word of God"? The Greek for "pure" is καθαρᾶς, which can mean "clean," "without admixture or blemish." Irenaeus uses the adverb and adjective elsewhere, always in the sense of being without blemish, or adulteration—whole, integral. In 4.17.4; 5.25.4, *purum sacrificium* is the sacrifice of the Eucharist that is without blemish. In 4.33.9 Irenaeus writes that the heretics have no martyrs, and that only the "Christ endures *pure* [Latin adverb] the opprobrium of those who suffer persecution." Then he adds that "she is often weakened, but she soon increases her members and becomes whole." Here he abstractly interprets *pure* to mean "integrally," inasmuch as persecutions do not harm her or blemish her; she retains her integrity. For further use of *pure* in Irenaeus, see Unger "Doctrina de Maria Virgine Matre," 111–15.

9. Cf. 1 Cor 15:53, 54; cf. 2 Cor 5:4. In *Proof* 31, Irenaeus says very concisely, "So He united man with God and brought about a communion of God

and man, we being unable to have any part in incorruptibility, had it not been for His coming to us."

10. Gal 4:5; Rom 8:15. Irenaeus again states simply that the Son of God became man so that humanity might become a son of God. He also reinforces the basic elements of his Christology: the Son of God becomes man to save, as man, the work of His hands. See Behr, *Way to Nicaea*, 131–33. MacKenzie (*Irenaeus's Demonstration*, 157–66) regards this passage as evidence of Irenaeus's belief in the "pre-eminence of the Word."

11. Isa 53:8. See *AH* 2.28.5; also Unger, "Divine and Eternal Sonship," esp. 385.

12. Jer 17:9.

13. Cf. Matt 16:17; John 1:13; Matt 16:13, 16.

14. Yet another direct equation of "Son" and "God"; cf. above 3.6.1 and 3.16.7.

15. Irenaeus here makes one of his most concise statements on the full divinity of Jesus Christ.

16. Cf. Isa 53:8; Pss 109(110):3; 2:6.

17. Cf. Isa 7:14. Irenaeus puts the twofold generation of Jesus nicely. Cyril of Alexandria will later make a similar point; see *Letter to the Monks of Egypt* 18 (trans. J. A. McGuckin, *St. Cyril of Alexandria and the Christological Controversy* [Crestwood, NY: St. Vladimir's Seminary Press, 2004], 255). Cf. Steenberg, "Mary as Co-recapitulator," 124–26; G. O'Collins, *Christology: A Biblical, Historical and Systematic Study of Jesus* (Oxford: Oxford University Press, 1995), 166, 71–72.

18. Cf. Isa 53:2, 3.

19. Cf. Zach 9:9.

20. Cf. Ps 68(69):22.

21. Cf. Ps 21(22):7; Isa 53:1.

22. Cf. Ps 21(22):16.

23. Cf. Isa 9:6; Ps 44:3.

24. Cf. Dan 7:13, 26; Matt 24:30. In this and the whole paragraph, Irenaeus demonstrates an awareness of Christ's human nature and powers, alongside His divine nature and powers. He goes on to describe in further detail the twofold nature of Jesus. Cf. the notes to follow in the present chapter, and below, our n. 18 to chap. 21.

25. This passage is extant also in Greek from an excerpt by Theodoret, differing from the Latin in some points. With the Latin as a basis, we may examine its careful structure:

A. *Sicut* enim homo erat
ut temptaretur,

B. *sic et* Verbum
ut glorificaretur:

C. requiescente *quidem* Verbo
ut posset temptari

D. absorto *autem* homine
in eo quod vincit et

| et inhonorari et crucifigi | sustinet et… |
| et mori, | et resurgit et adsumitur. |

The contrast between A and B is clearly marked with *sicut* and *sic et*, that between C and D with *quidem* and *autem*. In A and B there are two final clauses, clearly recognized from the *ut* in Latin and ἵνα in Greek. It seems certain too that C and D are a further explanation of A and B, that C explains A, and D explains B. The difficulty in C and D is that the Greek has an infinitive with ἐν τῷ, which could be a final clause or a temporal clause in this context; but the Latin has a final clause in C, and what seems to be a temporal clause in D. Because the subordinate clauses in A and B are final clauses, one might expect final clauses in C and D, but a temporal clause could fit as well. A temporal clause would explain how the event actually happened, implying a final clause. And were they originally final clauses, they would imply a temporal aspect. In our translation we have settled for temporal clauses, but could admit the alternative. As for the tenses used, *requiescente* is a present participle, and so the infinitives it governs are present, but the meaning is clearly past if the clause is temporal. *Absorto* is past tense, and so the Greek infinitives should have been translated with a past, not a present, namely, the perfect indicative (not imperfect, as SC 210:344 suggests).

"Absorbed" is according to Lat.Iren. The Greek has συγγινομένου, which would mean "united with," but that does not fit the parallelism as the union is supposed here and something further is declared, as in C for *requiescente*. Further, since the contrast is here between Word and man, and since Word is the subject in C, man should be subject in D, and not Word, with man in the dative, as the Greek has it. Once more, the Greek excerpt is from Theodoret, and scholars have noted that he changed the phrasing in his quotations if he suspected the original of error. It seems that *absorto* here smacked for him of monophysitism, and so he changed the verb. Therefore, contrary to Grabe (250, n. a), Massuet (MG 7:941, n. 64), and others, but in agreement with SC 210 (n. 1 to p. 379) and Sagnard (SC 34, p. 336), we believe Lat.Iren. is likely correct. The idea of the Word "absorbing" the weakness of the human nature in Christ through His glorious power is common in Irenaeus; see 3.19.1; 3.20.1; 4.36.6; 4.38.4; 5.9.2. Because of the supposed impasse in Lat.Iren. and the Greek, J. A. Robinson ("Selected Notes of Dr. Hort on Irenaeus Book III," *Journal of Theological Studies* 33 [1932]: 162) made his suggestion of what the Greek might have been; but such guesswork is not needed. The Latin makes good sense in the context of this paragraph and of Irenaeus's thought.

As to the Word "remaining quiescent" (*requiescente*, ἡσυχάζοντος) in part C, Kelly (*Early Christian Doctrines*, 148–49) draws attention to this as one of the passages that evidence Irenaeus's awareness of "the problems involved in the union of divinity and humanity," despite his lack of abstract terms for these realities.

One final point: in part D the Latin seems to have omitted a verb, present in the Greek. We have added it with "show Himself kind." Cf. 3.18.3, where we saw that Christ's prayer on the cross was a demonstration of His patience and goodness.

26. Cf. Isa 7:14, 11, 12.

27. Cf. Isa 7:14. This again is a text beautiful in its conciseness, but the absence of the Greek original makes the exact sequence of clauses, and subsequently the meaning, somewhat doubtful. We print the Latin so the reader can see the studied construction and follow the discussion more easily:

> *Quod [signum] non postulavit homo [Ahaz],*
> *quia nec speravit*
> (a) *Virginem praegnantem fieri posse*
>   *quae erat virgo*
> (b) *et parere filium,*
> (c) *et hunc partum Deum esse nobiscum,*
> (d) *et descendere in ea quae sunt deorsum terrae,*
>   *quaerentem ovem quae perierat*
>   *(quod quidem erat proprium ipsius plasma),*
> (e) *et ascendere in altitudinem,*
>   *offerentem et commendantem Patri eum hominem....*

Speravit is certainly the main verb that governs *posse*, and this *posse* governs the other infinitives. Sagnard (SC 34, pp. 336, 337) errs in his translation by making *posse* a finite verb that governs *speravit* (!). He also translated the last two infinitives as Greek purpose clauses. But that is scarcely possible, as the *et* before *descendere* would have to be dropped; also, both *quaerentem* and *offerentem-commendantem* modify *partum*, or are in apposition to it, and call for the continuation of the accusative with infinitive construction, dependent on *posse*.

The little phrase *quae erat virgo* creates the real problem in the sentence. It could easily have been omitted without disturbing the sense. Yet Irenaeus adds it, as seems, to pinpoint the fact that he is speaking of a virgin conceiving precisely as virgin, and thus bearing a son. We take the phrase as modifying *praegnantem fieri*; the normal reading in view of the position and conjunctions in these clauses. In Greek it was most likely a participial construction. It seems similar in meaning to the *manente ea in virginitate* of *AH* 3.21.4. According to this reading, Irenaeus expressly affirms the doctrine that Mary remained a virgin while becoming pregnant and bearing her child. De Aldama (*María*, 259) also supported this punctuation and translation. Some have wanted to read the phrase with the following clause (Sagnard does so in his translation), thus emphasizing the virginity of Mary in giving birth to her child; but this is not acceptable, as it would necessitate the introduction of *et* before the phrase, and there is no MSS warrant for such an introduction. V. Dellagiacoma (*S. Ireneo di Lione: Contre Le Eresie*, 2 vols. [Siena: I Classici

Cristiani, 1968], 317) skips translating *quae erat virgo* and departs in other points from the construction of Irenaeus.

28. Cf. Eph 4:9, 10; Luke 15:4–6; Gen 2:7. Irenaeus often speaks of humanity as the lost sheep; cf. 3.23.8; 5.12.3; 5.14.2; 5.15.2; *Proof* 33.

29. Cf. Luke 15:24, 32; 1 Cor 15:20. This is a poignant expression of the solidarity of the human race with Christ, of the body of Christ as having ascended because Christ the Head has done so. This is an idea developed and stressed by St. Athanasius and St. Cyril of Alexandria; see D. Unger, "A Special Aspect of Athanasian Soteriology," *Franciscan Studies* 6 (1946): 175–81; idem, "Christ Jesus the Secure Foundation according to St. Cyril of Alexandria," *Franciscan Studies* 7 (1947): 18–25. G. Joppich (*Salus Carnis: Eine Untersuchung in der Theologie des hl. Irenäus von Lyon* [Münsterschwarzach: Vier-Türme-Verlag, 1965], 61 n. 27) objects to Sagnard's taking this as an exclusive expression about the body of the Church, with an allusion to Eph 4:16. True, Irenaeus is speaking more broadly: it is all human persons who are united with Christ through the incarnation. However, only those who share the Redeemer's life will actually ascend with Him in the resurrection, which means only those who are united with Christ in the body of which He is the head. This receives confirmation from the last sentence in the paragraph, about the many members in the one body.

30. Cf. 1 Cor 15:20, 23; Eph 1:22; 2:5ff.; Col 1:18; 2:12.

31. Cf. Col 2:19. SC 210 (n. 1 to p. 383) criticizes Sagnard (SC 34, pp. 336–39) for taking these participles in the present as of actual growth in the body. SC takes them as of future actions for the perfected state of the body. This is also incorrect. Irenaeus has said that the body will rise in due time, and he borrowed ideas from Col 2:19 but changed the perspective. *Confirmatum* is past tense (though in Paul it was present); so *coalescens* seems to have a past meaning here. Irenaeus is describing what takes place in the body as a preparation for the resurrection.

32. Cf. 1 Cor 12:18; Eph 4:16.

33. Cf. John 14:2.

34. Cf. 1 Cor 12:12; Rom 12:4. Irenaeus mixed figures here of a building and a body: many mansions, many members.

CHAPTER 20

1. Cf. 2 Cor 12:9. This is Irenaeus's way of saying that God could permit the evil of sin and its consequences because of the greater glory through the manifestation of His immense goodness. Elsewhere Irenaeus similarly notes God's virtues in this respect: *AH* 1.20.3; 4.37.7.

2. Cf. Jonas 2:1ff., 3:1ff. A useful discussion of Irenaeus's treatment

here of the Jonas story is to be found in G. Jouassard, "Le 'Signe de Jonas' dans le livre IIIe de l'*Adversus haereses* de saint Irénée," in *L'homme devant Dieu: Mélanges offerts au Père Henri de Lubac*, vol. 1, *Exégèse et patristique*, Théologie 56 (Lyon: Aubier, 1963), 235–46.

3. Jonas 3:8, 9.

4. Jonas 1:9. Jesus referred to the miracle of Jonas as a sign of His resurrection (see Matt 12:39ff.). For Behr (*Asceticism and Anthropology*, 49) Irenaeus's "from the beginning" indicates that there was never a time when humankind was not in the condition of being swallowed up by the whale. In Behr's words, "There is, for Irenaeus, no lost golden age of primordial perfection." For qualifications, see his n. 51 to p. 49.

5. Jonas 2:2.

6. 1 Cor 1:29. In the rest of this paragraph Irenaeus speaks of the effects of such vain boasting (with possible allusions to Gen 3:5). First, he makes a general positive statement about humanity's being habitually grateful to God, and never thinking that he possesses imperishability by his own nature; then he explains the effects of a proud mentality. To follow the discussion of the problems in the sentence, one must examine Lat.Iren. directly (no Greek is extant):

Ingratum enim magis eum hoc ei qui eum fecerat perficiens, ET dilectionem quam habebat Deus in hominem obfuscabat, ET excaecabat sensum suum ad non sentiendum quod sit de Deo dignum, comparans et aequalem se iudicans Deo.

Two problems arise from the text: first, what are the antecedents of the pronouns? Second, what is the subject of *perficiens, obfuscabat, excaecabat?* The last question is the most decisive, and in view of it there are two main interpretations of the passage. In the first interpretation (defended by Nautin, "Notes critiques," 35–36, but already implied by such earlier authors as Harvey), *hoc* is taken as ablative, and *homo* from the previous sentence is the subject. Man is the central figure in this context. *Hoc* must then be an ablative, namely, by the previously mentioned proud mentality, humanity makes itself ungrateful. But if *homo* is the subject of *perficiens*, then the two instances of *eum*, which certainly refer to humanity, must be changed to the reflexive *se*. Such a change in the reading of the Greek was made easily and often. In favor of this view is the fact that *perficiens* is quite in line with the immediately preceding participles that have humanity as subject, as one would expect; and in this view the rest of the sentence needs no changing. So we have translated. The second interpretation sees the proud mentality as central and takes it as subject; in that case the immediate subject is *hoc* (a neuter nominative). This view was accepted by Sagnard (SC 34, pp. 340, 341), and is defended in SC

210 (n. 1 to p. 387). The *eum* then remains unchanged, referring to humanity; but *sensum suum* must be changed to *sensum eius*, else it would read: "the
proud mentality obscured its mentality" (!). *Sensum eius* reads, "the proud
mentality obscured his [i.e., humanity's] mentality," which is still somewhat
awkward. Sagnard (SC 34, p. 340) has *comparans...iudicans* referring to
humanity just implied in *eius*. SC suggests the change to *comparantem...iudi-
cantem*, since in Greek these would modify an *eum* that would be part of an
accusative with infinitive construction for *ad non sentiendum*. SC appeals to *AH*
5.3.1 on how extolling himself against God makes humanity ungrateful. That
would certainly favor *hoc* as the subject of *perficiens*. There are, however, too
many other changes required by this reading.

This passage represents an important text for Irenaeus's anthropology.
Even from creation, imperishability and immortality are not humanity's "by
nature," but rather are gifts of communion with God. Of his own, man is always
"mortal and weak" (section 2).

7. In spite of the phrase *morum providentiam* in *AH* 3.25.1, we believe
with Grabe (251, n. m) that *morum* is here a corruption in Lat.Iren. for *mortis*.
The idea of death seems demanded in the context of humanity's passing
through all things, among which the resurrection is the climax and death the
beginning. Then, too, Irenaeus says that thus humankind experiences that
from which it is liberated, which is of course death. This is in keeping, too,
with the figure of Jonas in the preceding paragraph. Sagnard (SC 34, p. 340)
kept *morum*, but allowed *mortis* as a possibility. SC 210 (n. 1 to p. 389) accepts
and defends *mortis*, and also was observant in finding *AH* 3.23.1 (where there
is a reference to the previous passage) and 4.39.11 as parallels.

8. Cf. Luke 7:42, 43.

9. The Latin MSS have *operationes*, and the sentence has been punctuated and interpreted in two ways, one involving a change to *operationis*. The
accepted text reads: *Gloria enim hominis Deus, operationes vero Dei et omnis sapien-
tiae eius et virtutis receptaculum homo*. This would read, "For God is the glory of
humankind, but the works belong to God; and humankind is the receptacle
of His wisdom and power." The *vero* indicates a contrast. If we thus read *operationes* (as all the MSS but one have), the contrast is between God and God's
works. But this seems odd. The contrast would seem to have been between the
two subjects, God and humanity, as *enim* connects this sentence with the preceding, which centered on this contrast. Here we have a key to the problem.
In that preceding sentence we are told that humans will understand that God
is so powerful as to give the mortal (human) immortality, and that they will
understand the other powers (*virtutes*) that God has manifested in them. So
those *virtutes*, which are received by humans, are in this sentence the "opera-
tions," which should therefore also be presented as received by humanity.
Grabe (251, n. o) suggested changing *operationes* to *operationis*, for which we
now have the reading of the Salamanca MS. That puts the contrast where it

would be expected—as in our translation—with wisdom and power as an explanation for *operatio*. Sagnard (SC 34, pp. 342, 343) and SC 210 (n. 2 to p. 389) read it this way. Harvey (2:106, n. 7) followed the Latin as punctuated above, which makes sense in its own right but does not seem to fit the context.

10. Rom 11:32. For the allusions in the next sentence about having obtained mercy, see John 15:9–10; Rom 9:25; 11:30; 1 Pet 2:10.

11. "Opinion": Lat.Iren. has *gloria*. Editors rightly conjecture that this stands for the Greek δόξα, which has that derived meaning; but here it should have been translated by its primitive meaning of "opinion," which is called for by the context.

12. Rom 8:3.

13. For "imitator," see Eph 5:1; for "dwelt in humanity," see John 1:14. "Led them to the Father's law" is in Lat.Iren. *imponens* (*eum—hominem*) *in paternam regulam ad videndum Deum*. This phrase has puzzled scholars. Various interpretations have been given, with a variety of changes suggested; yet the text can, in fact, be defended as it stands. An examination of the sentence structure assists. Irenaeus makes the statement that Christ was made in the likeness of sinful flesh for a twofold purpose (*uti*): on the one hand, to condemn sin and cast it out; on the other, to invite (*provocaret*) humanity to be made according to His own likeness. Such a twofold purpose is then explained by the three participial clauses: by assigning humanity to God as His imitator; by leading humans to the Father's law so they can see God; and by granting them the power to receive the Father. The middle explanation is our translation of the problem clause. The construction will not bear saying it means Christ imposed the Father's standard on humanity for imitation. *Imponens in* with the accusative would not mean imposing something, but leading someone to or into something. It has such a meaning in 3.10.5, where it translates ἀναγαγεῖν, and it is used that way in 5.1.1, where the Greek most likely was the same. But what can *regula* be here? In 4.2.6 we have the combination *paternae legis*, which may represent the same Greek as our present *paternam regulam*. In 3.16.6, we read *regula iusti iudicii*, which means law, or the standard of just judgment that Christ will manifest on the last day. That fits this context and Irenaeus's thought elsewhere. This *regula* is a means for beholding God. In 4.2.6, God's law is a means for knowing Him; by accepting that law one comes to Christ (see section 7 of that chapter). According to 3.11.4, the Father's light came to humanity in Christ; and according to 4.39.1, the transgressors of the law of liberty (Christ's law) separate themselves from the Father's light. According to 4.20.2, where one encounters Christ the King, the Father's light is in Him, and it brings humanity to imperishability. It is quite Irenaean, it appears, to say that Christ leads humans to the Father's law, light, that they might see God. If a correction for *regulam* were needed, we might suggest it was *lumen*: the expression *paternum lumen* is frequent in the corpus, as in the passages just noted. See also 5.20.1, where the Church is said

to carry Christ's light, which is her preaching. In view of this we see no reason to change *regulam* to *regnum*, as defended by SC 210 (n. 3 to p. 391), though the idea would fit well enough.

This is a typical passage in Irenaeus on how God gradually leads humanity to glory through His incarnation, here presented as a necessary step in that approach.

14. Cf. Isa 7:14. The editors rightly add *dedit*, which was omitted by a scribe. It is needed because *eum* calls for a transitive verb; the context below as well as Isa 7:14 itself speaks of God's "giving" the sign.

15. Cf. Isa 35:4.

16. Rom 7:18.

17. Rom 7:24, 25.

18. Isa 35:3, 4. Irenaeus, however, has "us" in place of "you."

19. Isa 63:9.

20. Isa 33:20.

21. Irenaeus in fact ascribes this passage to Isaias; but in *AH* 4.22.1 and *Proof* 78, to Jeremias; and in 4.33.12 to *alii dicentes*; and in 5.31.1 simply to "the prophet." In 4.31.1 he uses the words without ascribing them to anyone. Since it is here alone that he ascribes it to Isaias, we think SC 210 (n. 2 to p. 395) correctly suspects this is a corruption for Jeremias, and so we have corrected the text. According to Irenaeus's style, moreover, if he had ascribed it to Isaias he would have added a word like *rursus*, as he had just quoted Isaias.

The passage is actually in no canonical book of the Bible. Justin, *Dial.* 72.4 (Goodspeed, *Die ältesten Apologeten*, 182) accuses the Jews of fraudulently removing it from Jeremias. Judging by Lat.Iren., Irenaeus never quoted it quite the same way twice. This seems a clear case of using florilegia. It is also a clear case of how Lat.Iren. did not bother checking back for translations already made, but simply made a new translation each time from the Greek of Irenaeus.

22. Mic 7:19 is the actual source, though Irenaeus ascribes it to Amos, from whom, however, as well as from Joel, he took the next quotation. We have thus corrected the text.

23. Amos 1:2; Joel 3:16.

24. Not only scholars but also the writers of the MSS have had difficulty with this clause. To be able to follow the discussion we need the full Latin text:

> Et quoniam ex ea parte quae est secundum Africum hereditatis
> Iudae veniet Filius Dei, qui est Deus—<ex qua erat et> [exquerat
> (c) ‖ exquirat (aqs, Erasmus)] et Bethlehem, ubi natus est
> Dominus—<et> immittet laudationem....

The correction *ex qua erat et* was suggested by B. Botte and followed by Sagnard (SC 34, pp. 346–48). It is recommended, as it stays close to the letters in the MSS. V has *et qui erat et*, which seems a fumbling attempt to understand his copy. The correction of Botte is also recommended for two other important reasons. First, it allows the entire clause (which we placed between dashes) to be taken as parenthetical, which it seems intended to be. This introductory section to the quotation from Habakkuk is a kind of thesis of what is coming therein; but it is obvious that the scriptural citation does not speak of Bethlehem. How then does that reference fit in? As Irenaeus explains in this parenthetical clause, Bethlehem belongs to that southern inheritance of Judah, and so Bethlehem is spoken of implicitly by the prophet. Second, Botte's reading allows the *veniet* clause to be followed by its partner clause, *immittet*. Whatever the Greek construction was, in Latin all that is required is to add *et* before *immittet* (*qui* might also work). Of all other suggested corrections, that most frequently followed by editors beginning with Grabe (252, n. k), and which was written by a second hand into the Clermont MSS, was *et qui erat ex*, which, however, does not fit the context. Contextuality is also grounds for objecting to the most recent correction, in SC 210 (n. 2 to p. 397), which is *et quoniam ex*. Since *et quoniam* occurs a number of times in this paragraph, and since the author presents a contrast of parts here, this is very nearly acceptable. But the contrast is not between the places mentioned but between Christ's being God and being man. In Irenaeus's explanation following the quotation from Habakkuk, he does not join them with *et quoniam* but simply *et ex monte*. SC's suggestion also requires too substantial a departure from the lettering of the MSS, which is not necessary at this location.

    25. Hab 3:3, 5.

CHAPTER 21

    1. The sign is "of the Virgin," as an objective genitive, namely, the Virgin conceiving and bearing the Emmanuel is the sign. See n. 26 to the present chapter below.

    2. Cf. Isa 7:14. Such persons wrote νεᾶνις rather than παρθένος. Justin, *Dial.* 67, (Goodspeed, *Die ältesten Apologeten*, 174–76) notes the same practice. Scholars acknowledge that the Hebrew has basically the meaning of an unmarried girl of marriageable age. The error of the translators was for Irenaeus not philological but theological, inasmuch as they wished to return to a more primitive and vague understanding of the prophecy which thus need not imply a virginal conception. See P. Bénoit, "Le Septante est-elle inspirée?" in *Vom Wort des Lebens: Festschrift für Max Meinertz zur Vollendung des 70 Lebensjahres* (Münster: Aschendorff, 1951), 41–49.

    3. The Latin here reads: [*tantum* (CV) ‖ *tantam* (AQS, Erasmus)] *dispositionem Dei dissoluentes quantum ad ipsos est*. The *tantam* seems preferable, modifying economy, for in the context Irenaeus is stressing the greatness of

the sign, and so seemingly also of the economy. *Tanta* modifying *dispositio* occurs in 3.23.1, below.

4. See ACW 55, pp. 4 n. 15, 117, on Theodotion's text and Irenaeus, and its bearing on the date of the composition of the *AH*. See also Justin, *Dial.* 71 (Goodspeed, *Die ältesten Apologeten*, 181–82). This tradition on the origin of the LXX was first given in what is today recognized as the forged "Letter of Aristeas," a Jewish official at the court of Ptolemy Philadelphus (285–246 BC). Forged though it may be, this letter existed already in the early second century, that is, not long after the work of translating was supposed to have been done. Scholars readily recognize a kernel of truth in its legend, namely, that the work of translating the Scriptures into Greek began under this Ptolemy about the middle of the third century before Christ. See J. E. Steinmueller, *A Companion to Scripture Studies 1* (New York: J. F. Wagner/B. Herder, 1968), 160ff.; K. G. O'Connell, "Texts and Versions," in *The New Jerome Biblical Commentary*, edited by R. E. Brown, J. A. Fitzmyer, and R. E. Murphy (London: Geoffrey Chapman, 1990) 68.63 (corresponding to 69.53 in the original 1968 edition). For a discussion of this passage in regard to the inspiration of the Scriptures, see ACW 55, pp. 4 n. 16, 117; and Bénoit, "Le Septante est-elle inspirée?"

"Were recognized" is *creditae sunt* in Lat.Iren., where the extant Greek has ἐγνώσθησαν, which is literally as we have translated. SC 210 (n. 1 to p. 405) defends the Greek, as the idea occurs again in the explanation to follow, and thinks *creditae sunt* is a corruption of *cognitae sunt*. Perhaps; but in view of the fact that Lat.Iren. had a penchant for drawing implicit yet unusual meanings out of a Greek word, this *creditae sunt* was likely original, connoting the sense of being "recognized." In *AH* 4.26.3 we read: *qui vero crediti sunt quidem a multis esse presbyteri*, which could mean that they were believed to be presbyters, or, and more probably, that they were recognized as presbyters, though they were unfaithful.

5. Cf. 4 Kgdms 24:1—25:1; Jer 39 and 52; 4 Esd 14:22–26, 37–47. This latter supposes a rewriting of the Scriptures by five scribes under divine guidance and the direction of Esdras. See also 1 Esd 7:1; 2 Esd 8:1–12. We have here a strange difference between the Greek and Lat.Iren: for "ruined" Lat.Iren. has *corruptis*, which, though it can mean "destroyed," is weaker than the Greek διαφθαρεισῶν, which means primarily "destroyed" in this strong sense. On the contrary, for "restore" Lat.Iren. has *rememorare*, which means to recall (from memory), as it does in 4.33.12, but there it translates μιμνήσκω. In our current passage, however, the Greek is ἀνατάξασθαι, which means "to put in order" and, in the middle voice, "to go through again" or "to rehearse." The two languages are not so far apart. In 4 Esdras, as noted above, the books are supposed to have been destroyed or ruined and were under Esdras rewritten. Sagnard (SC 34, p. 355) translated "corrompues." SC 210 (n. 2 to p. 405) defends "destroyed" and translates *rememorare* (SC 211:405) by "revenus." We

have employed words ("ruin," "restore") that can be taken in either the weaker or stronger sense.

6. Cf. Gen 46:2ff. "For He": the conjunction is in Lat.Iren. only *et*. SC 210 (n. 3 to p. 407) claims it should be *enim* or *etenim*. We have broken down what is a long sentence in the source. In Latin there are two *cum* clauses that support the conclusion *vere impudorate* (later in the paragraph: "in view of this, truly impudent"). The second *cum* clause relies on the first *cum*, as is evidenced by the subjunctive mood of its verb. Each of these clauses is followed by another that seems to explain it. The first is our "The Scriptures, then,..."; the second our "Moreover, this translation...."

7. Cf. Matt 2:13–15.

8. It is doubtful from what point in time Irenaeus is calculating this forty-first year of Octavian. He was sole ruler only after the defeat of Anthony, September 31 BC until AD 14. Irenaeus could not have counted from 31 BC, because he holds that Christ was nearer fifty years old when He died (see *AH* 2.22.6) and was at the beginning of His thirtieth year when He was baptized (*AH* 2.22.5). He must be counting from 40 BC, when, in the autumn, Octavian began to rule together with Anthony.

9. Grabe (256, n. 2) conjectured that Irenaeus did not know of the apostle James since he does not mention him by name, though he was the chief apostle in Jerusalem. Harvey (2:115, n. 2) notes that Irenaeus omitted him here because he is arguing from the Old Testament and James has but few OT quotations. But perhaps a more cogent, and obvious, reason is that Irenaeus is here concerned only with the Gospel writings; Peter is represented in Mark's Gospel and Paul in Luke's, as Irenaeus stated earlier (*AH* 3.1.1, above).

10. Cf. Gal 4:4; Heb 1:1.

11. Cf. Matt 4:17; 3:2; Luke 10:9.

12. Cf. Luke 17:21 (for "dwells within [men]") and Isa 7:14 (for "Emmanuel").

13. Cf. Matt 1:18ff. Irenaeus clearly explains that Mary was virgin in the conception of Christ. He summarizes the contents of Luke 1:35 and Matt 1:22ff. as proofs of this, which he quotes immediately. Cf. O. Bardenhewer, "Zur Mariologie des hl. Irenäus," *Zeitschrift für katholische Theologie* 55 (1931): 600–604, written against H. Koch. He says concisely and correctly that in Irenaeus the virginity of Mary is "Kern und Stern aller Mariologie." See also K. Adam, "Theologische Bemerkungen zu Hugo Kochs Schrift, 'Virgo Eva—Virgo Maria,'" *Theologische Quartalschrift Tübingen* 119 (1938): 171–89, esp. 174–77.

14. Luke 1:35. *Quod...Sanctum* is a stereotyped relative clause in Lat.Iren., meaning "the Holy One to be born." So Irenaeus here takes sides with those who so read this passage, and not with other popular interpretations, for example, "your child (that is, what is born of you) will be called Holy, the Son of God."

15. Matt 1:22, 23.

16. Isa 7:10–17. The lacuna indicated with ellipsis points represents words in Isaias but not in Lat.Iren. These must have fallen out here, since Irenaeus uses them later in his comments.

"The way the Lord puts to the test," with Lord as subject, is a unique reading; in the LXX it is an indirect object, as "God" is in Hebrew and in the Vulgate. But this reading is found also in Tertullian, *Adversus Iudaeos* 9.1, and Cyprian, *Epistola* 10 and *Testimonia* 2.9, according to Sagnard's critical apparatus (SC 34, p. 360). The variation may have crept in through a florilegium.

For "choose the good," Lat.Iren. in fact has "change the good" (*commutabit bonum*) in the first instance, supposing ἀλλάξεται. This seems to be a clear-cut case of misreading, for the LXX has ἐκλέξεται ("will choose"). This reconstruction was embraced by SC 211:413, and defended in SC 210, n. 4 to p. 413.

17. The "He" here is, following Irenaeus's chain of subjects, the Spirit speaking through the prophet.

18. This paragraph presents a clear statement on the twofold nature of Jesus as God and man as a single person. See our notes on Irenaeus's vision of the dual generation and thus two natures in Christ, above, n. 17 and n. 24 to chap. 19. He is unwilling to admit either that Christ was man without divinity, or divine being without full human reality.

19. Ps 131(132):11; cf. Luke 1:27. See also above, n. 11 to chap. 9.

20. Cf. John 1:13. Throughout this and the next paragraph Irenaeus maintains the virginity of Mary not only in the conception of Jesus but also in His birth. Mary is "a pregnant virgin" and Christ "born from the Virgin"; His is a "birth from the Virgin." All this Irenaeus sees prophesied in Isa 7:14. Ps 131(132):11 was "fulfilled in the Virgin's childbirth." Irenaeus makes capital use of this Psalm, which, though it is directly about David, nonetheless mentions a woman's organ, the womb. This is for Irenaeus an indication that the Messiah would be David's descendant through the maternal, rather than paternal, lineage. See section 6, to follow, about the "unexpected generation and childbirth," which is the miraculous and virginal birth of Emmanuel. It is particularly this paragraph that was examined by J. C. Plumpe, "Some Little-Known Early Witnesses to Mary's *Virginitas in Partu*," *Theological Studies* 9 (1948): 567–77.

21. Luke 1:41.

22. Ps 131(132):11 and 17; cf. Luke 1:69; 1:27.

23. Isa 7:11.

24. Eph 4:10.

25. Isa 7:14.

26. It was an "unexpected birth" because it was virginal, miraculous. Irenaeus's interpretation of the Isaian sign is insightful. It has often been repeated in later treatises, and one does well to note just where he places the

sign: it is precisely in the virginal birth of Emmanuel. The sign does not begin after v. 14, but is contained therein. Cf. our n. 1 to the present chapter. For Irenaeus, it is in the miracle of the virginal birth that the assurance of salvation is met: the miracle of humanity's redemption is foretold by prophetical allusions to, then assured in the actual witness of, the miracle of the virginal conception and birth of the Christ.

27. Cf. Dan 2:34, 45; Ps 84(85):12.

28. Isa 28:16.

29. John 1:13.

30. Cf. Exod 7:9, 10, 12; 8:15.

31. Cf. Matt 12:41, 42.

32. Cf. Matt 22:43.

33. Matt 16:16, 17. Irenaeus's argument amounts to this: the Son of God had to become man of a virgin, otherwise He would be a mere human being. The miracle of His birth vouchsafes the miracle of His divine generation, and thus His divine nature, even as it does His human; see Steenberg, "Mary as Corecapitulator," 123–24. In *AH* 3.19.1 we read, "Those are liable to death who bluntly assert that He is a mere man, begotten of Joseph." In *AH* 3.21.9 this is yet clearer: If Jesus had been born of Joseph, He would be a natural man, not God's Son, and so humanity would still be unredeemed. See also 4.33.4.

34. Cf. Matt 1:12, 16. In the critical text of Matthew, Joachim does not figure; but he was mentioned in the MSS of the second century, and Jerome discusses his later absence.

35. Jer 22:24, 25.

36. Jer 22:28–30.

37. Jer 43:30, 31 LXX (36:30, 31 in the Hebrew numbering).

38. Cf. Ps 131(132):11; Eph 1:10. In this chapter Irenaeus adduces various arguments from Scripture that Jesus had to be conceived of a virgin mother without the cooperation of Joseph. In the present section 9, he has argued from God's disinheriting King Jechonias and his descendants, according to Jeremias. In general his argument runs thus: Jesus had to be born King of Israel (he assumes this as certain); but if He had been born of Joseph, He could not have inherited the throne of David because that line was broken through the disinheritance of Jechonias and his descendants, of whom Joseph was one, and Jesus would have been so also if He had been born of Joseph. This flow of argumentation has been recognized by most scholars; but J. A. de Aldama ("Observaciones sobre dos pasajes de San Ireneo," *Revista Española de Teología* 22 [1962]: 401–3) put forward a potential difficulty: The Latin reads:

Qui ergo dicunt eum [Jesum] ex Joseph generatum, et in eo [Jesu] habere spem abdicatos se [haereticos] faciunt a regno, sub maledictione et increpatione decidentes [haeretici] quae erga Jechoniam et in semen eius.

In brackets we have indicated the antecedents, according to the traditional interpretation. The subjects of *habere spem* are the heretics; the
antecedent of *in eo* is the same as of *eum*, namely, Jesus. This would be the normal grammatical connection. The reflexive *se* would thus refer to the heretics,
who disinherited themselves from the reign of Jesus and from salvation, since
Jesus would not have been a legitimate king and could not have been Savior.
De Aldama, however, had found cases in Irenaeus where the pronouns were
misread: a reflexive where it should be a demonstrative pronoun, or vice
versa. He believed that here the context demands a demonstrative pronoun
and not the reflexive. Then, too, *in eo* does not refer to Jesus but to Joseph.
De Aldama would read it thus: "Those who say that Jesus was born of Joseph,
and that He (Jesus) placed His hope (for reigning) in Joseph (*in eo*), really
exclude them (*eos*, not *se*), that is, Joseph and Jesus, from the reign." He
claimed the question to hand in the passage is of inheriting the reign of
David.

It is true that in Irenaeus's argument the question is of physical descent
from Jechonias, but that argument was substantially finished with the quotation from Jeremias. After it Irenaeus infers (*ergo*) that by their tenet the *heretics*
disinherit themselves (*se*) from the reign of Jesus, in whom they hope futilely.
This is precisely why Irenaeus introduces the Spirit as foreknowing and con-
demning their false teaching. In de Aldama's view there seems no solid reason for Irenaeus to speak of the heretics having been pre-condemned under
the curse of Jechonias. They disinherit themselves from the reign of Christ
who must reign as King and recapitulate all things (cf. the end of the paragraph). It is unclear whether, according to de Aldama, *decidentes* refers to the
heretics or to Joseph and Jesus. It seems he refers this to the heretics, as must
be the case; but then it would be abnormal grammatically and logically not to
refer *abdicatos* also to them. These participles have the same subject. Again,
since the verb *habere* is governed by a present (*dicunt*), the subject would normally be the heretics. If it referred to Joseph and Jesus, one would expect the
past infinitive. Joseph and Jesus no longer have such hope, but the heretics
do, even at the time of Irenaeus. The clinching argument against de Aldama's
view is that in the context the reason for being disinherited is the physical
descent from Jechonias, who was disinherited by God's curse. Joseph was
disinherited by his physical birth from Jechonias's lineage, regardless of
whether Jesus was born naturally from him or virginally from Mary alone. The
non-virginal conception of Jesus from Joseph would not have altered this.
Irenaeus would be saying (uselessly) that Joseph too was disinherited even in
view of a virginal conception of Jesus, and that is precisely why Jesus had to be
born virginally, from Mary alone. This cannot be so. The pronoun must
remain reflexive: the heretics disinherit themselves by putting their hope in
Jesus, who, in their view of a conception from Joseph, was disinherited.

SC 210 (n. 1 to p. 427) seems unaware of de Aldama's view, but it wants to change *habere* to *habent*, making it parallel to *dicunt* and not governed by it, thus yielding the meaning that the heretics not merely say they put their hope in Jesus but actually do so. We fail to see any practical difference. The heretics who say they put their hope in Jesus actually also do so, as is surely implied.

39. Irenaeus combines Rom 5:19, 12, 14. This is a classic statement of the typological connection, both via similarity and opposition, between Adam and Christ.

Lat.Iren. begins the paragraph with *Et antiquam plasmationem.* He had spoken of the recapitulation of the entire Davidic line (section 9). Now he begins speaking of Christ's recapitulating even Adam (section 10). Thus, *et* must be translated by "even" or "also." It is not a mistake for *igitur*, or something similar, as if he were drawing a conclusion, as SC 210 (n. 2 to p. 427) argues.

On Irenaeus's notion of the sin of Adam and its consequences for all his descendants, see Orbe, *Antropología*, 253–314.

40. Gen 2:5; for the next clause, see Ps 118(119):73; Job 10:8.

41. John 1:3.

42. Gen 2:7.

43. The fact that Irenaeus says that Mary was "yet a virgin" when Christ was formed from her womb, has led some, for example, H. Koch (see n. 13 to the present chapter above), to conclude that Irenaeus denies implicitly the perpetual virginity of Mary. To the list of scholars who refuted him that we have already given above, we might here add A. Eberle, in his review of Koch's book (*Theologische Revue* 29 [1930]: 153–55); B. Capelle, "Adhuc Virgo chez Saint Irénée," *Recherches de théologie ancienne et médiévale* 2 (1930): 388–95. Irenaeus, as the parallelism about virgin soil shows, is concerned only with the fact that both Adam and Christ were made from matter that was virginal, by God alone, without the cooperation of a creature. What happened later does not concern him here. Whether Mary remained virgin after the conception and birth must be gathered from other places. Irenaeus certainly considers Mary as remaining virgin throughout her life; cf. 3.21.4 and our n. 13 to the present chapter. Indeed, if *adhuc* were against the perpetual virginity, it would be also against virginity in childbirth, because Mary would have been virgin only in the conception of Christ. But this is certainly against the doctrine of Irenaeus.

It seems a stretch to claim, as Sagnard did (see n. 1, SC 34, pp. 373–77), that this parallelism of origin from virginal soil between Eve and Mary presents something akin to the nineteenth-century Roman Catholic doctrine of the Immaculate Conception, as de Aldama (*María*, 81–93) already pointed out. The same guidelines that prevent us from reading a commentary on the perpetual virginity into this passage which speaks solely of the virginal conception and birth, must likewise keep us from treating it as a commentary on Mary's status as per sin and sinfulness.

44. The doctrine of recapitulation presented by Irenaeus here emphasizes the solidarity of the entire human race. See A. Ottorino, "Problemi di origine in S. Irénéo," *Divinitas* 11 (1967): 95–116.

CHAPTER 22

1. Gen 1:26. Here Irenaeus reveals that the "likeness" is, in part, a physical, material likeness, since this is what is secured through Christ's birth from a virgin. Kelly rightly observed that only if Christ has full human flesh, only if He as the "instrument of salvation" is the same as that which is to be saved, is His salvation effective; see Kelly, *Early Christian Doctrines*, 148; cf. *AH* 5.9.1.

In an unusually long note, SC 210 (n. 1 to p. 431) observes that in *AH* 3.21.10, Irenaeus argued against the Ebionite view that Jesus was conceived naturally by Joseph and Mary, and not virginally by Mary alone—so he argues for Mary's virginal conception of Jesus; but in the next section (our present 3.22.1ff.) he argues against the Valentinians, who claim that the Christ simply passed through Mary without taking anything from her—so Irenaeus argues that Jesus took His flesh from Mary. Irenaeus restates these two erroneous views concisely in *AH* 5.1.2. On the grounds that Irenaeus was a markedly consistent writer, SC argues that he should not have said anything of the Ebionite view in this second section; yet if we accept the clause of Lat.Iren., *hic autem non manu et artificio Dei*, he would be presenting the Ebionite view as against the virginal conception. As such, SC proceeds to correct the clause in a rather novel way: in place of *manu* we should read *Maria*, thus *non ex Maria artificio Dei*. But if Irenaeus presents a parallel construction here, as SC admits, then *manu* certainly should not be dropped; it is needed to make the clause parallel in construction to its pair, namely, that Adam was made *de terra et manu et artificio Dei*. At most one could say that the name of Mary, or the word *virgine*, might be added to match *terra*—but this is not necessary for Irenaeus's argument. He is speaking about the Valentinian, not the Ebionite, view and is arguing from the principle of recapitulation, namely, that Christ had to be like Adam and thus have the same human nature as all people. He did not have to state expressly that Christ was made of the Virgin, as Adam of the earth, by God's hand and skill. This has already been made clear in the thesis, the first sentence. It will be stated again and argued later in this paragraph and in that to follow; it was already argued and/or stated in *AH* 3.18.7; 3.19.1, 3; 3.21.10 (in this last while speaking of the Ebionites). It is implicitly contained in the parallel drawn in our current context. It is possible that *manu* here refers to the Holy Spirit, as it does elsewhere; this would then be an allusion to Luke 1.35.

2. Matt 5:5; cf. also *AH* 5.6.1; 5.9.1, on the composition of humanity.

For this topic, see Orbe, *Antropología*, 75–77; also the old but still very useful entry by F. Vernet, "Irénée (Saint)," in *Dictionnaire de Théologie Catholique*, edited by A. Vacant, E. Mangenot, and E. Amann (Paris: Librarie Letouzey et Ané, 1923), 7:2451–54. It has become well appreciated that Irenaeus alternates between a "bipartite" (body and soul) and "tripartite" (body, soul, and spirit) description of the human formation throughout his work. Here he is at his most succinct in proclaiming the body and soul as the natural possessions of the human person, the latter serving as the means by which the Holy Spirit is received into this formation in the fullness of life-giving communion with God. See Behr, *Asceticism and Anthropology*, 99–101.

    3. Gal 4:4. Irenaeus insists (cf. 3.21.10; 3.22.4, 10; 5.21.1, 2; 3.19.3) that Christ recapitulated the human race and thereby redeemed it by taking flesh from the Virgin. He here makes clear his association with Paul in this regard. Divine adoption is the synthesis of redemption; Mary, therefore, is seen as cooperating in salvation just as she cooperates in divine adoption. See the useful studies on these themes by J. M. Bover, "Un texto de san Pablo (Gal. 4.4 f.) interpretado por San Ireneo," *Estudios Eclesiásticos* 17 (1943): 145–81, esp. 170–81; also idem, "Sanctus Irenaeus Lugdunensis, universalis mediationis B. Mariae Virginis egregius propugnator," *Analecta sacra tarraconoesia* 1 (1925): 225–42. Likewise, B. Frzybylski, *De Mariologia santi Irenaei Lugdunensis* (Rome, 1937), 41–86 and 111, who, however, takes exception to some of Bover's conclusions.

    4. Rom 1:3, 4.

    5. Cf. Matt 4:2, 11; Exod 24:18; 3 Kgdms 19:8.

    6. John 4:6.

    7. Ps 68(69):27.

    8. Cf. John 11:35.

    9. Cf. Luke 22:44.

    10. Matt 26:38.

    11. John 19:34. This paragraph represents a remarkable early collation of texts in demonstration of Christ's humanity or human nature. Many of the same passages will resurface in the disputes over precisely this in the debates between Cyril and Nestorius and the larger christological disputations of the fifth century.

    12. Luke 3:23–38.

    13. Rom 5:14.

    14. Cf. 1 Cor 15:46. This whole sentence has created problems for scholars. We will need it also in the next note. It is present in Lat.Iren. as:

Unde et a Paulo "typus futuri" dictus est ipse Adam, quoniam futuram circa Filium Dei humani generis dispositionem in semetipsum Fabricator omnium Verbum praeformaverat; praedestinante Deo primum animalem hominem, videlicet uti ab

spiritali salvaretur. Cum enim praeexisteret salvans, oportebat et
quod salvaretur fieri, uti non vacuum sit salvans.

Having asserted that Paul called Adam the "type" of the one to come, that
is, of Christ, Irenaeus explains why he was so called, namely, *quoniam futuram
circa Filium Dei humani generis dispositionem...praeformaverat.* We retain *in semetipsum* ("with a view to Himself") as indicating the purpose—Christ as the goal of
this recapitulation, as He is the goal in the next clause: *uti ab spiritali salvaretur*
(in some MSS *ut a*). Yet there is some grounding for those (e.g., SC 210, n. 4 to
p. 439) who think Adam must figure explicitly in this clause since it is an explanation of his being the type of Christ; so they correct *in semetipsum* to *in eo*
(Adam), the type of mistake that a scribe might easily make. However, the
change from accusative to ablative is not to be overlooked. Further, if *in semetipsum* is retained, Adam must in any case be implied in the clause.

The Word planned beforehand, in Adam, the "future economy on
behalf of the human race." If *generis humani* is taken to mean the human race,
the genitive must almost necessarily be translated as if it were a dative of
advantage. That the economy was for the human race is a frequent idea in
Irenaeus, e.g., 3.12, 13; 4.20.7; 4.33.7; and it seems sure that here it must have
such a meaning. The expression occurs in Lat.Iren. forty-five times according
to our count; and in each case it means the human race, never human nature
in general or someone's (i.e., Christ's) individually. In six of those cases the
Greek is extant as ἀνθρωπότης, which has the meaning of "human race." We
have not followed the opinion of those who think that the expression here
refers to Christ's human nature, for example, SC, loc. cit.; as also Sagnard (SC
34, p. 379) with "l'économie d'Incarnation."

15. Before we begin the discussion of this last sentence (see the Latin *in
toto* at the beginning of the previous note), it will be necessary to look at the
construction. De Aldama ("Adam, typus futuri," 268ff.) claims that Irenaeus's
statement that Adam was called the type of the future one is explained by
what follow as three clauses. This can be misleading, for the clauses are not
coordinate, and so they do not explain the "type of the future" with the same
directness. As mentioned in our n. 14, the *quoniam* clause explains why Adam
was called the *typus futuri*, namely, because the Word designed the economy
for the human race beforehand, to be realized through God's Son. This is
explained by a participial clause: God destined the ensouled man (Adam) to
be saved by the spiritual man (Christ). Implied here is what was said elsewhere, that Christ had to have the same human nature as Adam. The last
clause (*Cum enim...*) is a conclusion: since the Savior existed beforehand,
from the beginning, it was necessary for the one who is to be saved also to
exist—otherwise the Savior would be purposeless.

Authors differ as to what precisely is the subject and what the predicate
in the final sentence. De Aldama takes Savior as the subject of *fieri* and *quod sal-*

varetur (i.e., man) as the predicate: "For, inasmuch as the Saviour pre-existed, it was necessary that He become that which was to be saved." This idea is indeed found in 3.18.7: *Oportebat…id ipsum fieri quod erat ille, id est hominem*; but in de Aldama's view *salvans* would here be the Word as such. But in Irenaeus the Word is *salvans* only as incarnate, or to-be-incarnate. It would be illogical for Irenaeus to say, then, that the Word-to-be-incarnate, since it preexisted, as God-man, should become man. Further, the last clause (*uti non vacuum sit salvans*) does not make sense in de Aldama's view: *vacuum* is neuter, and so cannot modify *salvans* (masculine). The term is often used in *AH* to describe the emptiness of the Valentinian *Pleroma* and the Aeons: they have no substance, are devoid of reality. There is to them an absence, as with darkness over against light (see *AH* 2.4.1, 3; 2.8.3; 4.18.1 [cf. Deut 16:16]; 3.23.7; 3.25.6); their being is useless, has no purpose, no meaning (2.30.5; 4.28.2); and, Irenaeus notes, God does not do things without purpose (*vacuum*) (4.21.3). De Aldama's view, that the Word as *salvans* would be purposeless unless He became what humanity is, is inconsistent with the thought of Irenaeus. This latter wishes to say the *Verbum incarnandum* would be purposeless if humanity (*salvandus*) did not exist. Nautin ("L'*Adversus haereses* d'Irénée, livre III," 194–96) and G. Jouassard ("La parallèle Eve-Mari aux origines de la patristique," *Bible et vie chrétienne* 7 [1954]: 20–22) rejected de Aldama's view, as did SC 210 (n. 2 to p. 439), against Sagnard (SC 34, pp. 378, 379). But, against SC, it is not merely the *Verbum* as such that was designed beforehand according to Irenaeus, but the *Verbum incarnatum*, only so is He *salvans*.

We give our assent to SC's observation that here, as already in *AH* 3.20.2, Irenaeus indicates the true reason why God would have permitted evil, even sin; namely, the Word-to-be-incarnate already was part of God's economic design, and in light of His ultimate power, even evil could be permitted.

The passage under review is among the most significant for Irenaeus's view on the incarnation in the economy. It has often been used to argue that the incarnation is dependent on redemption and would not have taken place if Adam had not sinned. See Unger, "Doctrina de Maria Virgine Matre," 114–24, where he attempted to prove the exact opposite, as others before him had done. We might here offer a summary of Irenaeus's argument. He explains that Christ took on genuine flesh from the Virgin, and the fact that He did is a proof that man's flesh can be saved and a guarantee that it will —a point he will develop at length in book 5. Christ therefore, as God-Man, recapitulated all flesh even from the time of Adam. Adam was called the type of Christ because the Word, who is the artificer of all things, designed that God's Son be the spiritual man who would save the ensouled Adam. Since God preordained this Word incarnate as Savior, man to be saved had also to exist, else the Savior would have been without purpose. It is certain that by "Savior" Irenaeus does not mean the Word as such, because he never considers the Word in such a way. The Word saves only inasmuch as He is incarnate already or, as in OT times, is

to become incarnate. Does Irenaeus then mean that Christ was willed as liberator from sin before humankind was willed? That would be the case if "Savior"
were synonymous with "redeemer from a state of sin." A Thomistic view on the
motivation for the incarnation might hold exactly this. But Irenaeus presents a
more basic meaning for Savior and save. These words are used in their meaning of preserving: salvation is essentially granting and preserving the well-being
that is imperishable life. In this light, in our passage, the Word incarnate was
Savior already apart from sin, as through Him the human race would receive
grace and eventually glory. Interpreted so, the passage contains at least in kernel the view that the Word was willed absolutely to be incarnate in the original
plan and design of the universe. This was the reading of A. d'Alès, "La doctrine
de la récapitulation en Saint Irénée," *Recherches de Science Religieuse* 6 (1916):
191; and of Vernet, "Irénée," 2470. Yet both suggest that Irenaeus is speaking of
a possible, hypothetical world of the order of intention alone, but that the
order of execution of God's economy includes sin and redemption. For
Irenaeus it seems certain, however, that the order of intention must correspond
to the order of execution. In the universe that God willed there was first willed
the Word incarnate, who, because of intervening sin, would not be merely *salvans* but also *liberans*, as Irenaeus holds elsewhere. Other scholars suggest that
Irenaeus is speaking of the eternal existence of the Savior in God's mind, but
maintain that the motive of redemption is so tied up with that of the incarnation that if there had been no need of redemption there would have been no
Christ-Savior. Such scholars seem to read this into Irenaeus; thus, P. Galtier, *De
Verbo Incarnato et Redemptore* (Paris, 1926), 477; A. Verrièle, "Le plan du salut
d'après saint Irénée," *Revue des Sciences Religieuses* 14 (1934): 502, 516; L.
Escoula, "Le Verbe Sauveur et Illuminateur chez saint Irénée," *Nouvelle Revue de
Théologie* 66 (1939): 388 n. 3. For the thought of Irenaeus it is necessary to look
also at *AH* 5.14.1. Some scholars read these passages as witnesses to the view that
the incarnation was willed by God in the universal design of creation prior to
the advent of sin, with the consequent need of redemption; and that foreknowledge of this was not the spur for the incarnation itself. See Houssiau,
Christologie, 195–99; Wingren, *Man and the Incarnation*, xiv, 6, 18, 90–92, 201;
Ochagavía, *Visibile Patris Filius*, 18–120; Orbe, *Antropología*, 486–88, 91–93, 97,
502–15, 26.

      16. The present section is among the most important passages for
Irenaeus's views on Mary. It has been read in every manner of analysis, from a
general admission of her obedient assent, to Kelly's profession of a "universal
motherhood" (*Early Christian Doctrines*, 494). Neither extreme is wholly acceptable; but it must be noted that if Irenaeus tends toward either end of the spec-
trum, it is to the latter. Mary is understood as having an active, dynamic role
to play in human salvation, intimately connected to that of her Son. It is
notable that this passage of cardinal Marian significance is also one of important christological ramification. Irenaeus here presents his clearest descrip-

tion of the function of recapitulation (via the analogy of tied and untied knots)—and he does so in reference to Mary, not Jesus. On Mary's role in the recapitulation, see Steenberg, "Mary as Co-recapitulator," 117–37. Hoffman's study on the status of women in Irenaeus draws particular attention to the present passage, noting that "in many ways she is equated with Christ in the recapitulation process (and is considered morally and spiritually *superior* to Adam)" (see Hoffman, *Women and Gnosticism*, 95 [emphasis in the original]).

17. For Mary's obedient consent and faith, see Luke 1:38. "Consistently" is *consequenter*, a strong conjunction that puts Mary squarely into Christ's economy of recapitulation. Otherwise stated, Mary's role in that recapitulation is a logical consequence of Christ's being the type of Adam.

18. Gen 2:25; for the following, see Gen 1:28. Irenaeus explains that Adam and Eve were not ashamed because they were still young, an idea he presents also in 4.38.1–4 and *Proof* 12. For classic reflections on what Irenaeus may have meant here, see Orbe, *Antropología*, 195, 214, 18–25. J. Vives ("Pecado original y progreso evolutivo del hombre en Ireneo," *Estudios Eclesiásticos* 43 [1968]: 561–89, esp. 562–64) argues against O. Cullmann and A. Benoît that Irenaeus does not minimize the guilt of disobedience in Adam through this childhood imagery, though he does say that he was inexperienced and placed primary blame on the devil. For a more recent examination of what Irenaeus means by calling Adam and Eve "children," see Steenberg, "Children in Paradise," 1–22. Whether Irenaeus intends the term to be taken in a purely moral or metaphorical sense, or whether he genuinely believes the primal humans to have been some manner of physiological youths, is a hotly disputed topic among scholars. Most read the former, but some strongly argue for the latter position; see R. F. Brown, "Necessary Imperfection," 17–25; and C. R. Smith, "Chiliasm and Recapitulation in the Theology of Ireneus," *Vigiliae Christianae* 48 (1994): 318, 322.

Irenaeus reads Gen 1:28 as part of the initiatory phase of the divine economy of humanity's growth into salvation and thus draws attention to the matter of temporal implication in its contents. Humanity must *first* grow, *then* multiply. This he draws out in the present passage, and yet more strongly at 4.11.1, suggesting in both locations the economy of maturation and growth in which his vision of gradual human perfection is framed. For more on this matter, see Bacq, *De l'ancienne à la nouvelle alliance selon s. Irénée*, 96 n. 2; Behr, *Asceticism and Anthropology*, 37 n. 12; Steenberg, *Irenaeus on Creation*, 96–100.

19. Cf. Heb 5:9, where this phrase is used of Christ. By applying it to Mary, Irenaeus makes her role all the more emphatic. One notes here that Mary is both like and unlike Eve. They are like in that both are still virgins though already married; that is, both are wives (Irenaeus explains the relationship of espousal and marriage in what follows; see our n. 20, below). They are unlike in that Eve disobeyed, with the result that she brought death to herself and the entire race; Mary was obedient, and so became the cause of salva-

tion to the whole universe. Hoffman (*Women and Gnosticism*, 96), in reading this passage, calls Mary the "mother of all" Christians.
See our n. 43 to chap. 21 for discussion on the matter of Mary's virginity. In the present passage Irenaeus omits *adhuc* for Mary, clearly on purpose, as Capelle ("Adhuc Virgo chez Saint Irénée," 391) keenly observed. De Aldama stresses the same point as demonstrating that, in the mind of Irenaeus, Mary continued as perpetual virgin. However, since Irenaeus did use *adhuc* with reference to Mary in *AH* 3.21.10, and since he uses it of her in the next paragraph, it seems that he did not regard its presence as militating against the idea of perpetual virginity. Irenaeus is interested in the virginal origin of Jesus, rather than in Mary. And yet she is integrally necessary in this work of God, and so she is considered as having cooperated not merely physically but morally as well, through faith and obedience, in bringing about the incarnation, which was redemptive. Thus, she is "the cause of salvation of the entire human race." See *Proof* 33 on Mary's obedience in the work of recapitulation; cf. Steenberg, "Mary as Co-recapitulator," 129–37.
Lat.Iren. uses the reflexive pronoun *sibi*, indicating that Mary became the cause of salvation for herself first. Since Lat.Iren. certainly misread some of the pronouns in his Greek copy (αὐτός for ἑαυτός, and vice-versa), de Aldama (*María*, 282 n. 67) thinks it possible, if not in fact probable, that *sibi* should really be *ipsi* (thus, Eve). But the parallel with Eve excludes this change. Eve is said to have become the cause of death to herself (*sibi*) and the whole race. Here *sibi* cannot be a misreading for *ipsi*, because there was no other woman to which *ipsi* could refer. And since it must be *sibi* here for Eve, it can scarcely be other than *sibi* in the parallel clause about Mary.
20. For Eve's marital status see Gen 2:25; 3:8, 17, 20, 21; for Mary, see Matt 1:18; Luke 2:5. Irenaeus appeals to the law (the reference must be Deut 22:23ff.) that one who is espoused and still a virgin can be called a wife. He does not quote directly, but makes the application while loosely using the words of Deuteronomy. Since Lat.Iren. has the pluperfect for *desponsata erat* and *desponsaverat*, some consider that he is here applying these to Eve and then to Mary in the next clause. But Irenaeus seems to be speaking of Mary, then drawing a conclusion with respect to her person. Eve was never considered merely espoused to Adam, for which reason Irenaeus said earlier that Eve "had a man"; but of Mary he said a man had been destined for her beforehand—she was at that moment only espoused. On this point the two women are different, but the point of comparison is that both had a husband, both were wives, yet both were still virgins. See the long discussion in SC 210 (n. 1 to p. 441). Irenaeus's careful precision in this comparison is noteworthy.
The whole passage is a typical example of Irenaeus reading scriptural prophecy as deliberately set forth in preamble to the events surrounding the incarnation and salvation through recapitulation. It is not simply that Mary's espousal to Joseph while still a virgin could, according to the law, be yet con-

sidered a relationship of husband and wife; rather, the law was imbued with this reading from the beginning *precisely so that* Mary's situation could later be explained. Cf. his similar treatment of Jonas (3.20.1, 2), whom Irenaeus reads as being swallowed by the whale specifically so that future generations might learn to be submissive to God; and his reading of the prophecy of Habakkuk 3:3–5 (at *AH* 3.20.4), whom Irenaeus considers to have referred to "God's feet" as a deliberate foreshadowing of Christ that could be deployed against the heretics. So too his comments in 3.15.1 on God deliberately revealing some things only to Luke, so that in accepting these the heretics would be forced also to accept his larger testimony on the Church; and on the Holy Spirit inspiring Matthew to refer to "the generation of Christ" (rather than the generation "of Jesus") because the Spirit foresaw "the perverters" of this message—that is, those who "say that Jesus is the one who was born of Mary, but that Christ is the one who descended from on high" (3.16.2). John is understood to have "foreseen the blasphemous rules which divide the Lord" (that is, which claim He is two beings), and so he writes 1 John 2:18–22 (see *AH* 3.16.5). So also Paul who, "foreknowing through the Spirit the subdivisions of these evil teachers, and wishing to cut off from them every occasion for contention," penned Rom 8:34 and 6:9 on the united divinity and humanity of Christ (see *AH* 3.16.9).

21. "Return-circuit" is *recircumlatio* (CV), but in some MSS *recirculatio* (AQS and Erasmus). For the nuanced difference in this context, see de Aldama, *María*, 279 n. 58. Such a term has been coined by Irenaeus to express the role of Mary in the work of recapitulation, which latter term is reserved to Christ. See Unger, "Doctrina de Maria Virgine Matre," 77–80. SC 210 (n. 2 to p. 441) translated "retournement."

22. Irenaeus's explanation of the tying of a knot creates some problems. The Latin reads:

> in Evam recirculationem significans: quia non aliter quod colligatum est ["tied together"] solveretur, nisi ipsae compagines ["cords"] adligationis [of the tying or knot] reflectantur retrorsus, uti primae coniugationes ["cords"] solvantur per secundas, secundae rursus liberent primas, et evenit primam quidem compaginem [cord] a secunda colligatione [cord] solui, secundam vero colligationem primae solutionis habere locum.

As is well appreciated, Lat.Iren. frequently employed synonyms in Latin for the same Greek word, even within a single sentence. In the above, we have placed the English equivalents in brackets so it will be apparent where we consider that the Greek word may have been the same, or at least have had an equivalent meaning. Authors, translating *compagines* by "knot" (wrongly; see below), have always assumed that there is talk here of more than one knot; namely, a second knot is necessary to unlock the first, and this must then be first untied in order that one might unloose the first knot. Nautin ("L'*Adversus haereses*," 1953, 196–99) correctly observed that Irenaeus is speaking of one knot only—an opinion accepted by SC 210 (n. 1 to p. 443). Sagnard's translation (SC 34, p. 381), "l'assemblage des neuds," cannot be correct for *compagines adligationis*, also because the governing noun is plural while the genitive is singular, which he turns around. It is certain that in the application of the illustration to Eve and Mary there is but a single knot, which Eve tied, but Mary untied. How then to explain the plural in Irenaeus's illustration? Lat.Iren. uses both *compagines* and *coniugationes*. These seem, in fact, to be used synonymously for cords and do not represent a plurality of knots. *Adligatio* is the knot or the tying. In Col 2:19, which Lat.Iren. quotes with the translation *compagines et coniunctiones*, the terms refer to sinews and ligaments of the body, according to the Greek, and not to joints and ligaments. Both *coniugationes* and *compagines* could be, and it seems were, used by Irenaeus for straps or cords. One releases a knot by going through the same processes as for tying, but in reverse order.

23. Cf. Matt 19:30; 20:16. This creative reading of "the first shall be last and the last shall be first," as relating to Mary's recapitulation of Eve's actions, appears unique to Irenaeus.

24. Ps 44(45):17.

25. Col 1:18.

26. Cf. 1 Cor 15:20–22; Luke 3:23–38. Christ is here the "beginning" not merely in reference to point of time but also as the first principle.

27. This is a classic passage in the early Christian witness for Mary's role in the work of redemption. Irenaeus makes Mary the cause of salvation for Adam and Eve explicitly, presenting her mediation by explanation of the likeness and opposition to Eve.

Scholars have long discussed the source of Irenaeus's teaching on Eve and Mary. Justin and Tertullian have the same basic idea, but all three have different emphases and developments. On the early patristic discussion of Mary as mediatrix, see M. C. Steenberg, "The Mother of God as Mediatrix in Orthodox and Roman Catholic Thought," *Sobornost/Eastern Churches Review* 26, no. 1 (2004): 6–26; and the wealth of information in L. Gambero, *Mary and the Fathers of the Church: The Blessed Virgin Mary in Patristic Thought*, translated by T. Buffer (San Francisco: Ignatius Press, 1999).

Chapter 23

1. Cf. Luke 15:4–7; Matt 18:12–14; Luke 19:10.

2. Cf. Gen 1:26.

3. Acts 1:7. For the allusion of the next sentence, see Eph 1:5, 9.

4. Cf. Gen 3:1ff.

5. Irenaeus insists that God had to redeem humankind, not because this was owed to the devil or to humankind, but because by it are revealed His own wisdom and power.

6. Cf. Matt 12:29; 2 Tim 1:10.

7. Cf. Gen 3:5.

8. Gen 1:26.

9. Cf. n. 42 to chap. 18 above, for "justly."

10. Cf. Gen 3:17.

11. The "elder" indicated here has not been identified by scholars, though Irenaeus's phrasing is similar to that in *AH* 5.33.4, where he again refers to one "of the elders," there with explicit reference to Papias. Cf. SC 210, n. 3 to p. 451.

12. Cf. Gen 3:17–19.

13. Gen 3:14. Irenaeus is careful to note that only the serpent, the devil, is here directly cursed by God (as, above, the earth had been). Adam and Eve receive punishments for their disobedience, but the serpent receives the curse. Irenaeus sees cursing and ultimate destruction as tied together: that which is cursed shall eventually be destroyed by virtue of the curse, and so "the whole curse...fell upon the serpent." God does not wish this same end to come to His handiwork, humanity, and so Adam and Eve are chastised—however severely—but not cursed, "that they might not perish altogether." It is notable, therefore, that Irenaeus distinguishes degrees of guilt in the transgression: Adam and Eve are beguiled, but he takes care to note that "God took compassion upon man, who, through want of care no doubt, but still wickedly, became involved in disobedience" (4.40.3). As he shall say just a few paragraphs below our present passage, God "at first placed the curse on [Satan], that it might fall on humanity as a secondhand rebuke. For God hated him who had seduced humankind; but He gradually, little by little, had pity on the one who had been seduced" (3.23.5). The devil who deceives humanity is set, from this early point in scriptural history, for destruction. Humanity is chastised in accordance with its need for correction (with "the discipline that leads to imperishability," as Irenaeus describes it in *AH* 5.35.2), but he shall not ultimately pass away. There is a parallel to this manner of reading in the *Psalms of Solomon*, 13:7: "The discipline of the just for things done in ignorance has no similarity to the destruction of sinners."

14. Matt 25:41.

15. "Originally" is *principaliter*, which in the context seems to refer to the fact that hell was made at first, or in the beginning, for the devil. The underlying Greek is likely ἀρχαίως, which is less prone to confusion. Sagnard (SC 34, p. 389) translated it by "essentiellement," which does not contradict Irenaeus's thought, yet does not stress the proper aspect of this claim. The

same may be said of SC's "principalement," which stands for the guessed Greek προηγουμένως.

16. Irenaeus thus insists on the eternal punishment of hell, but also insists that it was originally made for Satan, the true enemy of Christ, the author of all apostasy from God. This becomes a cardinal theme of *AH* 5 and is developed more fully there.

17. Cf. Gen 4:7.

18. Gen 4:9.

19. Cf. Gen 4:11. Lat.Iren. has *a se peccatum attulit*. Since *adferre* means "to carry to," "to offer," Grabe (264) changed the preposition to *ad*. Harvey thinks *a se* means "of his own accord," and ANF 1:456 follows this lead. "Die Sünde abgeleugnete" in *Bibliothek der Kirchenväter* (Kempten: Kösel; Munich: Pustet, 1911–31), 3:313 seems better, as it leaves the text intact and makes sense. SC 211 has "parce qu'il avait, de lui-même, apporté le péché," which is similar to Harvey's, and Sagnard had much the same (cf. SC 34, p. 391). "Fratricide" is *parricidio* in Lat.Iren., which means literally the murder of parents, but was used in legal jargon for murder in any degree of affinity.

To say that Cain bore a curse "too," seems to relate him back to Satan, who is seen here to have influenced Cain's activities. But Cain took a greater portion of the initiative upon his shoulders in the murder than Adam and Eve had done in eating of the tree (Scripture makes no mention of the serpent having invited Cain to the crime), and so his punishment is a direct curse, just as it had been for the devil, who had dreamed up the wicked intention of convincing Adam and Eve to sin. Cf. our comments above, n. 13 to the present chapter, on the matter of cursing in Irenaeus's interpretation.

20. Cf. Gen 3:4ff., 8ff.

21. Ps 110(111):10; Prov 1:7; 9:10.

22. Cf. Gen 3:7, 10. Philo, *Quaestiones et solutiones in Genesin* 1, 41 (ed. Loeb, pp. 23–24), spoke similarly of the roughness of the particular leaves chosen by Adam (Harvey [2:128, n. 1] quotes him: *Quod quamvis fructus...ficulneus suavior caeteris est, at folia duriora*; cf. Lat. ed. Mercier, p. 106); yet the meaning of this action is for him quite different. Cf. Theophilus, *Ad. Autolycum* 2.25.

23. "Guileless and childlike": the MSS of Lat.Iren. have *indolem et puerilem amiserat sensum*. Literally this may be translated, "He lost his natural disposition and childlike mind." *Indolis* is used only once more in *AH* (in 2.22.5), with *prima* in a context of youth, where it most likely means the first disposition, or sign of youth. At best this sounds odd, and so the guessing begins. One would expect an adjective in place of the noun, so two adjectives would modify *sensum*. But what could *indolem* be a corrupt reading of that would fit here and would have a suitable Greek corresponding word? B. Botte ("Notes de critique textuelle sur l' 'Aduersus haereses' de saint Irénée," *Recherches de théologie ancienne et médiévale* 21 [1954]: 176) suggested that *indolem*

is a corruption of *indolum,* which would mean "guileless, innocent." SC 210 (n. 1 to p. 459) thinks that does not fit properly in the context. But SC, fortunately, discovered the use of Gen 2:25 also in *Proof* 14, of the state of sinlessness before the fall. Surprisingly, here there are two adjectives modifying the one noun "mind"; the second adjective, as in our case here, is "childlike," and the first is "sincere" or "innocent," according to the Armenian translation. SC thinks the Greek was ἀκέραιος. This word is used in *AH* for people who are simple, unlearned. In 1.Pref.2 it is translated once by *rudis,* and once by the comparative *simpliciores.* This would certainly fit nicely. But if that were the Greek word Irenaeus had written, what was the original Latin from which the corrupt *indolem* arose? SC suggests *innocentem,* which is possible, in view of other gross mistakes that Lat.Iren. or some scribe made elsewhere. Still, that seems far-fetched. *Indocilem,* which can mean "untaught" or "ignorant," could have been a simple scribal error.

24. Cf. Gen 3:21. Irenaeus here creatively offers a reading of Adam's response to his sin, which finds in his actions after the transgression multiple positive signs of repentance. On partaking of the fruit of the tree, Adam's and Eve's "eyes are opened" (cf. Gen 3:7) and they become aware of their actions, and their first response is to flee (cf. Gen 3:7–14), having sewn round their waists fig-leaf garments. But this is not a departure that represents a sinful disavowal of guilt, rather the contrite act of childlike humans overcome by the gravity of their deed, ashamed to stand before God, whom they know they have disobeyed. Irenaeus sees a sign of hope precisely in the fact that Adam hides himself, rather than run off to sin again (which is what the devil does, moving from Adam and Eve to Cain; cf. *Proof* 17). Adam is overcome by the burden of what he has done, which he now understands through the knowledge of good and evil made active in him by the fruit of the tree. It is too much for his immature mind to grasp, and so he cowers in shame and fear before God, who thus comes to seek him out. *AH* 5.15.4 makes clear that Irenaeus views this as a foreshadowing of the future economy of Christ; for "the same Word of God has come to call man, reminding him of his deeds, living in which he had been hidden from the Lord. For just as at that time God spoke to Adam in the evening, searching him out, so in these last times, by means of the same voice, searching out his posterity, He has visited them."

The matter of the fig-leaf garments is also a signal, for Irenaeus, of Adam's genuine repentance, as the present passage explains in detail. The fig leaves represent not only repentance but actual penance: Adam wishes to suffer the pricks of the leaves as a response to his own transgression. God's response, in changing the garments of leaves to those of skins, is a sign of His compassion: He lessens the severity of the penance in His mercy toward His creature. See Steenberg, *Irenaeus on Creation,* 179–83. For a slightly different reading, of solid merit, which sees Adam's response as in some manner preventing him from the receipt of God's gift of increase and growth until the fig leaves are exchanged for skins, see Behr, *Asceticism and Anthropology*, 118–19; idem, "Irenaeus *AH* 3.23.5 and the Ascetic Ideal," *St. Vladimir's Theological Quarterly* 37, no. 4 (1993): 311–13.

25. Gen 3:13.

26. Irenaeus's treatment here of Eve's actions is particularly insightful. In passing the "blame" for the transgression first from Adam to Eve, then from Eve to the serpent, the primal humans do not, by Irenaeus's reading, compound their sin. He reads this not as an attempt to avoid responsibility for their deeds, but as the truthful ascription of guilt and sinful activity. Eve does not shuffle blame from herself to avoid admission of sin; rather, she points to the serpent who really was most at fault in the transgression. She "related what had actually taken place." As such, the reassignment of blame from Eve to the serpent makes clear, rightly and in truth, that the devil was chief operator in the transgression. This is quite in accord with Irenaeus's comments above on the curse being spoken against the serpent and the earth, and not the human persons (cf. our nn. 13 and 19 to the present chapter), and finds its full description in the final sentence of our present paragraph. It also lays the groundwork for Irenaeus's treatment of Satan and his role in human sinfulness, which will become the object of his sustained treatment in *AH* 5.21–24. The notion of God coming "little by little" to have pity on humankind finds a parallel in the *Psalms of Solomon* 13:10: "For the Lord will spare His saints, and their transgression He washes away by discipline."

27. Cf. Gen 3:23, 24. See also *AH* 5.2.12, and *Proof* 16.

28. Who these "some" were is not known. There is a very close parallel to the present passage in Theophilus, *Ad. Autolycum* 2.25: "The tree of knowledge was itself good, and its fruit was good. For the tree did not contain death, as some suppose; death was the result of disobedience. For there was nothing in the fruit but knowledge, and knowledge is good when one uses it properly." With respect to Theophilus's treatment, Grant has proposed Apelles, of Marcionite background, as a possibility for the "some" in his remark, and this may apply also to Irenaeus; see R. M. Grant, *Theophilus of Antioch: Text and Translation*, Oxford Early Christian Texts (Oxford: Clarendon Press, 1970), 67 n. 1. For an explanation of the reasons given by Irenaeus for the expulsion from paradise, see Orbe, *Antropología*, 339–61; Wingren, *Man and the Incarnation*, 26–38; and M. C. Steenberg, "To Test or Preserve? The Prohibition of Gen 2.16–17 in the Thought of Two Second-Century Exegetes," *Gregorianum* 86, no. 4 (2005): 723–41.

29. Cf. Gal 2:19; Rom 6:2, 10.

30. Cf. Gen 3:15; Luke 10:19ff. This is the first of three places in the *AH* where Irenaeus makes use of or quotes and interprets Gen 3:15. The other two are 4.40.3 and 5.21.1 (though there is also an allusion in 2.20.3). To understand any of these passages correctly and completely it is necessary to consider all three. Unger dealt with them extensively in "Doctrina de Maria

Virgine Matre," 120–38. Here we shall restrict our remarks to what is pertinent to the present section.

Irenaeus does not directly quote Gen 3:15 in the present passage, but makes use of its ideas and makes application to the parties involved. As is his wont, he interprets the prophecy by later Scriptures (Ps 90[91]:13; and Luke 10:19). Gen 3:15 has three parts: first, the enmity between the serpent and the woman; second, the enmity between their offspring; third and finally, the battle and its outcome. Irenaeus states the first theme straightforwardly; then he condenses the remaining two by the wording of the LXX: *observantes invicem.* His wording of *semen eius* is in reference to the woman. The two "sides" in the battle are the serpent on the one, the woman and her offspring on the other.

31. Cf. Gal 3:19; Luke 10:19. Irenaeus explains the *observantes invicem* as a kind of battle between the two sides, but that the final victory will be won by the woman's offspring is explained in what follows. In the final battle will figure the offspring of the woman, whose sole will be bitten—an idea that must come from Irenaeus's interpretation of what a serpent can do to a human being. That the bite is not fatal is certain from the remark that the man (Christ) has the power to tread on the head of the enemy, which will be fatal for the serpent. The word allusion here is to Luke 10:19, which Irenaeus combines with some terms from Gen 3:15. On the opposing side is the one who bit and killed and hindered the steps of humankind, obviously the devil-serpent, who, as Irenaeus has it, worked havoc on humanity through the centuries. Some of these verbs may have been inspired by the prophecy of Jacob for Dan in Gen 49:16ff., though there the horse is bit, making the rider fall. "Steps" is *ingressus,* which is not "entrance," as Sagnard has it (SC 34, p. 395).

The serpent's attack continued only until the coming of the woman's offspring, whom Irenaeus identifies as Mary's child, of whose power he had already spoken. Now he states that this child was destined beforehand (by the will of God, as first revealed in Gen 3:15) to trample on the head of the serpent. This is the fatal action that brought victory, as described later. Here again Irenaeus uses words from Luke 10:19. Eve is not considered the woman of this prophecy. Indeed, elsewhere Irenaeus insists that Eve is Mary's opposite. This latter was the cause of salvation for all, but Eve not only did not cooperate in this, but she hindered it by actively bringing death to all. She cannot, along with Mary, be the victorious woman.

32. Ps 90(91):13.

33. There are here a number of scriptural allusions: "death that held sway" (Rom 5:14); "deprived of power" (1 Cor 15:24, 26). "Made man cold" is *frigidum reddebat,* which would imply that he was deprived of life: spiritual life through sin, physical life through death. Lat.Iren. seemed to have had some difficulty with the Greek verbs in this sentence. *Significans* controls the *quia* clause (the conjunction should have been *quoniam*), namely, the verbs *evacuaretur* and *conculcaretur. Quod...erigeretur et dilataretur* is a relative clause

explaining the action of sin. *Quod frigidum reddebat* is entirely parenthetical, describing what sin had done to humankind originally. The indicative mood in which it stands makes clear that it is not controlled by *significans*. Finally, the three participles (*insiliens, adligans, subiciens*) explain Christ's action in the last times, and so they depend on *conculcaretur* as temporal clauses. We disagree with SC 210 (n. 2 to p. 465) that these participles were originally infinitives that some unskilled scribe changed.

34. Cf. Luke 10:19. The "last times" are not the period after the second coming of Christ, as some have held. In Irenaeus they are the entire period after Christ's ascension until His second coming, though the final confrontation at the eschaton is of special importance.

35. Cf. Rev 12:9; 20:2. "Lion": Harvey (2:129, n. 4) guesses that dragon, written in Greek majuscule letters, was misread as *leon*. That change could, per se, have been made; however, in the context it lacks probability, since Irenaeus is commenting on Ps 90(91):13, where both beasts are mentioned. He notes the lion in this line, the dragon in the next.

36. And so another example of divine irony, which Irenaeus always likes to stress. The one who conquered humankind was again conquered by a human being.

37. 1 Cor 15:26.

38. 1 Cor 15:54, 55.

39. Cf. Luke 15:4–7; Matt 18:12, 13.

40. Cf. *AH* 1.28.1. "Combination" is *connexio*; his heresy was a complexus of all heresies.

41. 1 Cor 15:22. On Tatian inventing his error by himself, see Hippolytus, *Refutatio* 8:16 (GCS 3:236). Some question has arisen over just how Irenaeus regarded Tatian in relation to the other heretics presented in his polemic, and specifically whether he viewed Tatian as influenced by Valentinianism. That he did was accepted for a time, but has come to be rejected by most scholars. For a survey of the question and the responses put forward by scholars, see E. J. Hunt, *Christianity in the Second Century: The Case of Tatian* (London: Routledge, 2003), 20–36.

42. Rom 5:20.

43. How did the devil have humanity as the beginning and the object of his own apostasy, which had taken place in the heavens prior to the formation of the human creature? One must recall that Irenaeus holds Christ, the Word incarnate, as predestined in the original plan of the universe as Mediator of grace and glory, and humanity was then willed that the Savior would have before Him the object of His salvation (cf. above, 3.22.3). If the devil thought of humanity and through that apostatized from God, as here, it was the God-man of whom he had to think and whom he envied (cf. also *AH* 5.21.3), as he wanted the worship that would be paid to Christ (cf. 5.21.1, 4; 5.28.2). Through Christ he also envied the blessings to be had by all humankind. See

Unger, "Christ's Rôle," 124–28. In this, Irenaeus's stress on the preeminence of the Word, which we have seen evidenced and emphasized throughout book 3, presents one of its most creative implications.

44. "Overcome": All the Latin MSS have *vicit*; there was no reason for Grabe (266) and Harvey (2:130, n. 6) to change it to *vidit*, which makes no sense.

45. See *AH* 5.19.1 and its continued language of *advocata*. By obedience Mary became Eve's advocate, but by sin and false doctrine, the heretics become advocates for Satan. Irenaeus is fond of such advocate language: he employs it also in 3.17.3 as a proper title for the Spirit, and again in *Proof* 33, once more as a description of Mary's relationship to Eve. Such language is well suited to Irenaeus's recapitulative vision of the human economy and race, implying, in his usage, a relational connection between human persons that transcends the limitations of time, and even the barrier of death.

Chapter 24

1. This paragraph presents a kind of summary of what Irenaeus has written thus far in Book 3. The first sentence, which in Lat.Iren. constitutes the whole paragraph, is long and complicated, and so we have broken it down into shorter independent sentences. Throughout, there are a number of puzzling problems of reading, of word meaning, but especially of the connection of clauses; particularly whether there is an independent clause in the paragraph, and, if so, what it is. The Latin is necessary to address these issues, but it is too lengthy to quote in full. We present a truncated citation on which to base our subsequent discussion:

> (A) Traductis igitur omnibus qui nefandas inferunt sententias de…; (B) et ipsis ostensionibus eversis, his qui…de substantia Domini nostri et de dispositione,…falsa docent, (C) praedica-tione[m] autem Ecclesiae undique constante[m],…et testimonium habente[m] a prophetis…(quemadmodum ostendimus),…et [per] universam Dei dispositionem et [per] eam…solidam oper-ationem, quae est in fide nostra: quam perceptam ab Ecclesia custodimus.…

It is certain that (A) and (B) are subordinate, ablative absolute clauses. (C) might be the independent clause, but it has no finite verb—the participles are in the accusative. Scholars from far back have tried to find a verb in the context that might stand as the independent verb. Massuet took *ostendimus* from the parenthetical remark, and even wished that *quemadmodum* were absent to make this construction easier. But the phrase is typical of Irenaeus in such a construction. There is a finite verb present, namely, *custodimus*, in a subordinate clause. It is a thoroughly Irenaean thought to say that we safeguard the preaching of the Church, as it is to say that we safeguard the faith, as is actually expressed in the relative clause here. In the long study Unger did on this section ("Life in the Church: St. Irenaeus, *Adversus haereses* 3,24,1," *Laurentianum* 13 [1972]: 294–315), he thought one could understand this verb as governing *praedicationem* by an ellipsis. Since then, and in light of attention paid to *AH* 5.19.1, it seems clear that Irenaeus used in both places accusative absolutes. Such a construction is a very literal rendering of the Greek, where it is legitimate, though rare with personal pronouns not accompanied by a particle. These three participles, then, are accusative absolutes. True, even accusative absolutes were used only in dependent clauses; but the very fact that Irenaeus used them here in contrast to ablative absolutes (as he did in 5.19.1) makes it possible that he took them to represent independent clauses, and so we need not look for a finite verb to govern them. This may have been in imitation of an independent use of an accusative with infinitive. SC 210 (n. 1 to p. 473) took an altogether different approach. SC insists that the *autem* after *praedicationem* indicates a contrast to the preceding ablatives and makes it certain that the accusative participles should also be ablatives, and so changes them as such, against all MSS evidence.

What about an independent clause? SC holds that the relative *quam...custodimus* is that clause; but for this the relative *quam* needs to be corrected to *hanc*, which SC thinks came from the fact that Lat.Iren. misread an original ταύτην, and the *et quae* in the next clause must represent the definite article. Though it is true that faith is central in Irenaeus's thought in the next section, we find it odd that he would have had three causal dependent clauses, with a number of minor clauses added to the third, and that only from the last of these would he take the subject for his independent clause. One would have expected faith to be introduced in a more dominant construction. *Autem* is of course a problem for taking the *praedicationem* clause as independent. It is, however, not impossible that Lat.Iren. misread an original δή as δέ. We have so assumed. This is a rather simple change compared with others made by Lat.Iren. elsewhere, and that SC here supposes. Irenaeus uses *constare* often, but only twice in the sense of "it is clear" (2.9.1; 2.28.2).

2. "Own human race": Once again we encounter the ambiguity of this phrase, *propter hominem suum*, already discussed above (n. 21 to chap. 17). Some would take this to refer to Christ's own human nature; others to the broader nature of humankind. Either is possible, both are meaningful, and each is in line with Irenaeus's theology elsewhere. We have translated with the latter, which in the context seems most appropriate. The human race is called Christ's own in opposition to the Gnostic teaching that the human race was not created by the supreme Father and was therefore not the property of

God's Son. According to Irenaeus, the Son of God came into His own world and to His own race through the incarnation, because the Word created this world and its inhabitants. It was the economy that was *propter hominem suum*, and that was not merely for the individual human nature of Christ, but for the whole race.

3. "The beginnings" refers to the era of the prophets, that is, the Old Testament; "the middle times" are those of the apostles, beginning with Christ's coming; "the end" is the postapostolic period until the second coming. These three terms occur again in 3.25.5. His wording is similar to that of Plato, who wrote in his *Laws*: "O men, that God who, as old tradition tells, holdeth the beginning, the end and the center of all things that exist, completeth his circuit by nature's ordinance in straight, unswerving course" (*De legibus* IV, 715E; see Loeb Classical Library, Plato, *Laws*, vol. 1; in the next chapter, *AH* 3.25, Irenaeus quotes Plato directly from this passage). God's economy is once again presented as a single whole with many stages.

4. "Secure working" is *solidam operationem*. Here CV have *solitam*, but the idea of an "unusual working" of the Spirit would be unusual in Irenaeus. The idea of a secure working for a faith that will be secure is common: see *AH* 1.4.1; 1.13.4; 2.28.2; 3.21.3; 4.1.1; 4.6.2; 4.32.2. Lat.Iren. uses *solidus* in only one other place (2.10.3), but it has here the strong witness of AQ and Erasmus. It might stand for various Greek words, but most likely for βεβαίαν, a word used for *firmus*, and *firmus* is used often in Lat.Iren. with a variety of words related to preaching and truth. See also *Proof* 16, 98, for the association of security with preaching and faith. In Unger's study "Life in the Church," 300–303, he took this clause as parallel with *praedicationem*; namely, that "we safeguard" the preaching and the "secure deeds." However, with the acceptance of the accusative absolutes and the dropping of *custodimus* as the governing verb for *praedicationem*, this clause cannot be parallel to that containing the latter, because it would need its own participles, which it does not have. Furthermore, though we still think it is entirely in accordance with the mind of Irenaeus that *operationem* here means the good deeds that spring from faith, it seems better to look upon this *operatio* as that of God or the Spirit, since ministries of the Spirit are highlighted in what follows. Further, since Irenaeus stresses elsewhere (4.26.2, 5) the importance of the bishops in the transmission of the truth and the safeguarding of the faith, and that this is in virtue of a charism of the Spirit, it is entirely appropriate that the *operatio* here includes this ministry of the Church, through which the Spirit works. Hence, the stress to follow on the Spirit in the Church as the source of nourishment and drink. This *operatio* is explained immediately as a rejuvenating of faith itself and of the Church.

5. "Deposit": All the Latin MSS have *dispositum*, which means something that has been arranged in, or organized in, or furnished in. Since in the context this is faith in the Church, one might see some sense to the word here. Yet editors have always (with the exception of Sagnard; cf. SC 34, p. 398)

corrected the word to *depositum*, which certainly fits more easily, especially since it must be a noun, not an adjective. See Unger, "Life in the Church," 304. Irenaeus may have been influenced here by 2 Tim 1:14. In *AH* 3.4.1, Lat.Iren. had called the Church the *depositorium dives*, for the apostolic truth. Faith is thus considered a deposit in the Church. Though Lat.Iren. used the term *vas* in the sense of an instrument as well as a vessel, in this place it can mean only a vessel that contains some liquid. This is characterized as a *vas bonum*. We translated *bonum* with "suitable." That it holds a liquid, metaphorically, is gathered from what follows about the water; and from the context it is clearly water, and not wine or some liqueur, as Sagnard (SC 34, n. 1 to p. 399) suggested.

6. For "under God's Spirit" Lat.Iren. has *semper a Spiritu Dei*. Scholars have fit this into the clause in various ways. We take *semper* to modify *iuvenescere*, and not *dispositum/depositum*, which, we noted, must be a noun. Likewise, *a Spiritu* cannot effect *depositum* as a noun. It too is related to *iuvenescens*. But since this is an intransitive verb, *a Spiritu* is not to be read as an ablative of agent ("it is rejuvenated by the Spirit"), but the preposition *a*, supposing ὕπο has the meaning "under the influence of."

Irenaeus here gives beautiful expression to the perennial youthfulness and freshness of faith, which is nonetheless the same, universal faith handed down from the beginning. Whether the Greek had a connotation of "youth" is hard to tell, as Lat.Iren. is unpredictable in such precisions of implication. He may have had simply a verb meaning making new (cf. *AH* 3.11.8; 3.17.1). SC 210 (n. 1 to p. 473) discovered a kind of parallel to this in the letter of the churches of Vienne and Lyons. The author, which our notes above indicate is most likely Irenaeus himself, writes of the mother martyr Blandina: "but the blessed, as a noble athlete, rejuvenated (ἀνενέαξεν) herself by her confession" (Eusebius, *HE* 5.1.19 [GCS 3:408]).

7. We have followed Lat.Iren., namely, we have retained *hoc* (attested to by all the MSS) at the beginning, with *munus* as the antecedent: "this, God's gift," which is faith, given to the Church. SC 210 (n. 2 to p. 473) thinks *munus* is the Spirit Himself and so *hoc*, which would refer *munus* back to faith, cannot be correct. It was changed to *huic*, modifying *Ecclesiae*. Of course, *munus Dei* is the Spirit in *AH* 3.17.2, where John 4:10, 14 is used. However, Irenaeus did not have to take *munus Dei* here directly and exclusively of the Spirit. It is faith that is operative through the Spirit. In that sense, *munus Dei* is appropriate and coherent and is still given to the Church, which is central in the passage. SC had to change also *et in eo* to *et in ea*, again referring it to the Church. In Lat.Iren. the nearest antecedent is the neuter *munus*. The type of guesswork done by SC is fine, but should not be undertaken unless the text of the MSS cannot be read as they stand in common witness.

"Life-breath" is an allusion to Gen 2:7, about God's breathing the breath of life into Adam and thus making him a living being. "God's gift" by

which this is done in the Church is faith given by the Spirit and made operative under His influence. It is not the Spirit directly, as SC 210 (n. 2 to p. 473)
seems to hold. With the Spirit working through faith, it is still correct to view
Him as the life-giving principle, active in the soul.

8. Irenaeus now gives four titles to the Spirit. He is first of all the
"Communion of Christ." Christ sent Him, and now He dwells in the Church
and in Christians, uniting them with Christ and with each other. Irenaeus may
have taken this imagery from 1 Cor 1:9: [you] "were called to the communion
of His Son, Jesus Christ our Lord"; and 2 Cor 13:13: "communion of the Holy
Spirit." Elsewhere Irenaeus writes that the Spirit mediates our communion
with Christ and God (see *AH* 4.14.2; 5.1.2).

9. "The pledge of imperishability" derives from 2 Cor 5:5; 1:22; Eph
1:14. Since several of the groups against which Irenaeus wrote denied the
imperishability of the body, Irenaeus seems to have chosen this title carefully
and intentionally. See Unger, "Life in the Church," 309ff.

10. "The strength of our faith" is *confirmatio fidei*. The Latin *confirmatio*
occurs in only one other place in the *AH* (2.18.7), for a strengthening of the
Aeons. It is used in Phil 1:7 (as a warranty for the Gospel of Paul) and in Heb
6:6 (as a warranty for an oath). In Col 2:7 we find *confirmati fide*, which might
have given Irenaeus his impetus.

11. "The ladder" is an allusion to Gen 28:12ff., about Jacob's vision of a
ladder reaching to the heavens with the angels ascending and descending.
Irenaeus uses this passage also in *Proof* 45, when writing on the prophets' foretelling of Christ, where the ladder represents the cross by which we ascend to
heaven and by which we can communicate with the Father through the Son.

12. 1 Cor 12:28. If one uses also vv. 4–11, about the various ministries
that the Spirit works, it is plain how Irenaeus could speak of the "rest of the
Spirit's ministries." As we remarked earlier, it is likely that Irenaeus has in mind
the succession of the bishops as the means through which the Spirit transmits
the truth in the Church. See 4.26.5.

13. This sentence is a forceful practical conclusion aimed at the
heretics.

14. There is, Irenaeus claims directly, no such entity as a Church independent of the Spirit, or any such reality as the Spirit working independently
of the Church. They are as inseparable as soul and body. The Spirit is the truth,
and thus He safeguards the truth in the Church, as Christ had promised (John
14:16; 15:26); He gives the charism of the truth to the bishops (see *AH* 4.26.2);
He is where the Church is, and the Church is where He is; but (*autem*) He is
Himself the truth. As such, He guarantees the truth for those who are in the
Church. This phrase seems to have been taken directly from 1 John 5:6:
"because the Spirit is truth."

15. In this fifth sentence Irenaeus draws further conclusions (*quapropter*):
those who do not partake of the Spirit do not receive the Church's nourish-

ment, nor have they the saving waters of Christ. "Limpid spring" is the Spirit, who pours forth graces from Christ. The allusion to John 7:37ff. is certain, and possibly Irenaeus has John 19.34 in mind as well. He here follows, yet modifies, what must have been a fairly standard early interpretation of this passage, namely, that the spring of waters is Christ Himself. See also 5.18.1. This view is used also in the letter of the churches of Vienne and Lyons (cf. Eusebius, *HE* 5.1.22 [GCS 3:410]). In the letter of Barnabas we also read, "The outpouring on them [the people] in the community of the Spirit from the abundant fountain of the Lord." These people are said also to have taken of the deeply implanted favor of the gift of the Spirit (see chaps. 1.2, 3 [ACW 6:37]). According to another interpretation, which Origen originated, the Christians themselves are the fountains of water, because of the Spirit they have received from Christ. See R. E. Brown, *The Gospel according to St. John: Introduction, Translation, and Notes*, 2 vols., Anchor Bible 29, 29A (Garden City, NY: Doubleday, 1966, 1970), 1:320–24; H. Rahner, "Flumin de ventre Christi: Die patristische Auslegung von Joh. 7.37–38," *Biblica* 22 (1941): 269–302.

In this paragraph, Irenaeus employs vivid maternal imagery with respect to the Church. This latter is "mother," whose breasts "nourish unto life." This comment has been noted by many, not least Unger and Kelly (*Early Christian Doctrines*, 194). We must be careful not to read too much into Irenaeus's words, but this comment clearly demonstrates his ecclesiological vision of Church as parental protector of the faithful. More advanced, later teachings on "Mother Church" can rightly be seen to have at least some grounding in Irenaeus's thought.

16. The first part of this sentence is surely a use of Jer 2:13. With two participial clauses in Lat.Iren., Irenaeus describes the actions of the disbelievers and the results for them in relation to the Church and the Spirit—the two things intimately connected throughout the paragraph: they flee from the faith of the Church, and they reject the Spirit. The two movements are seen as inseparable. If the heretics do the one, they automatically do the other. See Irenaeus's comments, just above, on the Church being where the Spirit is, and the Spirit where the Church is (see also our n. 14 to the present chapter).

17. Cf. Eph 4:14ff.; 2 Pet 2:17ff. Cf. Irenaeus's remarks in *AH* 1.10.2 as to the futility of such sophistry in terms of attempted damage to the faith.

18. Cf. Matt 16:16ff.; 7:24–27.

19. Cf. Matt 7:7; Luke 11:9.

20. Cf. Eph 3:19. Humanity's ability to know God is discussed at length in book 2.

21. Cf. Gen 2:7; Ps 32(33):6; Prov 8:30; Job 10:8. In this parallel of Word and Wisdom, it is obvious that Wisdom is the Holy Spirit, as elsewhere in the corpus. For more on this identification of Wisdom and the Spirit in Irenaeus, see J. Fantino, *La théologie d'Irénée: lecture des Ecritures en réponse à*

l'exégèse gnostique—une approche trinitaire (Paris: Editions du Cerf, 1994), 287–91; O'Collins, *Christology*, 39–40.

22. Various scholars have suggested that *non* belongs in this Latin phrase, which seems correct. The next sentence, which contains the illustration of the present phrase, about a god *not* caring for the creation, confirms this. Lundström accepted the revision; see S. Lundström, *Studien zur lateinischem Irenäusübersetzung* (Lund: Gleerup, 1943), 129.

23. On the improvidence of the Epicurean gods, see Diogenes Laertius, book 10, 123ff. (Diogenes Laertius, *Lives of Eminent Philosophers* 10.123ff., translated by R. D. Hicks, Loeb Classical Library 185 [Cambridge, MA: Harvard University Press, 1948], 648, 650), who notes that, according to Epicurus, the gods are absolutely happy in themselves and cannot be bothered with humanity.

CHAPTER 25

1. "A care for morals" is *morum providentiam*, that is, one who is interested in observing morals. See *AH* 3.20.2 for *morum agnitionem* (as per Erasmus); however, this was corrected to *mortis agnitionem* and so is not directly parallel, as has often been thought.

Irenaeus here notes that God is active in the world, contrary to his characterization of the Epicurean god above in 3.24.2. Yet it is worth remembering Irenaeus's earlier qualifications on God's involvement: the Father "is far removed from those affections and passions that have their place in humans" (2.15.3). So God's involvement is qualified by assertions of his impassibility. See Gavrilyuk, *Suffering of the Impassible God*, 50.

2. The reference here is clearly to the followers of Marcion, as is made clear in section 3 below.

3. The construction in this sentence is obscure. ANF 1.459 rendered it "seem imperfect, as not saving all; [for it should do so,] if it be not accompanied with judgement." *Bibliothek der Kirchenväter* (Kempten: Kösel; Munich: Pustet, 1911–31) 3:318 has, "Wenn es nicht alle erlöst ohne Rücksicht auf das Gericht." Evidently, Irenaeus wanted to say that God, to be God, must be both good, namely, willing to save all men, and just, namely, saving only those who meet His judgment. SC 211:485 has "De la sorte, ni la bonté ne lui manque du fait de la justice...." Gavrilyuk (*Suffering of the Impassible God*, 54) has recently noted the value of this passage for an understanding of divine impassibility in the patristic tradition: "Without emotions expressing God's condemnation of evil, God would be neither just, nor merciful, nor good, nor intelligent." As we have already seen, these "emotions" are in fact the expressions in the cosmos of God's transcendent and unchanging care for humankind. As with so many patristic sources, it is for Irenaeus God's eternal

impassibility that renders Him capable of existing passionately as man in Christ, in a redemptive manner. See also T. G. Weinandy, *Does God Suffer?* (Notre Dame, IN: University of Notre Dame Press, 2000), 94–95.

Irenaeus's language throughout this paragraph, especially as regards his terminology of God's "judicial power," finds a strong parallel in Tertullian, *Adversus Marcionem* 2.17. Both authors make the point that if God does not possess in His character some sentiment that judges and punishes sin, then He is deficient as regards the genuine reality of His justice. So when each argues, as we have seen Irenaeus do on numerous occasions throughout book 3, that God is impassible, such statements must be qualified with the information put forward here. The divine impassibility does not divest God of states of emotion, but qualifies the divine emotions and their realizations. See Gavrilyuk, *Suffering of the Impassible God,* 54–55.

4. Cf. *AH* 1.27.2–4.

5. Matt 5:45.

6. Plato, *Laws* 4.717E, translated by R. G. Bury, Loeb Classical Library 187 (Cambridge, MA: Harvard University Press, 1926), 292; cf. our remarks on Irenaeus alluding to this passage, n. 3 to chap. 24 above.

7. Plato, *Timaeus* 3.29E (Plato, *Timaeus, Critias, Cleitophon, Menexenus, Epistles,* translated by R. G. Bury, Loeb Classical Library 234 [Cambridge, MA: Harvard University Press, 1929], 54).

8. Cf. *AH* 1.4.1–5; 1.27.2–4.

9. Cf. Dan 13:55, 59.

10. "Conglomeration" is *collectio,* namely, of heretical notions. It does not seem, as Harvey (2:136, n. 4) suggests, that it is a translation of the Greek ἐνθύμημα, which is an imperfect syllogism. For "abortion" the MSS all have *aborsio,* which editors have usually corrected to *abortio,* used by Irenaeus elsewhere. Sagnard (SC 34, p. 408) retains *aborsio,* which spelling was used in ecclesiastical Latin; see A. Blaise, *Dictionnaire Latin-Français des Auteurs chrétiens* (Turnhout: Brepols, 1954), s.v. *aborsio.*

11. "Spirit" was one of the many names given to Achamoth; cf. *AH* 1.4.1; 1.5.3.

12. Cf. *AH* 1.30.3.

13. Cf. Gal 4:19. Christians are born "legitimately" into the Church through baptism, and Christ is formed in them.

14. Irenaeus makes it plain that all the heretics could have the hope of returning to the Church, naturally, through repentance, which must include penitence and forgiveness. In the theology of Irenaeus, there are no sins that cannot be forgiven by the Church.

15. With all the energy and zeal of his heresiological polemic; with all his penchant for satire, parody, and exaggeration; with his repeated charges of homicidal, perverse, and immoral teachings among his foes, Irenaeus never lets his purpose and mission be lost. The aim of the man whom Hoffman long

ago called "the saint of peace" (Hoffman, *Irenaeus: A Leaf of Primitive Church History Corrected and Re-Written* [London: Thomas Scott, 1876], 37) is always correction. He has already made this point explicitly in 3.2.3, and it has been the underlying focus of all that has come since. And here, the great peacemaking Irenaeus ends, true to his name, with a prayer for the salvation of the heretics.

BIBLIOGRAPHY

ABEY, G. "Les missions divines de saint Justin à Origène." *Paradosis* 12 (1958): 184–86.

ABRAMOWSKI, LUISE. "Irenaeus, Adv. Haer III, 3, 2: *Ecclesia Romana* and *Omnis Ecclesia*; and ibid. 3, 3: Anacletus of Rome." *Journal of Theological Studies* 28 (1977): 101–4.

ADAM, KARL. "Theologische Bemerkungen zu Hugo Kochs Schrift, 'Virgo Eva—Virgo Maria.'" *Theologische Quartalschrift Tübingen* 119 (1938): 171–89.

ALDAMA, JOSÉ ANTONIO DE. "Adam, typus futuri (S. Ireneo, Advers. haer. 3,22,3)." *Sacris Erudiri* 13 (1962): 266–80.

————. "Observaciones sobre dos pasajes de San Ireneo." *Revista Española de Teología* 22 (1962): 401–3.

————. *María en la Patrística de los Siglos I y II*. Biblioteca de Autores Cristianos 300. Madrid: Biblioteca de Autores Cristianos, 1970.

ARMSTRONG, GREGORY T. *Die Genesis in der Alten Kirche: Die drei Kirchenväter*. Tübingen: Mohr Siebeck, 1962.

BACQ, PHILIPPE. *De l'ancienne à la nouvelle alliance selon s. Irénée: unité du livre IV de l'Adversus Haereses*. Paris: Editions Lethielleux, 1978.

BARDENHEWER, O. "Zur Mariologie des hl. Irenäus." *Zeitschrift für katholische Theologie* 55 (1931): 600–604.

BEHR, JOHN. "Irenaeus *AH* 3.23.5 and the Ascetic Ideal." *St. Vladimir's Theological Quarterly* 37, no. 4 (1993): 305–13.

————. *Asceticism and Anthropology in Irenaeus and Clement*. Oxford: Oxford University Press, 2000.

————. *The Formation of Christian Theology*. Vol. 1, *The Way to Nicaea*. New York: St. Vladimir's Seminary Press, 2001.

————. *The Mystery of Christ—Life in Death*. New York: St. Vladimir's Seminary Press, 2006.

BENOÎT, A. "Irénée et l'hérésie, les conceptions hérésiologiques de l'évêque de Lyon." *Augustinianum* 20 (1980): 55–67.

BÉNOIT, P. "Le Septante est-elle inspirée?" In *Vom Wort des Lebens: Festschrift für Max Meinertz zur Vollendung des 70 Lebensjahres*, 41–49. Münster: Aschendorff, 1951.

BENTIVEGNA, G. "L'angelologia de S. Ireneo nella prima fase dell'opera di salvezza; l'economia 'secundum providentiam.'" *Orientalia christiana periodica* 28 (1962): 5–48.

BÉVENOT, MAURICE. "Clement of Rome in Irenaeus's Succession-List." *Journal of Theological Studies* n.s. 17 (1966): 98–107.

BLANCHARD, YVES MARIE. *Aux sources du canon, le témoignage d'Irénée.* Cogitatio fidei. Paris: Cerf, 1993.

BOTTE, B. "Notes de critique textuelle sur l' 'Aduersus haereses' de saint Irénée." *Recherches de théologie ancienne et médiévale* 21 (1954): 165–78.

BOVER, J. M. "Sanctus Irenaeus Lugdunensis, universalis mediationis B. Mariae Virginis egregius propugnator." *Analecta sacra tarraconoesia* 1 (1925): 225–42.

—————. "Un texto de san Pablo (Gal. 4.4 f.) interpretado por San Ireneo," *Estudios Eclesiásticos* 17 (1943): 145–81.

BROWN, R. E. *The Gospel according to St. John: Introduction, Translation, and Notes,* 2 vols. Anchor Bible 29, 29A. Garden City, NY: Doubleday, 1966, 1970.

BROWN, ROBERT F. "On the Necessary Imperfection of Creation: Irenaeus' Adversus haereses IV, 38." *Scottish Journal of Theology* 28, no. 1 (1975): 17–25.

BROX, NORBERT. "Ein vermeintliches Irenäus-fragment." *Vigiliae Christianae* 24 (1970): 40–44.

BUELL, DENISE KIMBER. *Making Christians: Clement of Alexandria and the Rhetoric of Legitimacy.* Princeton, NJ: Princeton University Press, 1999.

CAPELLE, B. "Adhuc Virgo chez Saint Irénée." *Recherches de théologie ancienne et médiévale* 2 (1930): 388–95.

CHADWICK, HENRY. *The Early Church.* Baltimore: Penguin, 1967.

CHAPMAN, JOHN. "La chronologie des premières listes épiscopales de Rome, I." *Revue Bénédictine* 18 (1901): 399–417.

—————. "La chronologie des premières listes épiscopales de Rome, II." *Revue Bénédictine* 19 (1902): 13–37.

—————. "La chronologie des premières listes épiscopales de Rome, III." *Revue Bénédictine* 19 (1902): 145–70.

—————. "St Irenaeus on the Dates of the Gospels." *Journal of Theological Studies* 6 (1905): 563–69.

COMBY, JEAN. *Irénée—Aux origines de l'église de Lyon.* Lyon: Profac, 1977.

CROSS, F. L., ed. *The Jung Codex: A Newly Rediscovered Gnostic Papyrus.* London: A. R. Mowbray, 1955.

CUNNINGHAM, M. P. *Aurelii Prudentii Clementis Carmina.* CCSL 126. Turnholt: Brespols, 1966.

CURRAN, JOHN T. "St. Irenaeus and the Dates of the Synoptics." *Catholic Biblical Quarterly* 5 (1943): 34–46, 160–78, 301–10, 445–57.

D'ALÈS, ADHÉMAR. "La doctrine de la récapitulation en Saint Irénée." *Recherches de Science Religieuse* 6 (1916): 185–211.

————. "Le doctrine de l'Esprit en Saint Irénée." *Recherches de Science Religieuse* 14 (1924): 497–538.

DANIÉLOU, JEAN. *The Angels and Their Mission According to the Fathers of the Church.* Translated by D. Haimann. Westminster, MD: Newman Press, 1957.

DELLAGIACOMA, VITTORINO. *S. Ireneo di Lione: Contre Le Eresie.* 2 vols. Siena: I Classici Cristiani, 1968.

DILLISTONE, F. W. *The Christian Understanding of Atonement.* London: SCM Press, 1984.

DONOVAN, MARY ANN. *One Right Reading? A Guide to Irenaeus.* Collegeville, MN: Liturgical Press, 1997.

EBERLE, A. Review of H. Koch, *Adhuc Virgo. Theologische Revue* 29 (1930): 153–55.

ESCOULA, L. "Le Verbe Sauveur et Illuminateur chez saint Irénée." *Nouvelle Revue de Théologie* 66 (1939): 385–400, 551–67.

FANTINO, JACQUES. *L'homme, image de Dieu chez saint Irénée de Lyon.* Paris: Editions du Cerf—Thèses, 1986.

————. *La théologie d'Irénée: lecture des Ecritures en réponse à l'exégèse gnostique—une approche trinitaire.* Paris: Editions du Cerf, 1994.

FRZYBYLSKI, B. *De Mariologia santi Irenaei Lugdunensis.* Rome, 1937.

GALTIER, P. "La redemption et les droits du Démon dans S. Irénée." *Recherches de Science Religieuse* 2 (1911): 1–24.

————. "Les droits du Démon et la mort du Christ." *Recherches de Science Religieuse* 3 (1912): 344–55.

————. "La mort du Christ et la justice envers le démon." *Recherches de Science Religieuse* 4 (1913): 60–73.

————. *De Verbo Incarnato et Redemptore.* Paris, 1926.

————. "'...Ab his qui sunt undique...' (Irénée, 'Adv. Haer.,' III, 3, 2.)." *Revue d'Histoire Ecclésiastique* 44 (1949): 411–28.

GAMBERO, LUIGI. *Mary and the Fathers of the Church: The Blessed Virgin Mary in Patristic Thought.* Translated by Thomas Buffer. San Francisco: Ignatius Press, 1999.

GAVRILYUK, PAUL L. *The Suffering of the Impassible God: The Dialectics of Patristic Thought.* Oxford Early Christian Studies. Oxford: Oxford University Press, 2004.

GOODSPEED, EDGAR J. *Die ältesten Apologeten.* Göttingen: Vandenhoeck & Ruprecht, 1915.

GRANT, ROBERT M. *Gnosticism: A Source Book of Heretical Writings from the Early Christian Period.* New York: Harper & Brothers, 1961.

————. *Gnosticism and Early Christianity.* Rev. ed. New York: Harper & Row, 1966.

————. *Theophilus of Antioch: Text and Translation.* Oxford Early Christian Texts. Oxford: Clarendon Press, 1970.

————. *Irenaeus of Lyons.* Early Church Fathers. London: Routledge, 1997.

GUTJAHR, F. S. *Die Glaubwürdigkeit des Irenäischen Zeugnisses über die Abfassung des vierten kanonischen Evangeliums.* Graz: Leuschner and Lubensky's, 1904.

HEFNER, PHILIP. "Theological Methodology and St. Irenaeus." *Journal of Religion* 44 (1964): 294–309.

HEINE, RONALD E. "The Role of the Gospel of John in the Montanist Controversy." *Second Century* 6 (1987): 1–18.

HITCHCOCK, F. R. M. *The Treatise of Irenaeus of Lugdunum Against the Heresies.* London, 1916.

HOFFMAN, DANIEL L. *The Status of Women and Gnosticism in Irenaeus and Tertullian.* Lampeter: Edwin Mellen Press, 1995.

HOH, J. "Zur Herkunft der vier Evangelisten-symbole." *Biblische Zeitschrift* 15 (1918): 229–34.

HOUSSIAU, ALBERT. *La christologie de saint Irénée.* Louvain: Publications universitaires de Louvain, 1955.

————. "Le baptême selon Irénée de Lyon." *Ephemerides Theologicae Lovanienses* 60, no. 1 (1984): 45–59.

HUNT, EMILY J. *Christianity in the Second Century: The Case of Tatian.* London: Routledge, 2003.

JOPPICH, G. *Salus Carnis: Eine Untersuchung in der Theologie des hl. Irenäus von Lyon.* Münsterschwarzach: Vier-Türme-Verlag, 1965.

JOUASSARD, G. "La parallèle Eve-Marie aux origines de la patristique." *Bible et vie chrétienne* 7 (1954).

————. "Le 'Signe de Jonas' dans le livre IIIe de l'*Adversus haereses* de saint Irénée." In *L'homme devant Dieu: Mélanges offerts au Père Henri de Lubac.* Vol. 1, *Exégèse et patristique,* 235–46. Théologie 56. Lyon: Aubier, 1963.

KELLY, J. N. D. *Early Christian Doctrines.* Rev. ed. New York: Harper, 1978.

KLEIST, J. A. *The Didache, The Epistle of Barnabas, The Epistles and the Martyrdom of St. Polycarp, The Fragments of Papias, The Epistle to Diognetus.* ACW 6. London: Longmans, Green, 1948.

————. *Reread the Papias Fragment on St. Mark.* St. Louis University Studies, Series A. St. Louis, MO: St. Louis University Press, 1948.

KOCH, H. *Adhuc Virgo: Mariens Jungfrauschaft und Ehe in der altkirchlichen Überlieferung bis zum Ende des 4 Jahrhunderts.* Beiträge zur historischen Theologie. Tübingen: Mohr Siebeck, 1929.

————. *Virgo Eva—Virgo Maria: Neue Untersuchungen über die Lehre von der Jungfrauschaft und der Ehe Mariens in der ältesten Kirche.* Arbeiten zur Kirchengeschicht 25. Berlin/Leipzig: de Gruyter, 1937.

KOTTER, B. *John of Damascus—De fide orthodoxa.* Patristische Texte und Studien 12. Berlin: de Gruyter, 1973.

KÜRZINGER, J. "Irenäus und sein Zeugnis zur Sprache des Matthäusevangelium." *New Testament Studies* 10 (1963–64), 108–15.

LUNDSTRÖM, SVEN. *Studien zur lateinische Irenäusübersetzung.* Lund: Håkan Ohlssons Boktryckeri, 1943.

MACKENZIE, IAIN M. *Irenaeus's Demonstration of the Apostolic Preaching: A Theological Commentary and Translation.* Aldershot, England: Ashgate, 2002.

MCDONNELL, KILLIAN. "Quaestio disputata: Irenaeus on the Baptism of Jesus." *Theological Studies* 59 (1998): 317–19.

MCGUCKIN, JOHN A. *St. Cyril of Alexandria and the Christological Controversy.* Crestwood, NY: St. Vladimir's Seminary Press, 2004.

METZINGER, A., H. HÖPFL, and B. GUT. *Introductio Specialis in Novum Testamentum.* Rome, 1948.

MEYER, BEN F. *The Early Christians: Their World Mission and Self Discovery.* Wilmington, DE: Michael Glazier, 1986.

MINNS, DENIS. *Irenaeus.* Outstanding Christian Thinkers. London: Geoffrey Chapman, 1994.

MOHOLY, J. F. "Saint Irenaeus: The Father of Mariology." *Studia Mariana* 7 (1952): 129–87.

NASRALLAH, LAURA. *"An Ecstasy of Folly": Prophecy and Authority in Early Christianity.* Harvard Theological Studies 52; Cambridge, MA: Harvard University Press, 2003.

NAUTIN, PIERRE. "L'*Adversus haereses* d'Irénée, livre III: Notes d'exégèse." *Recherches de théologie ancienne et médiévale* 20 (1953): 185–202.

————. "Notes critiques sur Irénée, Adv. haer III." *Vigiliae Christianae* 9 (1955): 34–36.

OCHAGAVÍA, JOAN. *Visibile Patris Filius: A Study of Irenaeus's Teaching on Revelation and Tradition.* Orientala Christiana Analecta 171; Rome: Pontifical Institute of Oriental Studies, 1964.

O'COLLINS, GERALD. *Christology: A Biblical, Historical and Systematic Study of Jesus.* Oxford: Oxford University Press, 1995.

O'CONNELL, K. G. "Texts and Versions." In *The New Jerome Biblical Commentary,* edited by R. F. Brown, J. A. Fitzmyer, and R. E. Murphy, 68.63. London: Geoffrey Chapman, 1990.

ORBE, ANTONIO. *La Unción del Verbo,* vol. 3. Estudios Valentinianos 3. Rome: Gregorianum, 1961.

————. *La teología del Espíritu Santo.* Estudios Valentinianos 4. Rome: Libreria Editrice dell'Univeristà Gregoriana, 1966.

————. *Antropología de San Ireneo.* Madrid: Biblioteca de Autores Cristianos, 1969.

————. "Los hombres y el creador según una homilia de Valentin (Clem. Strom IV 13,89,1–91,3)." *Gregorianum* 55, no. 2 (1974): 339–68.

————. "¿San Ireneo adopcionista? En torno a *adv. haer.* III,19,1."
Gregorianum 65, no. 1 (1984): 5–52.

————. "El Espiritu en el bautismo de Jésus (en torno a san Ireneo)."
Gregorianum 76, no. 4 (1995): 663–99.

OSBORN, ERIC. *Irenaeus of Lyons.* Cambridge: Cambridge University Press,
2001.

————. "Irenaeus on God—Argument and Parody." *Studia Patristica* 36
(2001): 270–81.

OTTORINO, A. "Problemi di origine in S. Irénéo." *Divinitas* 11 (1967):
95–116.

PERUMALIL, A. C. "St. Matthew and His Critics." *Homiletic and Pastoral Review*
74 (1973–74): 31–32, 47–53.

PLUMPE, JOSEPH C. *Mater Ecclesia: An Inquiry into the Concept of the Church as
Mother in Early Christianity.* Studies in Christian Antiquity 5, 5.
Washington, DC: Catholic University of America Press, 1943.

————. "Some Little-Known Early Witnesses to Mary's *Virginitas in Partu.*"
Theological Studies 9 (1948): 567–77.

PUECH, H. C., and G. QUISPEL. *Evangelium Veritatis.* Zurich: Rascher Verlag,
1956.

RAHNER, H. "Flumin de ventre Christi: Die patristische Auslegung von Joh.
7.37–38." *Biblica* 22 (1941): 269–302.

REYNDERS, BRUNO. *Lexique comparé du texte grec et des versions latine, arménienne et syriaque de l'Adversus Haereses de saint Irénée.* Louvain: L. Durbecq,
1954.

RINGGREN, HELMER. "The Gospel of Truth and Valentinian Gnosticism."
Studia Theologica 17, no. 2 (1963): 51–65.

RIVIÈRE, J. *The Doctrine of the Atonement: A Historical Essay.* 2 vols. St. Louis:
Herder, 1909.

————. "La doctrine de saint Irénée sur le role du démon dans la redemption." *Bulletin d'ancienne littérature et d'archéologie chrétiennes* 1 (1911): 178–88.

————. "La mort du Christ et la justice envers le démon." *Recherches de
Science Religieuse* 4 (1913): 57–60.

ROBERT, A., and A. TRICOT. *Guide to the Bible.* New York: Desclée, 1960.

ROBINSON, J. A. "Selected Notes of Dr. Hort on Irenaeus Book III." *Journal
of Theological Studies* 33 (1932): 151–66.

ROBINSON, JAMES M. *The Nag Hammadi Library in English.* San Francisco:
Harper, 1991.

RORDORF, W., and A. SCHNEIDER. *L'évolution du concept de tradition dans
l'église ancienne.* Traditio Christiana 5; Frankfurt: Peter Lang, 1982.

SABATIER, A. *The Doctrine of the Atonement and Its Historical Evolution.*
Translated by Victor Leuliette. London: Williams & Norgate, 1904.

SAGNARD, FRANÇOIS M. M. *La gnose valentinienne et le témoignage de saint
Irénée.* Études de Philosophie Médiévale. Paris: J. Vrin, 1947.

SCHÜSSLER FIORENZA, E. "Word, Spirit and Power: Women in Early Christian Communities." In *Women of Spirit: Female Leadership in the Jewish and Christian Traditions*, edited by Rosemary Radford Ruether. New York: Simon & Schuster, 1979.

SLUSSER, MICHAEL. "Theopaschite Expressions in Second-Century Christianity as Reflected in the Writings of Justin, Melito, Celsus and Irenaeus." D.Phil., University of Oxford, 1975.

————. "Docetism: A Historical Definition." *Second Century* 1 (1981): 163–72.

SMITH, CHRISTOPHER R. "Chiliasm and Recapitulation in the Theology of Irenaeus." *Vigiliae Christianae* 48 (1994): 313–31.

SMITH, DANIEL A. "Irenaeus and the Baptism of Jesus." *Theological Studies* 58 (1997): 618–42.

STEENBERG, M. C. "Children in Paradise: Adam and Eve as 'Infants' in Irenaeus of Lyons." *Journal of Early Christian Studies* 12, no. 1 (2004): 1–22.

————. "The Mother of God as Mediatrix in Orthodox and Roman Catholic Thought." *Sobornost/Eastern Churches Review* 26, no. 1 (2004): 6–26.

————. "The Role of Mary as Co-recapitulator in St Irenaeus of Lyons." *Vigiliae Christianae* 58 (2004): 117–37.

————. "To Test or Preserve? The Prohibition of Gen 2.16–17 in the Thought of Two Second-Century Exegetes." *Gregorianum* 86, no. 4 (2005): 723–41.

————. "An Exegesis of Conformity: Textual Subversion of Subversive Texts." In *Discipline and Diversity*, edited by K. Cooper and J. Gregory, 27–35. Studies in Church History 43. Woodbridge: Boydell & Brewer, 2007.

————. *Irenaeus on Creation: The Cosmic Christ and the Saga of Redemption.* Leiden/Boston: Brill, 2008.

————. "Scripture, *graphe*, and the Status of Hermas in Irenaeus." *St. Vladimir's Theological Quarterly* 53, no. 1 (2009): 29–66.

————. *Of God and Man: Theology as Anthropology from Irenaeus to Athanasius.* London: T&T Clark/Continuum, 2009.

STEINMUELLER, J. E. *A Companion to Scripture Studies 1.* New York: J. F. Wagner/B. Herder, 1968.

TIESSEN, TERRANCE L. *Irenaeus on the Salvation of the Unevangelized.* London: Scarecrow Press, 1993.

TIMOTHY, H. B. *The Early Christian Apologists and Greek Philosophy—Exemplified by Irenaeus, Tertullian and Clement of Alexandria.* Assen: Van Gorcum, 1973.

UNGER, DOMINIC J. "Christ's Rôle in the Universe According to St. Irenaeus." *Franciscan Studies* 5 (1945): 3–20, 114–37.

―――. "A Special Aspect of Athanasian Soteriology." *Franciscan Studies* 6 (1946): 30–53 (part I) and 171–94 (part II).

―――. "Christ Jesus the Secure Foundation according to St. Cyril of Alexandria." *Franciscan Studies* 7 (1947): 18–25.

―――. "St. Irenaeus and the Roman Primacy." *Theological Studies* 13 (1952): 359–418.

―――. "Sancti Irenaei, Lugdunensis Episcopi, Doctrina de Maria Virgine Matre, Socia Iesu Christi Filii Sui ad Opus Recapitulationis." In *Maria et Ecclesia: Acta Congressus Mariologici Mariani in Civitate Lourdes Anno 1958 Celebrati*, 4:67–140. Rome: Academia Mariana Internationalis, 1959.

―――. "Life in the Church: St. Irenaeus, *Adversus haereses* 3,24,1." *Laurentianum* 13 (1972): 294–315.

―――. "The Divine and Eternal Sonship of the Word According to St. Irenaeus of Lyons." *Laurentianum* 14 (1973): 357–408.

UNNIK, WILLEM CORNELIS VAN. *Newly Discovered Gnostic Writings: A Preliminary Survey of the Nag Hammadi Find.* Studies in Biblical Theology 30. London: SCM Press, 1960.

VERNET, F. "Irénée (Saint)." In *Dictionnaire de Théologie Catholique*, edited by A. Vacant, E. Mangenot, and E. Amann, vol. 7. Paris: Librarie Letouzey et Ané, 1923.

VERRIÈLE, A. "Le plan du salut d'après saint Irénée." *Revue des Sciences Religieuses* 14 (1934): 493–524.

VIVES, J. "Pecado original y progreso evolutivo del hombre en Ireneo." *Estudios Eclesiásticos* 43 (1968): 561–89.

WEINANDY, THOMAS G. *Does God Suffer?* Notre Dame, IN: University of Notre Dame Press, 2000.

WHITE, VICTOR. "Chief Druid and Chief Bishop: A Parallel in Caesar's *Gallic War* with Irenaeus *Against the Heresies*, III, 3." *Dominican Studies* 4 (1951): 201–3.

WINGREN, GUSTAF. *Man and the Incarnation: A Study in the Biblical Theology of Irenaeus.* Translated by Ross Mackenzie. Edinburgh: Oliver & Boyd, 1959.

WRIGHT, D. F. "Clement and the Roman Succession in Irenaeus." *Journal of Theological Studies* n.s. 18 (1967): 144–54.

YOUNG, FRANCES M. *Sacrifice and the Death of Christ.* London: SPCK, 1975.

INDEXES

SCRIPTURE

AUTHORS

GENERAL INDEX

Abraham, 33, 133, 138, 165; God's
covenant with, 45, 49, 66
Adam, 24–25, 88, 102, 103; and
Christ, 176–77, 193, 194, 197;
eschatological redemption of,
15–16, 25, 105–10; fig-leaf
garments, 108, 205–6; God's
covenant with, 9, 57, 60, 78;
repentance, 108, 205; second-born,
177; sin and punishment, 197, 199,
203, 205; as type of one to come,
15, 104, 196, 197
Aeons, 5, 49, 83, 96, 159, 163, 197
Against the Heresies: Book 3: central
theme, 6–7, 12–13; content outline,
16–26; previous critical editions,
1–6; summary of text, 6–16
Ahaz, 94, 99–100
Alexander I, Pope, 33
Alogoi, 151
Anacletus, Pope, 32, 128, 129
Angels, 49–50, 53, 65, 137, 153;
Cherubim, 56, 149
Anicetus, Pope, 33, 36
Anna, 18, 51, 74, 144
Antichrist, 21, 40, 42, 81, 83
Antioch, 126
Apelles, 206
Apostles: perfection of, 61–62, 152;
proclamation of truth, 17, 32,
36–38; and tradition, 10, 12, 36,
130; *see also* specific apostles, e.g.:
Peter
Apostolic gospel. *See* Gospel
Apostolic succession, 7, 10–11, 16, 20,
32–34, 58, 128–30; truth and, 11,
17, 34–38
Aquila of Pontus, 97
Ascension, 18, 182

Baptism, 70, 85, 167, 168; of Christ,
18, 21–22, 140–41, 146, 189
Barnabas, 66, 69, 70, 72, 214
Basilides, 31, 137
Bethlehem, 187
Blandina, 162, 212

Cain, 25, 204, 205
Cana, miracle at, 19, 54–55, 82,
164–65
"Catholics" (as name), 158
Cerdon, 35
Cerinthus, 19, 31, 34, 52
Cherubim, 56, 149
Christ: and Adam, 176–77, 193, 194;
ascension, 182; baptism of, 18,
21–22, 74, 140–41, 146, 189; birth,
18; death and resurrection, 9, 21,
23, 189; dual nature, 100, 190;
eternity of, 170; firstborn, 161–62,
176–77; four dimensions of Christ's
nature, 21; mediator of faith in one
God, 131; mediator of grace and
glory, 208; non-virginal birth, 23,
53, 92–94, 98, 100–102, 191, 192,
194; one and the same Lord, 6,
12–13, 21, 159; suffering, 88–91; as
Word of God, 21, 23, 77–84, 87–92,
163–64; *see also* specific headings,
e.g.: Incarnation; Virgin birth
"Christians" (as name), 158
Church: Jerusalem Church, 126, 152;
Mother Church, 116–17, 214;
succession of Churches, 126; *see
also* Roman Church
Circumcision, 66, 69, 71
Clement of Rome, Pope, 32–33, 128
Communes, 158
Cornelius, 63

242